Daily
Meditations
with
F.B. Meyer

Al Bryant

Daily
Meditations
with
F.B. Meyer

WORD BOOKS
PUBLISHER
WACO, TEXAS

ISBN 0-8499-0148-0
Library of Congress catalog card number: 79-63938
Printed in the United States of America

To
all
those
who sincerely seek
to live the life
F. B. MEYER
wrote about and
sought to share

Preface

ONE OF F. B. Meyer's most ambitious efforts in devotional writing was his *Our Daily Homily* series, which has recently been reissued under the title, *Great Verses Through the Bible*. While this is an excellent volume, it dissipates much of the impact of Meyer's incisive pen because of its chronological progression through the Bible, selecting a key verse from each succeeding chapter which Meyer called "gems of thought from every chapter in the Bible." Single gems are beautiful, but they make a greater impact in clusters. And this is what we have sought to do in this compilation—cluster Meyer's incisive thoughts on a given subject and center on that theme for a month.

We have chosen to arrange these meditations around monthly themes to give the reader an opportunity to digest Meyer's thoughts on a particular aspect of the Christian life or doctrine. For reasons sometimes obvious (e.g., "The Thankful Life" for November) and sometimes less apparent, we have arranged the meditations as follows:

January—The Surrendered Life
February—The Life of Prayer
March—Discipleship, The Life of the Learner
April—The Life of Faith
May—The Suffering Life
June—The Witnessing Life
July—The Dedicated Life
August—The Day-by-day Christian Life
September—The Spirit-filled Life
October—The Worshiping Life

November—The Thankful Life

December—The Expectant Life (the Second Coming of Jesus)

While many of these meditations are adapted from *Our Daily Homily,* we drew upon others of his published works as well in this compilation. F. B. Meyer has been described as "a man of dignified appearance, compassionate heart, ceaseless industry, prolific pen, and graceful style" by Arthur Clark in *The New International Dictionary of the Christian Church.* Here is a distillation from his "prolific pen" and "compassionate heart" for today's reader. As you consider his deep thoughts on these important monthly subjects, we trust that you will grow spiritually, enjoying the companionship of this spiritual giant.

The Surrendered Life

January

As we have therefore opportunity, let us do good unto all men, especially unto them who are of the household of faith.
Galatians 6: 10

1

A NEW YEAR is opening before us, and there is some satisfaction in feeling that this will give us an opportunity for a brand new start. Each true heart in which there is a spark of the divine life turns eagerly toward the unblemished page, the untrodden way, the new year. We turn not with wonder simply, or with hope, but with the fervent resolve to let the dead past bury its dead, and to live a nobler, fuller, sweeter life in the days that remain for us.

But it is of little purpose merely to wish and to resolve. We must deal with mistakes and sins which have dogged our footsteps in the past. If we could turn our backs upon these, and make a new start, we could then expect the coming year to make us better men.

The Lord taketh pleasure in them that fear him, in those that hope in his mercy.
Psalm 147: 11

2

THE LORD watches us more closely than we realize. At each turn, his eye is upon us; and when we manifest some trait of obedience or devotion, it sends a thrill of pleasure through His heart. Of course our standing is always in His grace. We love only because He first loved. Our comeliness is placed on us by our King. And when we are at our best we always need the sprinkling of the precious blood. But still it is the constant teaching of Scripture that we may please

January

God. This was the testimony borne of Enoch before his translation, and the apostle exhorts us to walk worthily of the Lord, unto all pleasing. He tells us not to entangle ourselves in the affairs of this life, that we may please Him who hath chosen us to be his soldiers.

How well it would be if this were the aim of every day, the purpose of every sermon, the motive of every act. It were easy to be baptized in the waters of death, if only on emerging we might stand beneath the open heavens, while a voice said, "This is my beloved child, in whom I am well pleased." Let us strive for this. Let our eye be ever fixed on that beloved face, checking any act that might threaten to bedim it, carrying out all that might bring over it a smile of loving appreciation and thankfulness.

And see how the verse closes: "them that fear him . . . those that hope in his mercy." Not only does God take a personal interest in each step of the obedient soul, but He gives them hope who fear (revere) Him. Our hope is in Him—in no one else!

3

The kingdom of heaven is like unto treasure hid in a field; the which when a man hath found, he hideth, and for joy thereof goeth and selleth all that he hath, and buyeth that field.

Matthew 13: 44

THERE is a beautiful illustration of the truth of these words in the life of Justin the Martyr, who died for the gospel in the second century. As a young man he earnestly sought for truth, specially that which would arm him with self-control. He took up one system of philosophy after another, trying them as a man might explore mine after mine for silver. Finally, he found that every effort was futile. At length, wandering in despair on the seashore, he met an aged man, a Christian, who spake as none had ever done to his heart, and pointed him to God in Christ. Beneath those words, that afternoon, he understood the fear of the Lord, and found the knowledge of God.

Thomas longed for evidences of the Resurrection, and Christ came to him. The eunuch, as he sat in his chariot reading the book of Isaiah the Prophet at chapter 43, desired to know the truth, and

January

Philip was sent to him. To Saul of Tarsus, groping at midnight, there came fuller revelations than ever Gamaliel gave, through Stephen and Ananias, led by the Spirit of God.

But you must be prepared to sacrifice all. He who seeks diamonds, or pearls, or gold, will leave his native land, and what other men hold dear, and center his whole attention on his search. Not otherwise must it be with those who would understand the fear of the Lord, and find the knowledge of God. They must be willing to count all things but loss, to sell all they have, to buy the field with its treasure-trove.

When the Lord bringeth back the captivity of his people.
Psalm 14: 7

4

IT IS wonderful to notice the many ways in which the Lord brings us back to Himself. We may have been carried into captivity by a host of anxieties or a horde of worries; by temptations like the sons of Anak; by pride and other evils, as when David found that the Amalekites had carried off his belongings into captivity. Then God comes to the rescue: sometimes by a drawing felt throughout the soul; sometimes by a little word dropped by another; sometimes by an incident from a biography. Any one of these acts upon us as the sunbeams on frost—there is a meeting and yielding, a desire to get alone, confession of waywardness and wandering, and earnest petitions for renewal of the blessed past. Thus the Lord "bringeth back the captivity of His people" (Ps. 53: 6).

Are you a captive, pining in some distant bondage? It is not surprising that you hang your harp upon the willows, and weep as you remember Zion—how you went with the throng, and even led them to the House of God, with the voice of joy and praise. And as you contrast the past and the present, it is well that your soul is cast down. But when the Lord brings again your captivity, Jacob shall rejoice, and Israel shall be glad.

Would it not be well to look out for your brother Lot if he has been carried off down the long Jordan Plain? Should you not arm

January

and go to his rescue, as Abraham did? Perhaps the Lord would turn your captivity, if you sought to turn the captivity of others; and Melchizedek would meet you with the bread and wine.

For he is our God; and we are the people of his pasture, and the sheep of his hand.

Psalm 95: 7

THE SENSE of God's proprietorship is the true basis of our consecration. We must realize His rights over us before we can freely give Him His due. Those rights are well-grounded in their sweet logic; but among them all, this claim of creation is one of the chief. God has a right to us because He has made us.

We are Christ's by creation, by purchase, by toils and tears, by the gift of the Father. The Good Shepherd owns us, though we do not always acknowledge His ownership, or repay His pains and wounds for us. Look up into His face and say, "I am Yours by a myriad ties, and am bound to You for evermore. Lead me where You wilt; guide me where You choose; count me as one of Your people; feed me on Your pasture lands; make as much of me as You can, this side of heaven; number me with Your saints in glory everlasting."

"With bowed heads and open hearts," says Dr. Westcott, "may we offer ourselves. We can do no more, and we dare do no less."

I will walk within my house with a perfect heart.

Psalm 101: 2

THIS IS the hardest place to walk in perfectly. It seems easier to walk perfectly among strangers than in one's own house. But you may rest assured that a man is really no better than he is to his own.

January

You must not gauge your worth by what the outside world thinks and says, but by the estimate of those who see you in the ordinary relationships of the home.

To be perfectly courteous to those whom you are meeting at every meal; to hold yourself under perfect control when worried by tiny insidious jars, and stung by almost invisible gnats; to maintain always the perfect girding of the loins; to have the head always anointed and the face always washed; to realize God's ideal, love's ideal, and your own. This requires the utmost grace God can give. To die once is easy; to live always with an undivided heart, this is difficult.

Understand that in the home-life God is educating and training you for the greatest victories. There you are learning the deepest lessons in sanctification. You need not run to conventions, sermons, and holiness meetings; if you would resolve to walk in your house with a perfect heart, you would discover how far from perfect you are, and how you are the least of His saints. Seek the perfect heart in your home-life; for then God will come unto you, and dwell beneath your roof, and the story of Bethany would be reduplicated for your household and yourself.

A tranquil mind. . . .

Proverbs 14: 30, RSV

7

IF WE WOULD have a tranquil mind, we must resolutely put from us the ambition to get name and reputation among men, to exert wider influence for its own sake, and to amass large accumulation of money. Directly we begin to vie with others, to emulate them, or compare our position and influence with theirs; directly we allow strong desires to roam unchecked through our nature; directly we live on the breath of popular applause, we are like those who step from the pier on a rocking boat—all hope of tranquility is at an end.

"In God's will," Dante said, "is our peace." When the government is on His shoulder, of its increase and of our peace there is no end. Would you have your peace flow as a river?—then rest in the

January

Lord, be silent unto Him; fret not thyself; turn away from the things that are seen and temporal; set your face to those that are unseen and eternal. Live in the secret place of the Most High, and hide under the shadow of the Almighty. Say of the Lord that He is your fortress and high tower. Put God between yourself and everything. Let the one aim of your life be to please Him, and do the one small piece of work with which He has entrusted you. Look away from all others to Him alone. And learn to look out on others with a tender sympathetic gaze, turning to prayer about them and everything else that might ruffle and sadden. Let all your requests be made known unto God, so shall His peace keep heart and mind.

8	*Stormy wind fulfilling his word.*

Psalm 148: 8

AS IT RUSHES through the forest, the hurricane tears down the rotten branches, and makes way for the new shoots of the spring; and as it searches out the intricacies of the crowded alleys and courts it bears away the fever germs, and changes the atmosphere. Do not dread it, if you meet it rushing across the ocean and churning up the mighty billows on its way; know it to be your Father's strong servant, intent on fulfilling some errand on which it has been sent.

Stormy winds sometimes invade our lives. "All had been so fair and blessed with us. The south wind, blowing softly, had led us to suppose that we might make for another harbor. But not long afterwards the tempestuous Euroclydon beat down on us, blowing us far off our course, and threatening us with destruction." But even under those circumstances, dare to trust. That stormy wind cannot separate you from God; for through its mad fury His angels will visit you, His care will surround you, His purpose will be fulfilled of bearing you onward, as the Apostle was borne toward Rome, with its opportunities of witness-bearing (Acts 27).

The great matter to remember is to run before the wind. Let its course be yours. Yield your will to God's will; and even though it takes you far off your course, dare to believe that it is the quickest and best way of attaining the harbor which God has prepared. There is nothing terrible in fire, or hail, or stormy wind, when we see God behind them.

The king's heart is a stream of water in the hand of the Lord; he turns it wherever he will.
Proverbs 21: 1, RSV

9

MADAME Guyon says that there are three classes of souls that may be compared to rivers flowing toward God as their ocean.

1. Some move on sluggishly and feebly. These are often discouraged, dwell much in the outer and emotional, and fail to seek God with their whole strength.

2. Some proceed decidedly and rapidly. These have large hearts, and are quick in their responses to God's Spirit.

3. Some press on in headlong impetuosity.

This comparison of our hearts to streams filled with torrents from the hills is a very beautiful one, and is capable of great expansion.

Streams need fresh supplies of water from the hills: and our hearts are in constant need of freshets from the everlasting fountain of God's nature.

Streams must fulfill their ministry in all weathers: and we must continue patiently in faith and well-doing, whatever be our circumstances or emotions. If we fail, the whole land will be smitten with drought.

Streams end in merging their waters with the ocean tides: so God will one day be all in all.

Will you let God lead your heart wherever He will? Just as a farmer will cut irrigation ditches in different directions to conduct the flow of the water, so will you not let God lead your life? You can be a stream: He must give the water. Only be content, like the riverbed, to lie deep hidden beneath the waters; not noticed or thanked by those that stoop to drink the refreshing draughts. It is impossible for the water to pass through you without nourishing your own soul.

January

10

Trust in the Lord with all thine heart; and lean not unto thine own understanding. In all thy ways acknowledge him, and he shall direct thy paths.

Proverbs 3: 5–6

THY paths! Then, every man's path is distinct for him, and for no other. The paths may lie side by side, but they are different. They have converged; they may diverge.

We need to be divinely directed.—The man who stands above the maze can direct you through all its labyrinth by the readiest path. God who made you for your life, and your life for you, can direct you, and He only.

First: *Lean not to thine own understanding.*—A person is apt to pride himself on his farsighted judgment. We consult our maps and guides and the opinions of fellow travelers, to find ourselves at fault. We have to learn that our own understanding is not keen enough or wise enough to direct; we must adjure and renounce all dependence on it.

Second: *In all thy ways acknowledge Him.*—Let your eye be single; your one aim to please Him; your sole motive, His glory. It is marvelous how certainly and delightfully our way opens before us when we no longer look down on it, or around at others, but simply upward into the face of Christ. "It is a universal law, unalterable as the nature of God, that no created being can be truly holy, useful, or happy, who is knowingly and deliberately out of the divine fellowship, *for a single moment.*"

11

Commit your work to the Lord, and your plans will be established.

Proverbs 16: 3, RSV

THERE are four matters which we are to commit to God—ourselves, our burden, our way, and here, our works. This is the genesis of Christian work. We become conscious of the uprising of a noble purpose. We are not sure at first whether it is of God or not, till we have taken time to subject it to the winnowing fan of His good Spirit.

It is always wise to subject it to the fire of His criticism before it takes shape. Even then, however, all is not done. We must submit our plans before they are executed, our methods by which they are being executed, and the results of the execution, to the infinite wisdom of the heavenly Father.

What a comfort it is to commit our works to God! The servant of God who is carrying the responsibilities of a vast missionary enterprise. That preacher with his church and organizations. That promoter of philanthropic and helping agencies. Let them roll their works upon God and be content to take a subordinate place of acting as His agents and executors. The heart will be light and the hands free, if only we can learn the blessed secret of imposing the responsibility and anxiety of our efficiency, finance, and success on the Lord. Commit your works and see that they do not roll back upon you again. Put on the restraint of faith to make them keep their position. Reckon that God takes what you give; and when you have let your works go, be sure to cast yourself after them on His patient carefulness.

Remember that He desires to work in us to will and to work of His good pleasure. Do not worry, nor fret, nor be always looking for results. Do your best, and leave the rest to Him, who is our rearward. He will follow up our efforts and establish the work of your hands.

Doth the plowman plow all day to sow? . . . A man shall nourish . . . two sheep.
Isaiah 28: 24; 7: 21

| 12 |

THESE are two basic aspects of farming—the agricultural, "plowing"; the pastoral, "keeping sheep." Between them they also cover our service to men for Christ's sake. Some of us are engaged in plowing. In the short November days, when the last leaves are falling drearily from the trees, and the skies are covered by dense and dripping clouds, we go forth weeping, with our plow or bearing precious seed. In loneliness, depression, and fear we tread the furrows, and return crying: "Who hath believed our report and to

January

whom is the arm of the Lord revealed?" (Isa. 53: 1). Or we are called to *keep the flock,* drenched at night by dew, scorched during the day by the sun's heat, seeking the straying, defending the attacked, tenderly nursing the weak and sick. In either of these avocations we must often become weary, and faint in our minds looking forward to finishing the work and relaxing. "Surely," we softly whisper to ourselves, "we have earned a rest!" But that is exactly what the Master does not intend, because He knows the subtle temptations of our hours of ease. When we come in from the field, He does not say, "Come and rest"; He meets us on the threshold, as we are tired and stained from our labor, saying, "Make ready and serve *me* . . . *and afterwards* thou shalt eat and drink."

13	*Therefore if thou bring thy gift to the altar, and there rememberest that thy brother hath ought against thee.*
	Matthew 5: 23

THERE is a marked difference between memory and recollection. Memory resembles a great box or chest into which a man casts his letters, accounts, and diaries. Recollection is the readiness, more or less, to lay one's hand on what he requires. Often amid the accumulation of years we are unable to find what we want. We know that it is somewhere in our possession, but search as we may we cannot find it. Everything that happens to us, that we see, read, or hear, is kept in the archives of memory, but often we cannot recall it—we cannot recollect.

There are times, however, when our power of recollection is greatly quickened. They tell me that one who is drowning sees the whole of his life flash before him, even to the smallest incident. In such cases recollection and memory have been equal to each other in their recall. Another moment of quickened recollection is that in which we stand before God, "when thou bringest thy gift to the altar and rememberest. . . ." As the Divine Light plays upon our past life it reveals many things which had passed from our mind. Conscience is a keen quickener of our powers of recollection. By confession we can keep that conscience clear.

January

And if thy hand offend thee, cut it off: it is better for thee to enter into life maimed, than having two hands to go into hell, into the fire that never shall be quenched.
Mark 9: 43

14

OUR LORD had just come from the Mount of Transfiguration. The great scheme of the world's redemption was clear to His mind and heart, and His sacrificial death in Jerusalem called to Him. No lamb ever went to the altar more willingly than He; and with that fire of love burning in His heart He calls on all who love Him to present themselves living sacrifices, even though in the process they should be exposed to salt, with its searching sting, and fire, its consuming flame.

Of course, it is best to retain the precious members of our body in perfect purity and righteousness. They are not only natural, but most important assets to the working force of a successful life. No one has a right to perform this amputation unless it is the only alternative to death or uselessness. A skilled mechanic repairing a machine inadvertently caught his fingers in the machine, and found his arm being drawn between mighty rollers. Not a moment was to be lost; he caught up a hatchet lying near, and with a blow severed his arm at the elbow. He was just in time to save his life. Such hours come to us all. It may be a friendship not compatible with the high ideals of family life, or a habit, sapping our nervous energy, or a form of amusement. Whatever hinders us in our best moments must, if we cannot master it and compel it to keep within bounds, be yielded to the knife.

And if thy foot offend thee, cut it off: it is better for thee to enter halt into life, than having two feet to be cast into hell, into the fire that never shall be quenched.
Mark 9: 45

15

OUR LORD was well advised, when He said, "Cut it off." The one swift, irrevocable blow is the easiest and most painless in the end. We must often expose ourselves to more anguish in our effort to retain and restrain, than to remove absolutely and forever. If an engagement must be broken off, it is easiest when miles of land and sea sever the lovers.

If the pursuit of art or medicine causes trains of thought which are unwholesome, let there be an honest attempt to master the wrong, replacing it by the right, and to see everything under the holy light of God's creatorship; if these fail, it would be better to renounce the profession for some other mode of life. So with books, amusements, associations, and much else that enters into our daily life.

There are great compensations for us, if we dare to follow the ideals that beckon to us from the lofty pinnacles above us. As in the physical sphere, it is well known that when a sense or a limb is lost, the nervous energy glows with more vigor and thrill through the remaining members, so that the blind excel as musicians and the dumb become more dextrous with their fingers. It is even so with the soul. Surrender all that impedes your highest life, and its fountains will burst forth in an abundance that will make the desert rejoice and sing. Is not this better than being cast into Gehenna? Better anything than to be a castaway, flung from the hands of Christ as unclean.

But which of you, having a servant plowing or feeding cattle, will say unto him . . . when he is come from the field, Go and sit down to meat?

Luke 17: 7

FROM THIS parable we are surely to infer that our Master says in effect: "You have been working for Me, but I have missed you. You have been so engaged in guiding your plow, or guarding your sheep, that you have forgotten to look into My face. You have allowed the hours to pass without addressing Me, or listening for My voice and now I want you to be quiet, and to direct to Me the full volume of your heart's confidences. Minister to Me." This is a parable for Sunday evening when the toils of day are over. Nothing will more certainly injure us than to yield to that relaxation of moral and spiritual fiber to which we are so prone, while nothing will so rest us, or afford such gratification to our Lord, as to turn to minister to Him. To put Him in His right place, and to adjust the focus of our soul by His priority to all other considerations. When Christ's work is done, turn to Christ Himself and minister to Him; be still before Him, prepare Him a feast of faith and love and joy, that He may come into His garden and eat His precious fruits.

After all this *we* may eat and drink (Luke 17: 8). Yes, He will gird Himself and serve us. When Christ is in His right place in our love and service; when our whole life is poured out as a sacrifice at His feet, then we can eat and drink, the heart is merry, prayer is easy, the Bible glistens with new light, service becomes an increasing joy, and we hear the voice of the Holy Spirit calling us to undertake new and original work (Acts 13: 2).

Jesus saith unto them, My meat is to do the will of him that sent me, and to finish his work.

John 4: 34

| 17 |

THE WRITER of the Epistle to the Hebrews (chap. 10) lays great stress on the concept contained in these words. He says that this yielding up of Christ's will to his Father's was consummated on the cross, and was the inner heart of our Savior's passion. "By the which will (surrendered and given back to God) we are sanctified (surrendered and given back to God)." He then proceeds to suggest that it is only as we enter into a living oneness with Jesus in this that we can pass from the outer court and have boldness to enter into the Holiest of all. This, he says, is the new and living way. Jesus entered into the Holiest because He gave Himself absolutely to his Father. We cannot expect to reach that degree of sanctification till we have become possessed of the same spirit.

It is a solemn question for each. Have we all stood at the cross, as the slave of old at the doorpost of his master's house, and said, "I love my Master. I will not go out free"?

But there is yet another condition. We can have no right to stand within the Holiest, except through the blood of Jesus, shed for sin on the cross. This is necessary before sinners can have boldness in the presence of Divine Purity.

January

When Rutherford was dying a natural death, instead of a martyr's death, he said, "I would think it a more glorious way of going home, to lay down my life for the cause at the cross of Edinburgh or St. Andrew's; but I *submit* to my Master's will. Oh, for arms to embrace Him!"

18 *Study to be quiet.*

1 Thessalonians 4: 11

A SIGNIFICANT title for the saints, which has been adopted at least by one great religious body. In every age God has had His quiet ones. Retired from its noise and strife, withdrawn from its ambitions and jealousies, unshaken by its alarms; because they had entered into the secret of a life hidden in God. We must have an outlet for the energies of our nature. If we are unfamiliar with the hidden depths of eternal life, we shall necessarily live a busy, fussy, frothy, ambitious, eager life, in contact with men and things. But the man who is intense on the eternal, can be quiet in the temporal.

The man whose house is shallow, but one room in depth, cannot help living on the street. But as soon as we begin to dwell deep— deep in God, deep in the watch for the Master's advent, deep in considering the mysteries of the kingdom, we become quiet. We fill our little space; we get our daily bread and are content; we enjoy natural and simple pleasures; we do not strive, nor cry, nor cause our voice to be heard in the street; we pass through the world, with noiseless tread, dropping a blessing on all we meet; but we are no sooner recognized than we are gone.

Get quiet, beloved soul; share your sorrow and complaint with God. Let not the greatest business or pressure divert you from God. When men rage about you, go and tell Jesus. When storms are high, hide yourself in His secret place. When others compete for fame and applause, and their greed might influence you, get into your closet, and shut your door, and quiet yourself. For if your voice is quiet to man, let it never cease to speak loudly and mightily for man in the ear of God. Oh, to be a Quietist in the best sense!

January

Peter said unto him, Lord, why cannot I follow thee now?
I will lay down my life for thy sake.

John 13: 37

19

PETER was well aware that some disaster was about to break in on his Master's life. He could not but realize that the One whom he loved with passionate devotion was passing into the shadow of a great eclipse; and the fear that they were likely to be permanently separated was unendurable. In the ardor of that hour he so minimized the thought of death, and all that it might involve, that he went out to court its dangers. Better to die once and now, he thought, if the Master is to die, than live long years apart from Him. His impulsive spirit could not brook delay: "Lord, why cannot I follow thee now? I will lay down my life for thy sake."

We have all felt that way! If only we could be freed once and for all from the clinging pain we must endure, or that thorn in the flesh, that gnawing, stinging problem from which there seems to be no deliverance. A sudden departure would be so much easier than the long waiting which now confronts us. It is far easier to rush into the battle, where the excitement and fever may be trusted to make us oblivious to pain, than to wait through long, icy nights on sentry duty. But this may be God's call for us.

Ye have not chosen me, but I have chosen you. . . .

20

John 15: 16

YE did not choose me." How surely He diagnoses the human heart. How inevitably He puts His finger on our greatest shame and sorrow. Like the world in which we lived, and which counted us its own, we chose "after the sight of the eyes and the hearing of the ears." But as for Jesus, when we saw Him there seemed no beauty that we should desire Him, and we turned away.

We did not choose Him—there you have the evil of the human heart, the film of blindness which sin casts on the sight, the deaf-

January

ness which dulls the ear; for to have missed Jesus is as though the pearl)hunter were unable to recognize the pearl of greatest price.

"But I chose you." He chose us probably because we were useless and helpless, and He wanted to show what supreme miracles His grace could achieve. The principle of God's election is to take what all others reject. It was for some such reason that He chose us. He knew all that we were, all that we should be. How He could have struck such a poor bargain passes all our understanding. But having chosen us, He is going to justify His choice, unless we definitely refuse to let Him have His way. If only we will *abide* in Him, though we be the least worthy of all His creatures, He will make something of us for the everlasting blessing of mankind, and the everlasting blessedness of our own souls.

21	*These words spake Jesus, and lifted up his eyes to heaven and said, Father, the hour is come; glorify thy Son, that thy Son also may glorify thee.* John 17: 1

JOHN 17 has been called the incense altar of the New Testament. It is full of the sweet fragrance of our Lord's intercession for His own. It is more than a prayer; it is a window into His interconsciousness. Four significant clauses give us the secret of His life here in chapter 17: "I have glorified thee on the earth"; "I have finished the work thou gavest me to do"; "I have manifested thy name to the men whom thou gavest me"; "I have kept them in thy name." The whole drift of His ministry was toward the Father. He anticipated, in fact, those great words of Paul, "Of him, and through him, and to him are all things: To him be the glory forever" (Rom. 11: 36).

The springs of His life were in the eternal throne. His influence during those early days of popularity, His words never paralleled in human speech, His works and miracles, His human love—everything, from the crowds on the hills of Galilee to the familiar love of the home at Bethany, He reckoned to have come to Him from His Father. In this we have an example, that we should follow in His steps. We also must find our fresh springs in Him as He found them in God. If any glory should ever fall to our lot, we must lay it at His feet and share it with those entrusted to our charge. All our Lord's prayers, all His deepest transactions with God while men slept, all His anguish, sorrow, and pain, were for God, for man, for any but Himself. He obliterated Himself that God might be all in all.

May be able to comprehend with all saints what is the breadth, and length, and depth, and height [of the love of Christ].

Ephesians 3: 18

22

ITS *breadth*. It is as broad as the race of man. It is like the fabled tent which, when opened in a courtyard, filled it; but when unfurled in the tented field, it covered an army. It claims all souls.

Its *length*. It is timeless and changeless. It never began; it will never stop. It cannot be tired out by our exactions or demands upon its patience.

Its *height*. Stand by the cradle, or lower yet, at the cross, and you behold it, like Jacob's ladder, reaching to the throne of God. A spiral staircase by which the guiltiest may climb from the dark dungeon into the palace.

Its *depth*. There is no sin so profound, no despondency so low, no misery so abject, but the love of Christ is deeper. Its everlasting arms are always underneath.

As we consider these things, we can almost hear the voice of God speaking to us as to Abraham: "Lift up now thine eyes, and look from the place where thou art, northward and southward, and eastward and westward; for all the land which thou seest, to thee will I give it, and to thy seed forever. Arise, walk through the land in the length of it, and in the breadth of it; for I will give it unto thee." When we separate ourselves from our Lots, this land is ours. It is an undiscovered continent on which we are settled; but every year we may push our fences outward to enclose more of its infinite extent.

January

23

Who shall also confirm you unto the end, that ye may be blameless in the day of our Lord Jesus Christ.
1 Corinthians 1: 8

THE AGENT of this blameless life is God Himself. None beside could accomplish so marvelous a result. What are we? Pure snow trampled into mud; jet-black ink, liable to make a permanent stain. But even *we* can be made blameless, not only yonder, but also here and now. This is a marvel that only the finger of God could effect. But He does it by condescending to indwell our souls. Our sanctification is due to the indwelling presence of God. As He condescended to fill Solomon's Temple with His glory, so He waits to infill spirit, soul, and body of those who believe.

The mightiest forces are the stillest. Whoever heard the day break or detected the footfall of the Spring through the woods? Who thinks of listening for the throb of gravitation, or the thud of the forces that redden the grape, golden the corn, and cover the peaches with bloom? So God works in the hearts He loves. He does not strive, nor cry, nor cause His voice to be heard. When we think we are making no progress, and that nothing is happening, He is most at work. The presence of ozone in the air can only be detected by a faint color on a piece of litmus paper, and God's work in the soul is only apparent as the bloom of perfect health spreads upon the face.

24

Know ye not that they which run in a race run all, but one receiveth the prize? So run, that ye may obtain.
1 Corinthians 9: 24

WHEN I was in school, I can remember running "spur-of-the-moment" races, when we began fairly well clothed. As we ran, and found ourselves slowly losing ground, however, we would tear off one article after another in our anxiety to reach the goal. The course would be littered with coats, ties, and other articles. Similarly, in the great race of life, the flight of the year should be marked by the weights and sins that we have laid aside. Each new year would be enriched by the needless extravagances we had learned to live without. We should run lighter, meet the stormy waves with less encumbrance, and stand a better chance of reaching the goal, to stand among the rarer spirits on the higher ranges.

Such running implies sacrifice, and this is the attitude with which we must face the opening of the New Year. This would give us a new start indeed!

It is sown in weakness; it is raised in power.
1 Corinthians 15: 43

25

WEAKNESS and brokenness are very attractive to God. He is attracted by our need, more than by our beauty. Every shepherd will tell you that it is the weary and the weak, the lambs and the ewes with young, that he cares for. Every mother will confess that there is an infinite fascination in the tiny baby, who is more helpless and exacting, but less self-sufficient than others of her brood. So it is with God. If you should be defeated and troubled, and at the end of your resources, you are at the very beginning of God's power.

He that dwelleth in the secret place of the most High shall abide under the shadow of the Almighty.
Psalm 91: 1

26

TO ABIDE under the shadow of the Almighty reminds us of our Lord's words: "How often would I have gathered thy children together, even as a hen gathereth her children under her wings, and ye would not!" (Matt. 23: 37). John Bunyan says that the hen has four calls: the call when night is near; the call for food; the call of peril; and the call of brooding love when she wants to feel her

January

chicks under her wings. Today God is calling to each of us, saying: "Come, My children, make the secret place of My presence, of My environment, of My constant keeping, your home; for he that dwelleth in the secret place of the most High shall abide under the wings of God."

The promise is clear: "He shall give his angels charge over thee, to keep thee in *all* thy ways"—business ways, social ways, the ways of service into which God may lead us forth, the ways of sacrifice or suffering. Let us simply and humbly ask for the fulfillment of the promises in this Psalm. He will answer your prayers. He will be with you in trouble. He will satisfy you with many years of life, or with living much in a short time, and He will show you the wonders of His salvation.

27	*Whether therefore ye eat, or drink, or whatsoever ye do, do all to the glory of God.*
	1 Corinthians 10: 31

WHAT counts in God's sight is not the work we do, but the way in which we do it. Two men may work side by side in the same factory or store; the one, at the end of the day, shall have put in a solid block of gold, silver, and precious stone, while the other has contributed to the fabric of his life-work an ephemeral, insubstantial addition of wood, hay, and stubble, destined to be burnt. What is the difference between the two? To the eye of man, there is none; to the eye of God much; because the one has been animated, in the lowest, commonest actions, by the lofty motive of pleasing God, and doing the day's work thoroughly and well, while the other wrought to escape blame, to secure the commendation of man, or to win a large wage. Never be ashamed of honest toil, of labors, however trivial or menial, which you can execute beneath the inspiration of noble aims; but be ashamed of the work which, though it makes men hold their breath in wonder, yet, in your heart, you know to have emanated from earthly, selfish, and ignoble aims.

Even when we were dead in sins, hath quickened us to-gether with Christ, (by grace ye are saved;)
Ephesians 2: 5

28

GOD'S love was not daunted by our sins. In the day that we were born, we were cast out in the open field, dead in trespasses and sins, and to the abhorring of our person. But He loved us even then. His great love was not diverted by the spectacle of our loathsomeness. He knew what we were, and what we should be, and how much pain and sorrow we would cost Him; but He loved us still. He foresaw our failures and backslidings, and lapses into the darkness of shadow; but none of these things were able to quench His love. So rich was He in mercy that He could afford to be prodigal of His wealth.

It is a great comfort to know that God loved us when there was nothing to attract His love; because He will not be surprised by anything He discovers in us, and He will not turn from us at those manifestations of evil which sometimes make us lose heart. He knew the worst from the first. He did not love us because we were fair, but to make us so. We cannot understand it; but since He began He will not fail nor be discouraged until He has finished His work.

As thou hast sent me into the world, even so have I also sent them into the world.
John 17: 18

29

THOUGH Jesus forsook His own interest in His human life, there were many things which were inalienable and of which He could not dispossess Himself. He knew that He had been the only Be-loved, before the world was made. He knew that He had ever been one with God, and ever would be. He knew that the love which had existed between the Father and Himself was now to be shared by a multitude that no one could number.

Though we may obliterate ourselves in our love for others, and have no thought of our own glory and honor, yet it is ours to know,

January

blessedly and increasingly, that we were chosen in Christ before the foundation of the world, that we are loved with an unchanging love, and that in Christ we are enriched unto the measure of God's unchangeable fullness. Oh! why do we not more deeply share the self-obliteration of Christ for others, that we may stand on these glorious heights beyond the reach of doubt or fear? The true mother is never fulfilled in her life until she has seen her children and children's children. So it is with Christ. It is only as He sees His joy glowing in myriads of redeemed souls, and finds His love reproduced in others, that He is fulfilled and satisfied.

30	*And to know the love of Christ, which passeth knowledge, that ye might be filled with all the fulness of God.*
	Ephesians 3: 19

CHRIST'S fullness is measureless. There is no limit to the infinite nature of our Lord. The fullness of deity is resident in Him. Only God the Father knows Him, and no other being, saint or seraph, beside. An angel with drooping wing might be imagined as reaching the furthest limit of space and beholding the last of the stars; but it is impossible to conceive of any limit whatsoever to the love, or power, or patience of Jesus. The ocean is shoreless. The height is unsearchable. The depth is bottomless. Such is Jesus that there is no common standard by which to compare Him with the greatest and noblest and eldest-created spirit in the universe of God. You might compare such a one with an aphid on a leaf, for they are alike, finite; but you cannot compare the finite and the infinite.

All that fullness is for us. We are settlers on the continent of Christ's infinite nature, and we are at liberty to go on putting back the walls of our enclosure, so as to take in an ever-growing share of our inheritance. But we need never fear that we shall reach or touch its furthest limit.

January

And ye are complete in him, which is the head of all principality and power.

Colossians 2: 10

31

WHEN we have spent a million years exploring and appropriating the fullness of Christ, we shall know as little of its real contents as the pilgrim fathers knew of the America which has reared itself on the foundations which they laid. Though our capacities to receive out of Christ's fullness were increased a thousandfold, all their need would be as regularly and constantly met as at this present hour, because the nature of God awaits to feed them, and we may count on being filled up to the measure of the fullness of God.

That measure will always be beyond us. We may therefore rest in perfect satisfaction that we cannot exhaust it; and yet we may ever strive in our poor measure to attain more nearly toward it. The Mediterranean is ever losing volume by evaporation; and yet it is always full, because it can draw by the Strait of Gilbraltar of the Atlantic. And its tidelessness may well become the emblem of the peace and restfulness of that soul which has learned the secret of taking into itself the blessedness of Jesus.

The Life of Prayer

February

1	*Enoch walked with God. . . . By faith Enoch was translated . . . ; had this testimony, that he pleased God.* Genesis 5: 22; Hebrews 11: 5

WHAT AN epitaph on this ancient saint! It is as clear-cut today as when first recorded. We know nothing of Enoch but this brief record, but it tells us everything. It was not an act or a number of acts, but a high tone of life constantly maintained. Better to walk with God every day in calm, unbroken fellowship, than to have occasional rapturous experiences succeeded by long relapses and backslidings. The Hebrew might be rendered, "Enoch walked, and continued to walk."

Be sure to go God's way. He will not walk with you in your way, but you may walk with Him in His. To this He calls you. Each moment, and especially when two or three roads diverge, look up to Him and pray, "Which way are You taking that I may walk with You?" It will not be so hard to forsake inviting paths and exciting companions if only you keep your eyes fixed on His face, and the track of His footsteps determines your road beyond hesitation or dispute.

Be sure to keep God's pace. Do not run impetuously before Him. Learn to wait His time: the minute hand as well as the hour hand must point the exact moment for action. Do not loiter behind in idleness and apathy. Be loyal and true to His ideals, and quick to obey His least commands.

Be sure to wear God's light. He is in the light; the light is His chosen symbol; it ill becomes you to wear the unfruitful works of darkness. Put them off, and put on the armor of light. Walk with Him daily in stainless robes, washed in the blood of the Lamb. Then your fellowship will be with the Father, the Son, and the Holy Spirit—maintained with the binding ties of prayer.

February

And she called the name of the Lord that spake unto her,
Thou God seest me: for she said, Have I also here looked
after him that seeth me?

Genesis 16: 13

2

LAXITY in our Christian lives has, without doubt, something to do with our past failures. As long as the bright summer sun shines into the forest, the fungus has no chance to flourish; but when the sunshine wanes, in the months of autumn, the woods are filled with these strange products of decay. It is because we drift from God that our lives are the prey of numberless and nameless ills. Make the best of all new starts, and return to the more earnest habits of earlier days, or beginning from them now, give yourself to God, believing that He will receive and welcome you, without a word of condemnation or delay.

Form habits of morning and evening prayer, especially in the morning taking time for deep communion with God. Live in His Word until He speaks to you. Join with His people in worship, and find a place of Christian service there. Depend upon the Holy Spirit to enable you, keeping you true to your new resolves, causing you to be steadfast, immovable, and set on maintaining life at a higher level. In all these ways, let the beginning of this new year witness a new start for you.

3

Then said she, Sit still, my daughter. . . .

Ruth 3: 18

THE HABIT of reckoning on Christ is the key to a restful life. Not only to depend on His promises, but also to count on himself. A good man, one of those for whom some would even dare to die, is more than his words or assurances, because a case may arise not covered by either of them, and then we can fall back on what we know him to be. Christ is more than His spoken and recorded words. Boaz, in the story of Ruth, is a picture of our Kinsman-Redeemer, Jesus Christ. Just as Boaz turned Ruth's bitterness into blessing, so Christ does for His redeemed children.

February

Is there some great perplexity in your life? Is there a lurking evil in your life, which you have tried in vain to defeat? Is there some anxiety about one dearer to you than life, who is drifting beyond your reach? Is there a yearning for all that can be realized of deliverance from sin, the filling of the Spirit, the life and love of God? Go to the great Kinsman, find Him when you can speak to Him without interruption, tell Him everything. Hand it all over to Him, then go home and sit still.

If there is anything for you to do, He will tell you what it is, and give you the grace to do it. But if not, sit still, wait patiently, quiet yourself. He cannot forget, He will not procrastinate, He cannot fail. He is allowing no grass to grow under His feet. He is making haste, though He appears to tarry. And presently at the door there will be a shout of joy. Then the bridal bells shall ring out over an accomplished purpose, and your life shall be no more Marah, but Naomi, and bitterness shall be swallowed up in blessing.

4	*. . . As Moses entered into the tabernacle . . . the Lord talked with Moses.*
	Exodus 33: 9

THE MEANING of this verse seems to be that when Moses went into the Holy Place to speak with God he became conscious of the divine Voice that opened to him the thoughts and purposes of God in such a way that he was caught up in the current and borne back to God.

This is the true conception of prayer. *We* often go to God with *our* thoughts and desires, and having uttered them we go our way. We do not wait long enough to see the cherubim and the light of the Shekinah, or hear the divine Voice. Thus our prayers fail of their answer. We do not ask what is according to the will and mind of our Heavenly Father, and the heavens seem like brass to our pleas. We have not because we ask not, or because we ask amiss. We must ask in faith, nothing wavering.

The true conception of prayer is that it originates in the purpose of God, and passes from the Father to the Son, who is also the Head and Representative of His people. From Jesus it is brought into our hearts by the blessed Spirit, who unites the Head with each member of the mystical body; and from the saints it returns to the source from which it came.

If, then, we pray aright, we should wait before God until the Holy Spirit suggests what we should pray for, and indeed begins to plead within us for the saints. Silence, solitude, waiting before God; the return to God of His own thoughts; the being burdened with the weighty matters that lie heavily on the heart of Jesus—such is the noblest kind of prayer. It is those who wait upon the Lord who renew their strength, that mount up with wings as eagles; that run and are not weary, that walk and are not faint (Isa. 40: 31).

Unto thee will I cry, O Lord my rock; be not silent to me; lest, if thou be silent to me, I become like them that go down into the pit.

Psalm 28: 1

5

OH, that God would break the silence! If He would but say one word! If we might but hear that voice—deep as the sound of many waters, and tender as the call of love—just to say that He was there; that all which we believed was true; that He was satisfied and pleased; that our perplexities would work out right at last! It is so difficult sometimes to go on living day by day without one authoritative word; and we are prone to rebuke Him for silence, that He is still, that He holds His peace. "Be not silent to me, (lest I be like those) that go down into the pit."

But God has not kept silence. The Word was manifested. In Him the silence of eternity was broken. And if you and I are still, if our ear is cleansed, and anointed with the blood and oil, if we make a great silence in our heart, we shall hear Him speak.

'Tis not where torrents are born, nor amid snowcapped peaks, nor in the break of the surf; but in the heart, weaned from itself, isolated in chambers of sickness, cast among strangers, yearning for tender voices that cannot make themselves heard—there God is no longer still. He breaks the silence. "Comfort ye, comfort ye, my people, saith your God." "It is I; be not afraid." It is always easy to detect God's voice, because it is full of Jesus, who is the Word of God, and it is corroborated by Providence; but the heart must be still, and it must be listening!

February

6	*To draw nigh to hear is better than to give the sacrifice of fools.*

Ecclesiastes 5: 1, RV

THIS IS certainly half of our business, when we kneel to pray. It is a drawing nigh to hear. One has truly said that the closet is not so much an *oratory,* in the narrow sense of making requests, as an *observatory,* from which we get new views of God, and new revelations of Him.

We are all inclined to be rash with our mouths. We run hurriedly into the presence of God, leave our card as on a morning call, and then plunge into the eager rush of life. We have spoken to Him, but we have not paused, not stayed to hear what He would say in reply. We have suggested many things to Him, but have not sought for His comments, or reactions, in return. We do not take time to fix the heart's gaze on the unseen and eternal, or to abstract our mind from the voices of the world, so as to hear the still small voice that speaks in silence and solitude.

> Only the waters which in perfect stillness lie
> Give back an undistorted image of the sky.

7	*Blessed is the man whom thou chooseth, and causest to approach unto thee, that he may dwell in thy courts: we shall be satisfied with the goodness of thy house, even of thy holy temple.*

Psalm 65: 4

I WOULD be one of those favored ones, my Savior. There is nothing that the heart can conceive, which is to be compared with this blessedness. The light of nature, the joy of friendship, the fascination of art and books, can give no such delight as this approach unto You, this dwelling in Your courts. But the longer I know myself, the surer I am that You must *cause* me to approach, that *You* must put forth extraordinary means for making me *dwell.* So cause me to approach that I may dwell.

When your soul has put up such a prayer as this, be sure that an answer will come. You may be brought nigh by an invisible but all-penetrating attraction, as when the sun draws the earth, or the magnet the needle.

It was said by the great Charles Haddon Spurgeon that he was not conscious of spending a quarter of an hour of his waking moments without a distinct recognition of the presence of God. And this will be true of us if we will trust the great High Priest to bring us within the vail, and keep us there. He entered that we may enter. He abides that we may abide. He stands in the Holiest that He may cause us to have a place of access among those who stand before the face of God. The anointing which we receive from Him will teach us how to abide. This may well be adopted as a life-prayer: "Cause me to approach, that I may dwell in thy presence."

And when he had sent the multitudes away, he went up into a mountain apart to pray. . . .
Matthew 14: 23

8

ONE DAY, when "He was praying in a certain place, one of his disciples said to him, 'Lord, teach us to pray . . .'" (Luke 11: 1). It was a wise and good request, prompted by the Savior's own practice. He did not, in the first instance, command His disciples to pray; but He gave Himself to the blessed practice of prayer, and this made them eager to learn and practice the holy art. This is the best way of inculcating new and holy habits on those who surround us. Do not begin by exhorting them; begin by living before them a life so holy, so unselfish, so consecrated and devout, that they will voluntarily approach you, saying, "Give us your secret; tell us how we may do and become as you." A holy life provides our best pulpit.

We should daily ask the Master to teach us to pray. Each time we kneel in prayer we may well preface our petitions with the sentence: "We know not what we should pray for as we ought; but by Thy Holy Spirit, Lord, teach us to pray." And probably the Lord's answer will fall into suggestions, borrowed from the form and model of prayer which He gave His disciples. It is known as the Lord's Prayer; it should be called the Disciple's Prayer.

Address prayer to the Father, through the Son. Do not be self-

February

centered in prayer; but look out on the needs of others, incorporating them in every petition—*us, we, our*. Remember, you are speaking to your Father. His honor and glory should have the first and foremost place. If you desire first the hallowing of His name, and the coming of His kingdom, all your personal needs and desires will fall easily and naturally into their place, which will be a comparatively subordinate one. You will need forgiveness as often and as regularly as your daily bread. Also, be direct and definite in prayer.

9	*Have regard for thy covenant; for the dark places of the land are full of the habitations of violence.*
	Psalm 74: 20, RSV

WHAT a striking statement! Here is a broken heart, pouring out its wail into the ear of God about His sanctuary and city. His adversaries have broken into the sacred precincts, and have hewn down its exquisitely carved work with hammer and hatchet. They were as men who lift up the hatchet against a forest of trees. There is nothing more utterly sad than the lament, "We see not our signs: there is no more any prophet; neither is there any among us that knoweth how long" (v. 9).

But from it all the suppliant rises to a climax of insistent appeal, and bids God have respect unto the covenant, made centuries before with Abraham and his seed. This was an appeal which struck right home to the heart of God. He could not deny Himself.

Here is an attitude in prayer, which can only be taken when the soul has become intimate with God, and come to close grip with Him. When every other reason has been marshalled, and every argument alleged; when still the answer tarries, and the case is desperate, then turn to God, and say, "Thou canst not run back from the terms of the covenant to which You hast pledged Yourself. This is included in the bond of agreement. I claim that You should do as You have said."

The covenant is set out at length in Hebrews 8. It will cover all the exigencies of our lives. And by Galatians 3: 14 we may also place ourselves under the provision of the threefold covenant which God ratified with Abraham. In every trial, when desiring any bless-

February

ing, when the crashing blows of the adversaries' hatchet are heard, turn to God, and say, "Have respect unto the covenant, of which Jesus is the Mediator and His blood the seal."

Show me Thy ways, O Lord; teach me Thy paths. Lead me in Thy truth, and teach me.
Psalm 25: 4, 5

10

GOD does not show us the whole plan of our life at a burst, but unfolds it to us bit by bit. Each day He gives us the opportunity of weaving a curtain, carving a peg, fashioning the metal. We know not what we do, but at the end of our life the disjointed pieces will suddenly come together, and we shall see the symmetry and beauty of the divine thought. Then we shall be satisfied. In the meantime let us believe that God's love and wisdom are doing the very best for us. In the morning ask God to show you His plan for the day in the unfolding of its events, and to give you grace to do or bear all that He may have prepared. In the midst of the day's engagements, often look up and say, "Father, is this in the plan?" At night, be still, and match your actual with God's ideal, confessing your sins and shortcomings, and asking that His will may be more perfectly done in you, even as in heaven.

Thou, Lord, art good, and ready to forgive. . . .
Psalm 86: 5

11

WE ARE blinded by sin, and cannot believe that God is *ready to forgive*. We think that we must induce Him to forgive, by tears, promises of amendment, religious observances. There is in every heart such difficulty in understanding the unwearying patience and ever-yearning love of our heavenly Father. Oh, clasp this word to your heart! Say it over and over again—"Ready to forgive, ready to forgive!" At any moment of the sad history of the prodigal, had he returned, he would have found his old father as ready to forgive as

February

on the day, too long delayed, when he did return. The only pity was that he had not come long before.

You have fallen a hundred times, and are ashamed to come to God again; it seems too much to expect that He will receive you again. But He will, for He is *ready to forgive.* You feel that your sin is aggravated, because you knew so much better; but it makes no difference to Him, He is as *ready to forgive* you now, as when you first came. You are disposed to wait a little, till your sin has become more remote, till passion has subsided, till the inscription has faded from the wall; but you might as well go at once, God is as *ready to forgive* at this moment as at any future time. You are wounding Him greatly by doubting Him. He is ready, waiting, eager to forgive. You have only to call upon Him, and you would discover the plenteousness of His mercy. How ready Jesus ever was to forgive sinners. In this way He revealed God's heart!

12	*. . . Samuel cried unto the Lord for Israel; and the Lord heard him. . . . Moses and Aaron among his priests, and Samuel among them that call upon his name; they called upon the Lord, and he answered them.*

1 Samuel 7: 9; Psalm 99: 6

EVIDENTLY those who call upon the name of God compose a separate class. There are classes of prophets, pastors, teachers; and there are the mighty wrestlers with God, whose voices are familiar sounds in the divine presence chamber. It is a high honor to be included among them who call upon His name. If you cannot find your place in any other class, perhaps it is here. Possibly you have great gifts of prayer and intercession, which you have never rightly employed, to your own great loss, and the loss of others. Do not wait for God's Angel of Providence to shut you forcibly into a lonely chamber, and compel you to use your great gift.

I had a memorable interview with the late George Muller. He told me some of his wonderful experiences in dealing with a prayer-answering God. Just before Muller died he heard of the conversion of an old man, for whom he had prayed during fifty years. May not he, and such as he, be remembered in this holy category?

Oh, to be remembered among those who call on God's name! But always bear in mind the thrice-accentuated message of this Psalm

February

(vv. 3,5,9), that God is holy. It is only as we are cleansed from all filthiness of the flesh and spirit, that we can prevail in intercessory prayer.

Out of my distress I called on the Lord.
Psalm 118: 5, RSV

13

WHAT COULD we do without the resource of prayer? When surrounded with the cords of death, and held by trouble and sorrow, what help would there be for us who avoid the methods of self-deliverance which the men of the world do not hesitate to employ, if we might not go to our knees?

Only let us never forget the immense importance of those five great "ifs"—

John 15: 7, which touches our life in Him, and His in us, in unremitted fellowship.

Matthew 18: 19, which touches our life with others, that must be clear as crystal.

Matthew 17: 20, which concerns the vigor and health of our own soul-life.

1 John 5: 14, 15, which demands that we know God well.

John 14: 14, which winnows out from prayer all that is inconsistent with the name of Jesus.

Oh, for the deep-dwelling life, spent in the secret place, where earth's voices grow faint, and God's clear. Such a life is a perpetual appeal to God's nature for help—an appeal which awakens an instant response.

And therefore will the Lord wait, that he may be gracious unto you . . . blessed are all they that wait for him.
Isaiah 30: 18

14

GOD does not show us the whole plan of our lives at a burst, but unfolds our life to us bit by bit. Each day He gives us the oppor-

February

tunity of weaving a curtain, carving a peg, fashioning the metal. We know not what we do, but at the end of our life the disjointed pieces will suddenly come together, and we shall see the symmetry and beauty of the divine thought.

God's delays are not denials; they are not neglectful nor unkind. He is waiting with watchful eye and intent for the precise moment to strike, when I can give a blessing which will be without alloy, and will flood all after life with blessings so royal, so plenteous, so divine that eternity will be too short to utter all our praise.

15	*Call upon me in the day of trouble; I will deliver thee. . . .*
	Psalm 50: 15

TROUBLE such as Israel passed through in the Exodus comes but once in the history of a nation. From the brick-kilns and treasure-cities which they built, God's people called to Him with strong cryings and tears, extorted by unendurable sorrows. Still more did they need to cry for help when they stood between the Egyptians and the waters of the Red Sea. From the beach a nation's call rose to God. This was their day of trouble and heart-travail—a nation in throes of pain! Are you in trouble? Call upon God in the day of trouble; He will answer.

God's answers are often in the secret place of thunder (Exod. 19: 19). From his pavilion of cloud God spoke in tones of thunder that pealed over the heavily-breaking surf of the Red Sea. Several of the Psalms allude to the thunderstorm that rolled through the night of the passage through the deep. The march of Israel was to the roll of thunder. The peals of heaven's artillery struck dismay into the hearts of the alien; but it was as though the Father was speaking to His children, the people with whom He had His covenant.

God's answer to our prayer is often in thunder-tones that hurtle through the air. By terrible things in righteousness He answers us. When Jesus asked the Father to glorify His name, the quiet reply was, "I have . . . and will"; while He understood it, it sounded like thunder to the bystanders. Happy the child who in thunder-claps

February

detects the Father's voice, and in mystic characters of flame reads the Father's handwriting! While, at Sinai, the people trembled at the repeated thunder-peals reverberating above them, Moses went into the thunder-covert where God was. There is no fear in love, because perfect love casteth out the fear that gives torment.

They which receive abundance of grace and of the gift of righteousness shall reign in life by one, Jesus Christ.
Romans 5: 17

16

DO YOU reign in life? If not, the reason may be that you do not distinguish between *praying* and *taking*. There is a profound difference between praying for a thing and appropriating it. You may admit God's abundant grace is near you through Jesus Christ, and yet you may not quite see the necessity of learning how to take. Some people are always telegraphing heaven for God to send a cargo of blessing to them; but they are not at the dock to unload the blessing when it comes. How many of God's richest blessings for which you have been praying for years have come right close to you, but you do not know how to lay hold and use them? Notice— "they which *receive* the abundance of grace shall reign." The emphasis is not on grace, not on abundance, but on *receiving* it. The whole grace of God may be around you today, but if you have not learned to take it in, it will do you no good.

17

[Jesus said] ... men ought always to pray.
Luke 18: 1

WE SHOULD pray *at all seasons*. Prayer is never out of place. There is no conceivable circumstance in life where it would be inappropriate to pray. At a wedding or a funeral; as we begin our work or finish it; whether the wind blows from the cold north or the balmy south—it is wise and right to pray.

We should pray *in the Spirit* (Eph. 6: 18). It is well in prayer to

February

wait until the scum of our own choice and desire has passed off, that the yearnings of the Holy Spirit may rise and manifest themselves. We need to be in the Spirit, not only on the Lord's day, but always, that He may be mightily in us, teaching us the will of God.

We should pray *unselfishly*. "For all saints," said Paul, and "for me" (Eph. 6: 18). We should *watch*. Stand at God's door until He opens. Be on the alert. Wait on the watchtower. Many of God's ships pass in the night, and many of His gifts arrive at the wharf when those to whom they were consigned are asleep or gone.

We should *persevere*. God keeps us waiting that He may test and humble us, and know what is in our hearts. Delays are His winnowing fan, discriminating between the chaff and the wheat. What we asked so vehemently we did not ask wisely. When we pray according to his heart, He graciously sustains us. Persevere; you do not know how near you are to the blessing you have sought for years.

18	*And when he putteth forth his own sheep, he goeth before them, and the sheep follow him: for they know his voice.*

John 10: 4

DO YOU need guidance as to your path? Look unto Jesus; it is always possible to discern His form, though partially veiled in mist; and when it is lost, be sure to stand still until He comes back to find and re-establish the blessed connection. Do not look to impressions which often contradict one another, which rise and fall with variable fickleness, and are like eddies upon a flowing current; do not seek for guidance from friends who will differ from each other, and no two of which will give the same advice on the same grounds, but look away to Christ; throw on Him the responsibility of making you know the way you are to take; leave it to Him to make it so abundantly clear that you cannot do other than follow; even tell Him that you will stand still until He puts His arms under you, and carries you where He would have you be. Do not get anxious or flurried. Put the government of your life upon His shoulder, and leave Him to execute His plan.

February

Jesus answered him [Peter], Wilt thou lay down thy life for my sake? Verily, verily, I say unto thee, The cock shall not crow, till thou hast denied me thrice.

John 13: 38

19

PETER had made four mistakes. He miscalculated the might of the tempter. He had no conception of what the Adversary could do at his worst. It is a fatal mistake for any general to miscalculate or underrate the power of his opponents.

He miscalculated his own strength and relied upon the fervor of his emotion. He underestimated his need for that strengthening of the will and energizing of the spirit which fall within the province of the Holy Spirit, and are due to the grace of the risen Christ. It is not possible for mere human enthusiasm to sustain the soul, when it comes to close grips with the power of Satan.

He miscalculated the weapon by which to overcome. Beneath his upper garment he had a literal sword, and thought that when the hour came for conflict, that would be enough for him. We, too, have failed in this area. We have been enthused as we have chanted our battle songs, we have brandished the cold steel of strong resolve, crying as we did so, "Never again will we fail." And then the disillusioning processes set in, and we have sorrowfully proved that it is not by flesh and blood that a man can enter the kingdom.

He miscalculated the help that comes through prayer. So confident was he that he slept in the garden instead of praying. Three times the Lord came to remind them of the urgent need for watching, but His words were unheeded. Then the crash came, and Peter three times denied his Lord. Only after sorrow and repentance was he restored.

And they continued stedfastly . . . in prayers. . . . We will give ourselves continually to prayer. . . .

Acts 2: 42; 6: 4

20

THE DISCIPLES seem to have lived always in the atmosphere and attitude of prayer, doing all things as unto the Lord. But they rightly

February

felt that they should devote themselves more to prayer and less to the more "mundane" aspects of the early church. So they sought a division of labor that some might devote themselves to serving tables and ministering the alms, others might be free to devote themselves to prayer. This would keep the lines of communication open to heaven, drawing down its blessing and power, and would be the means of procuring strength and wisdom for their great responsibilities.

There are many courses of usefulness open to each of us in this world, and we must choose the one, not only most suited to our abilities and gifts, but in which we can best serve our day and generation. It may be that in our incessant activities we are neglecting the one method by which we may contribute most largely to the coming of our Father's kingdom. Notice that one word, "Give." It is as though the spirit of prayer were seeking natures so pure, so devoted, that without hindrance He might form Himself into them. Give yourself to Him for this!

"In that day," said our Lord, speaking of the day of Pentecost, "ye shall ask in my name." It is only when we are full of the Holy Spirit that we can experience the true power to plead with God, and use the name of Christ so effectively as to receive the richest blessings for ourselves and others. Much prayer; much blessing. Little prayer; little blessing. No prayer; no blessing. Give yourself to prayer!

21

. . . continuing instant in prayer.

Romans 12: 12

STONEWALL Jackson was once asked what he meant when he used the expression "instant in prayer." He replied, "I will give you my idea of an illustration, if you will allow it, and not think I am setting myself up as a model for others." On being assured that there would be no misjudgment, he went on to say: "I have so fixed the habit in my own mind that I never raise a glass of water to my lips without a moment's asking God's blessing. I never seal a letter with-

February

out putting a word of prayer under the seal. I never take a letter from the post without a brief sending of my thoughts heavenward. I never change my classes without a minute's petition on the cadets who go out and those who come in." "And don't you sometimes forget this?" "I think I can say that I scarcely do; the habit has become almost as fixed as breathing."

And if this was the habit of the servant, how much more of the Master? In the Gospels we are frequently told of his heavenward look: "... looking up to heaven, he blessed ..." (Matt. 14: 19). It was as though he were always looking up for his Father's smile, direction, and benediction; so that He could be assured that what He was engaged in was in the line of His Father's purpose, and that He might gain the needed power to act and wisdom to speak.

It is only thus that we shall be able to meet the hunger of our times. Our slender stores will not feed so great a multitude. But if we bring them to Him, and place them in His hands, and look up to heaven for His enablement, we shall break and break again until all be filled. But this habit can only be maintained by those who go into the mountain of prolonged fellowship.

Now unto him that is able to do exceeding abundantly above all that we ask or think, according to the power that worketh in us.

Ephesians 3: 20

22

IN THIS marvelous doxology the Apostle seems to have come to the limits of human speech, though not of thought or conception. Here the two seem to be on the point of parting company. The speech remains below, while the thought goes forth on its glorious way.

Paul had a wonderful glimpse of what God would do in answer to prayer. For notice—the power of God *without* is always commensurate with his power that works *within*. It is the same Greek word in each case. He is able to do exceedingly abundantly above our prayer or thought, according to the power that worketh in us. As lofty and overwhelming as the mountains are, it is probable that the depth below us is equal to the heights above us. So the power of God that waits to answer prayer in yonder heights, is equivalent

February

to the power of God the Holy Spirit, who makes intercession for us with groanings that cannot be uttered.

23	*And take the helmet of salvation and the sword of the Spirit, which is the Word of God.*

Ephesians 6: 17

HE IS equally necessary in service and in prayer. In conflict with Satan, whether in our experience or in the attempt to rescue souls from his accursed bondage, there is no weapon so useful as the Spirit's sword which is the Word of God. Our blessed Lord parried the devil's attacks by "It is written"; and we shall not improve on his method. The armor of the enemy is impenetrable to all blades save that which has been forged in the celestial fires of the Holy Spirit.

"Praying always with all prayer and supplication in the Spirit, and watching thereunto with all perseverance and supplication for all saints" (Eph. 6: 18). And if you would acquire the habit of intercessory and earnest prayer, so as to be able to watch thereunto and to persevere, pouring out supplications and entreaties, you can only do so in the Spirit. He alone can teach this holy art, or give this eager temper of soul, or perpetuate its practice. Let us earnestly seek it at His hand; for there is nothing that so refuses or ennobles, purifies or strengthens the Spirit, as this constant breathing out of prayer and breathing in of the fullness of God.

24	*No unclean person . . . hath any inheritance in the kingdom of Christ and of God.*

Ephesians 5: 5

IT WAS very easy for the Israelite (and for us) to become unclean without realizing it. To touch a corpse, to be in the same room as the

February

dead, to stumble over a grave, was enough to defile the Israelite and excommunicate him from the Tabernacle with its holy rites. Could anything more graphically set forth the contagiousness of sin? We cannot be in contact with those who are dead in trespasses and sins, or breathe air defiled by their filthy speech, or read books which contain their thoughts, without suffering in some way by it.

This is the reason why, at the end of the day, we often feel unable to pray, or hold fellowship with God; we are excluded from the most holy place, because of this defilement. Indeed there is only one way of escaping it, and that is in being covered, hermetically sealed, by the Spirit of God. "In whom ye were sealed unto the day of redemption" (Eph. 4: 30, RV).

For this reason also, we should perpetually seek fresh cleansing in the precious blood of Christ. He is represented in the heifer without spot, slain in its prime, whose ashes were mingled in running water to testify of their perpetual efficacy and freshness. If the ashes of the heifer availed for the purifying of the flesh, how much more shall the blood of Christ cleanse our consciences! Ask perpetually for the sprinkling of the blood of Jesus Christ, that you may have access with confidence into the Most Holy Place. Let us apply the ashes and the water of purification to each other. Jesus said: "If I then, your Lord and Master, have washed your feet, ye also ought to wash one another's feet" (John 13: 14).

Praying always with all prayers and supplication in the Spirit, and watching thereunto with all perseverance and supplication for all saints.
Ephesians 6: 18

25

THE CHRISTIAN warrior must use the two essential means of grace—the Word of God and prayer. Add to all the above the diligent use of the Word of God in our souls in the preparation of our words to others, and in dealing with the consciences of those with whom we come in contact. Let there be besides the perpetual use of the weapon of all-prayer, and there is no enemy born of hell that will be able to withstand us. We in the feebleness of human weakness, are strong in the Lord, and in the power of His might.

February

Daily meditate on your union with the ascended Lord. Reckon that in Him you have died to sin. Present your tempted members as instruments of righteousness unto Christ—and yours will be a course of unbroken victory.

26	*. . . Without ceasing I have remembrance of thee in my prayers night and day.*
	2 Timothy 1: 3

WE ARE to pray without ceasing; always praying, never fainting; asking, seeking, knocking. But there are some subjects concerning which God says, "Speak no more unto me of this" (Deut. 3: 26). In some cases these topics have to do with others, but more often with ourselves as in the case of the Apostle Paul when he asked for the "thorn" to be removed from him (2 Cor. 12: 9).

It is an awful thing when God says of certain individuals, "Ephraim is joined to idols; let him alone" (Hos. 4: 17); and when the conviction is wrought within us that the sin unto death has been committed, concerning which the apostle John said, "I do not say that he should pray for it." Such times come only rarely; so long as you feel able to pray for another, so long as no negative command has been given, you may be sure that God waits to be entreated, and that your prayer will assuredly be answered.

But have you not realized at times that God has said about some earthly boon you were craving, "Child, do not ask Me more"? He goes on, "I know what you want, and what is best for you. Seek first my kingdom, and all these things, literally or their equivalent, shall be added unto you." It is well when we have been praying eagerly, to allow God's winnowing fan to pass over our petitions, to winnow away all that is not in His mind to give, so that only those desires may remain which His Spirit has indicted, and which He is therefore pledged to bestow. If He does not give the exact thing you ask, He will give the Pisgah view (Deut. 3: 27) and more grace. He will say to you as He did to Paul, "My grace is sufficient for you; for my strength is made perfect in weakness."

February

The effectual fervent prayer of a righteous man availeth much.

27

James 5: 16

WHERE WE go wrong in prayer is that we are so self-willed. We set ourselves to pray for things; we vow to pray all night to bring God around to our way of thinking; we use strong cryings, tears, and protestations; we endeavor to work ourselves into a frame of faith; we think we believe; we shut the doors of our heart against the tiniest suggestion or suspicion that we do not believe. And then we are surprised if the fig tree does not wither, or the mountain remove. "Jesus answered and said unto them, Verily I say unto you, If ye have faith, and doubt not, ye shall not only do this which is done to the fig tree, but also if ye say unto this mountain, Be thou removed, and be thou cast into the sea; it shall be done" (Matt. 21: 21).

Where are we wrong? It is not hard to see. There is too much of self and the energy of the flesh in all this. We can only believe for a thing when we are in such union with God that His thought and purpose can freely flow into us, suggesting what we should pray for, and leading us to that point in which there is a perfect sympathy and understanding between us and the divine mind. Faith is always the product of such a frame as this. Be sure that you are on the line of God's purpose. Wait for Him till the impulses of nature have subsided, and the soul is hushed and still. Then the Spirit will lead you to ask what is in the will of God to give, and you will know instantly that the Spirit intercedes within you according to the will of God.

But let him ask in faith, nothing wavering. . . .

28

James 1: 6

CONCEIVE of all that the saints have thought. Imagine the unspoken prayers of the saints. Things that could not be uttered because speech failed; thoughts that had flashed back and forth

February

between the Father and His children, like love glances between those who can read each other's heart through the eyes. But God who inspired them, was able to do exceedingly abundantly above all.

He is not stingy in his gifts, begrudging us our measure, just coming to the brink of our emptiness. Where sin abounds His grace abounds much more. He not only feeds our hunger, but gives us twelve baskets full of fragments over and above.

Ask great things of Him, His work and His world; and believe that He will far exceed your furthest reach of desire. Your least word will stir and bring down a blessing, mighty as an avalanche, but soft as a summer rain.

| 29 | *Elias was a man subject to like passions as we are, and he prayed earnestly that it might not rain: and it rained not on the earth by the space of three years and six months.*
James 5: 17 |

WHEN WE read that Elijah was a man subject to the same passions as we, we are apt to suppose that here lies the driving force of his life. But the scripture makes it clear that it was not his passion, but his prayer which achieved the wonderful results. He prayed earnestly that it might not, or that it might, rain, and his prayers had power over the very course of Nature.

We need have no difficulty in accepting the fact of this great miracle. One commentator says that he can see no difference between a man asking a fellow man to water his lawn than to ask God to send rain. In each case the will of a man must operate on the will of another; and if it can operate on the will of man, why should it not operate also on the will of our heavenly Father? This, however, is not the main thought before us, but that Elijah, though capable of the same earnestness with which we are all endowed, refused to accomplish his life work by the employment of these lower energies. Rather, he set himself to obtain the results he sought through prayer. He was a man of like passions with ourselves, but he prayed earnestly. He turned his passion into prayer.

Discipleship—
The Life of the Learner

March

The Lord had said unto Abram, Get thee out of thy country . . . unto a land that I will shew thee. . . . So Abram departed, as the Lord had spoken unto him.

Genesis 12: 1,4

1

ABRAHAM, as this passage shows, first met the call of God with a mingled and partial obedience; and then for long years neglected it entirely. But the door still stood open for him to enter, and that gracious hand still beckoned him, until he struck his tents and started to cross the mighty desert with all that he owned. Sarah may have been broken down with bitter regrets, but Abraham did not falter. He staggered not through unbelief. "He was fully persuaded that what God had promised, he was able also to perform."

Moreover, already some glimpses of the "city which hath foundations" and of the "better country, the heavenly," had loomed upon his vision; and that fair sight had loosened his hold upon much which otherwise would have fascinated and fastened him.

Ah, glorious faith! This is your work, these are your possibilities! —contentment to sail with sealed orders, because of unwavering confidence in the love and wisdom of the Lord High Admiral; willingness to arise up, leave all, and follow Christ because of the glad assurance that *earth's best cannot bear comparison with heaven's least.*

And the priest shall cast salt upon them, and they shall offer them up for a burnt offering unto the Lord.

Ezekiel 43: 24

2

ALWAYS distinguish between salt and acid. Acid corrodes, burns, kills. Salt smarts, heals, saves. Some rejoice in what they call plain speaking; but they forget to speak the truth in love, and are like a

March

physician who goes around with wholesome but nauseous medicine, and whenever he sees a mouth open pours some down. It is necessary to wash the saint's feet; but be sure you do not do it with scalding water. If you have to tell men that they are enemies of the cross of Christ, do it with weeping. Let it be evident that you have no axe to grind, no selfish end to serve, no grudge to pay, when you rebuke others by life or word for things which ought not to pass unnoticed.

Salt may lose its savor. Housewives will tell you that if it is allowed to get damp, it will lose its taste and become quite useless. So we may lose all power of arresting sin because of one act of inconsistency or some secret sin, which produces indecision in our manner. We can be like Lot who remonstrated with the men of Sodom and urged his children to escape, but was tarred too deeply with the same brush for men to heed. Let us live daily such straight, strong, pure, noble lives that evil may be ashamed in our presence and slink away. Whatever you do, keep your savor.

3	*Fret not thyself because of evildoers, neither be thou envious against the workers of iniquity.*
	Psalm 37: 1

THE LAW for Christian living is not backward, but forward, not for experiences that lie behind, but for doing the will of God, which is always ahead and beckoning us to follow. On each new height to which we attain, there are the appropriate joys that befit the new experience. Leave the things that are behind, and reach forward to those that are before.

An old legend says that as Eve was leaving Eden she plucked a flower to take with her as a memento of its unfading loveliness; it withered, however, as she passed the garden gate. But she came upon other flowers that grew wild, or came of careful cultivation, that were as fair and fairer; and was not the face of her first-born son more bewitching in beauty than any flower picked from the soil of Paradise?

When we are weak and weary God throws bunches of flowers into our laps; but as we grow stronger, He weans us from the dear

March

delights of earlier years, and puts on a stronger regimen. Do not resemble a babe crying for its mother's breast. This is one of the childish things which we must put away, as we enter upon our maturer life; but, of course, the child cannot forecast the fruits and meats which are in store and will make it look askance at the milk that once seemed all-important. Don't fret because life's joys are fled. There are more in front. Look up, press forward, it is better on before!

Behold, thou desirest truth in the inward parts; and in the hidden part thou shalt make me to know wisdom.
                                                    Psalm 51: 6

| 4 |

BE TRUE in your opinions. We are likely to be warped in our opinions by considerations of what is popular, expedient, and likely to commend us to our fellows. The statesman is sorely tempted to listen to the wire-pullers of his party, the slogans of his constituency, the leading of some popular opinion-shaper, and to allow these to divert him from the path of conviction and conscience. How often have men like Pilate been led to act against their clear judgment by the insistence and fear of the mob. Like waves of the sea, they are driven by the winds and tossed. Like the weather-vane, they move around with the least puff of breeze. This is especially the temptation of religious leaders, who are assailed by many voices, such as, will it pay? Will it attract people, or alienate them? Will it be popular or the reverse? Life is pitiable indeed when such considerations have to be balanced.

Of course, we must speak the truth in *love*. Some seem to think that truthfulness, of necessity, involves rudeness and ruggedness of speech. But this need not be. The King of Truth was also the Good Shepherd, whose words were music, whose ways were mercy as well as truth, and whose glory comprised, in equal proportions, truth and grace.

March

<table>
<tr><td>5</td><td>Fret not thyself because of evil men, neither be thou envious at the wicked.</td></tr>
</table>

Proverbs 24: 19

FRET NOT because the future seems dark. After all, the troubles you anticipate may never really befall. It is a long lane without a turning. The dreariest day has some glint of light. How do you know that some spell of good fortune may not be about to befall you? In any case, worrying will not mend the matter. It can alter neither the future nor the past, though it will materially affect your power for bearing it. It will not rob tomorrow of its difficulties, but will rob your brain of its clear-sightedness and your heart of its courage. Turn from it to God with faith and prayer and look out for the one or two patches of blue which are in every sky. And if you cannot discover any where you are, dare to anticipate the time when God shall wipe away all tears, and give you a kiss like that which a mother gives to her tired, sobbing child who is too weary to go off to sleep.

<table>
<tr><td>6</td><td>My soul clings to thee; thy right hand upholds me.</td></tr>
</table>

Psalm 63: 8, RSV

THIS IS a marvelous saying. Literally rendered, the words are, "cleaves after thee"—contact and eager pursuit. The metaphor which underlies it is obviously borrowed from the psalmist's familiarity with the wilderness. It is a dry and thirsty land, where no water is: one says that he knows of a secret spring, whose waters are clear and cool, and offers to lead the thirsty one to its margin, lined with mosses and grasses. Instantly the soul starts in pursuit, and follows hard on the footsteps of the pioneer. "My soul followeth hard after thee. . . ."

So when we are athirst for God, He comes, and, in the person of Jesus, leads us to Himself. He is Guide and Gain, Prompter of the impulse, and Promoter of its satisfaction. He excites the desire, offers to show us its sufficient supply, and finally brings us to His own lovingkindness, which is better than life.

And they compel one Simon, a Cyrenian, who passed by, coming out of the country, the father of Alexander and Rufus, to bear his cross.

Mark 15: 21

7

IF WE MAY listen from the familiar way in which Mark speaks of the sons of this Cyrenian, whom the soldiers brutally compelled to carry our Savior's cross, we should assume that from this hour Simon became a Christian. He had little suspected such a thing in the early morning, when he left his lodging to attend to his business; but, being compelled to go to Calvary, he lingered there voluntarily through those anxious hours, and was led to feel that such a Sufferer, to whom even Nature paid such worship, was worthy henceforth to receive his loyalty.

But how many of us are carrying our cross because we are compelled to do so? There seems no alternative but to carry the dead weight of our cross with us everywhere, only wishing a hundred times each day that we might have release. Dear Christian friend, that cross is yet going to be the greatest blessing of your life if it leads you to the Crucified, and you find in Him what will transform your cross into the ladder which links earth with heaven, swaying beneath angel tread.

If Simon became a Christian, with what rapture must he have reviewed that incident in his life! How easy it would have been to carry the cross had he known Jesus as he came to know Him afterwards! He would have needed no compelling! So if you saw the will of Jesus in your cross, and that you were carrying it with Him, how much easier it would be! But that is so. He is in it. Bear it with Him; out of the cross will fall a shower of flowers.

There is no such thing as chance in our lives. It might have seemed mere chance that Simon was coming into Jerusalem at that moment. It was shown, however, to be part of the Eternal counsel. Dare to believe in the divine purpose which orders your cross.

March

8	*Salt is good: but if the salt have lost his savour, wherewith shall it be seasoned?*

Luke 14: 34

IT IS A sad comment on society that it needs salt. You do not think of salting life, but death, to keep it from rotting. This, then, was Christ's verdict on the society of His time. It had enjoyed the benefit of all the Greek intellectualism and Roman government could effect, and yet was like a carcass on the point of putrefaction. But is not this the state of all society, from which religion is banished, or where it has become a system of rites and dogmas? Go into any large factory or financial institution, or a tavern, where men feel able to talk freely, and there is too often the smell of the barnyard in the stories that pass around, and the jokes that pass from lip to lip.

Here is something that each of us can do. Perhaps we cannot speak: we cannot shed a far-reaching ray of light to warn from the black rocks, and guide to harbor: we seem shut away from the scenes of important Christian activity, but we can be good salt, checking the evil which would otherwise infect the air of our world, and breed disease in young and healthy lives.

9	*Called unto the fellowship of his Son Jesus Christ our Lord.*

1 Corinthians 1: 9

THE WORD for *fellowship* here is the same as that employed in Luke 5: 10, of James and John being *partners* with Simon. We have been called into partnership with the Son of God, in His redemptive purposes, His love and tears for men, and ultimately in His triumph and glory. He has entered into partnership with man, and we are now summoned into partnership with Him through the communion of the Holy Ghost. In the words of the Apostle, "our fellowship [or partnership] is with the Father, and with his Son Jesus Christ our Lord."

How fruitful of comfort is the thought that Christ's interests are ours, and that we are at liberty to draw upon His resources to the uttermost. Suppose a poor clerk were to be summoned from his desk into the office of a Rothschild, and informed that from that moment he was taken into partnership with the firm: would it not be less of an honor than this which has been offered to us? Association with a millionaire in money-making is infinitely less desirable than association with the Son of God in world-saving. And would that poor clerk feel any anxiety as to his share in meeting the immense liabilities of the concern? However great they might be, he would know that the resources of the firm were adequate, and he would be able to sleep easily at night, though millions were due on the morrow. Child of God, cannot your Father meet all His Son's commitments?

This call to partnership is from the Father. It is He who has chosen us for this high honor of cooperating with His Son. Will He have led us into such an association, and leave us to be overwhelmed by the difficulties of the situation He has created? It cannot be! He will supply all our need.

They that make them are like unto them. . . .
Psalm 135: 18

10

THAT MEN become like their ideals is a commonplace; and that the heathen resemble their deities is notorious. Men first impute to their deities their own vices, as the Greeks and Romans to the gods and goddesses of their Pantheon; and then endeavor to honor them by imitation.

But, in another sense, this is gloriously true of our relation to the Lord Jesus. If we make Him our ideal, and trust Him with all our hearts, His beauty shall dawn upon our face, and we shall be changed into His image, from glory to glory. We know that when He shall be revealed finally, we shall be like Him, for we shall see Him as He is; and, in a measure, this process of transformation is taking place in those who see Him by the eye of faith, and are becoming like Him.

March

We are doing more by our life than by our words. We cannot always speak for Jesus, but we may always live for Him. I was told the other day of a young girl, lately gone forth as a missionary, who cannot speak a word of the language of the foreign land to which she has gone. Her life or rather the life of Jesus in her, was exerting a far wider influence than she knew. This is the divine method: look and live; trust and be transfigured; abide in Him, and He shall abide in you.

Auskar, a missionary to the Scandinavians in the ninth century, when asked if he could perform miracles, replied: "If God were indeed to grant that power to me, I would only ask that I might exhibit the miracle of a holy life." But this is the most difficult of all. It is easier to die once for Jesus, than to live always for Him. Yet God's grace is sufficient. He will keep us as stars in His right hand.

11

Make love your aim. . . .

1 Corinthians 14: 1, RSV

WHAT A LIGHT must have shone on the Apostle's face as he concluded this exquisite idyll, this perfect poem of love (1 Cor. 13). The change in tone and rhythm must have caused his amanuensis to look suddenly up into his master's face, and lo! it was as the face of an angel when he exalted, "The greatest of these is love" (1 Cor. 13: 13). Why is love greatest?

Because it crowns the other two, and includes them.—Faith is the root; hope is the stem; love the perfect flower. You may have faith without hope, and hope without love; but you cannot have love apart from faith and hope.

Because it is most like God.—God's nature is not specially characterized by faith, because there is no uncertainty with His perfect knowledge; nor by hope, because there is no future to His eternal existence. But God is love; and to love is to resemble Him.

Because it will immeasurably outlast the other two.—Human knowledge, at best but the spellings of babes, will vanish in the perfect light of heaven. Eloquence will seem like the lispings of infancy.

March

Prophecies will have no place, because all the landscape of the future will be revealed. Faith and hope will be lost in realization. Love only is forever.

Because love brings the purest rapture.—"Where is heaven?" asked a wealthy Christian of his minister. "I will tell you where it is," was the quick reply: "if you will go to the store, and buy $100.00 worth of provisions and necessaries, and take them to that poor widow on the hillside, who has three of her children sick. She is poor, and a member of the church. Take a nurse, and someone to cook the food. When you get there, read the twenty-third Psalm, and kneel by her side and pray. Then you will find out where heaven is."

. . . In the wilderness shall waters break out, and streams in the desert.

Isaiah 35: 6

12

DESERT means *uninhabited*. It seemed a strange providence that took Philip to such an area (Acts 8: 26). He had been chosen to the honorable office of deacon, and there was probably plenty of work to do in connecting the scattered church. Moreover, Philip had just completed a most successful mission in Samaria, where the multitude had listened attentively to the things he had spoken; but now he was suddenly landed in a lonely desert, where only chance travelers could be encountered. Did he count it strange, and wish to get home to his four little daughters (Acts 21: 9)?

There are many deserts in life! The solitude of a new country, in which you do not know the language. The solitude of a sick-chamber, in which the earnest worker suddenly discovers the limitations of physical weakness. The solitude of small suspicion and dislike, which contrasts strangely with some large and devoted circle. God often brings us to such places. No flower can thrive in unbroken light.

But in every solitude, if we wait patiently on the Lord, there are opportunities of service. There is always some inquiring soul in need of the precise help we can give. There is an old story of some

March

monks to whom the Book of Revelation was being read. At the end each was asked to choose the promise he loved best. One said I will take this, "God shall wipe away all tears." Another chose, "To him that overcometh I will give to sit on my throne." The third replied, "I would choose, 'His servants shall serve Him.'" This latter was Thomas à Kempis, who afterwards wrote *The Imitation of Christ*.

13	*And lest I should be exalted above measure . . . there was given me a thorn in the flesh. . . .*
	2 Corinthians 12: 7

WE NEED not discuss the nature of Paul's thorn in the flesh. It is enough that he calls it "a stake," as though he had been impaled. It must have, therefore, been very painful. It must also have been physical, because he could not have prayed thrice for the removal of a moral taint, and been refused. It came from Satan, permitted by God, as in the case of Job, to buffet his servant. It is not unlikely that he suffered from weak eyes, or some distressing form of ophthalmia; hence the eagerness of the Galatian converts to give him their eyes (see Gal. 4: 15).

God does not take away our thorns, but He communicates sufficient grace. He always answers prayer, though not as we expect. Let the music of these tender words reach you, poor sufferer! "My grace is sufficient even for thee" (2 Cor. 12: 9). This promise is immediately followed by Paul's burst of praise: "When I am weak, then am I strong" (2 Cor. 12: 10). Sufficient when friends forsake, and foes pursue; sufficient to make you strong against an infuriated crowd and a tyrannical judge; sufficient for excessive physical exertion and spiritual conflict; sufficient to enable you to do as much work, and even more, than if health and vigor were not impaired, because the very weakness of our nature is the chosen condition under which God will manifest the strength of His.

Do not sit down before that mistaken marriage, that uncongenial business, that physical weakness, as though all life must be a failure; but take in large reinforcements of that divine grace which is given to the weak and to those who have no might. It is clear that Paul had reached such a condition, that it was a matter of deep congratulation to him to be deficient in much that men hold dear, and to have what most men dread. He rejoiced in all that diminished creature-might and strengthened his hold on God.

Thou art Peter, and upon this rock I will build my church; and the gates of hell shall not prevail against it.
Matthew 16: 18

14

WHAT A WONDER it is that Satan and man do not prevail against the saint! There is no way of accounting for it, except in God's election. Because God has chosen us for Himself, and redeemed us at great cost, He cannot afford to hand us over to the will of our enemies. He may allow our backs to be furrowed by the heavy scourge, because the servant must be as his Lord; but He will cut our cords in the day selected for our execution, and let us go free from the hand of our foes. So it was with Peter, and many a time with Paul.

Let us then walk with God. Fellowship with Him should be the daily bread of our souls. If we cultivate the fresh sense of fellowship with Him, we shall not yield to fear, be our foes never so venomous and their plans ever so insidious. A close walk with God is the sure way of escaping them. "The man of God sent unto the king of Israel, saying, Beware that thou pass not such a place; and the king of Israel sent to the place that the man of God told him and warned him of; and he saved himself not once nor twice."

This daily fellowship is only possible through the blood of Jesus, by which we draw nigh unto God; and it can only be maintained by constant watchfulness in little things. "Let us be very zealous over ourselves for the Lord, watching against the least shyness between the soul and Himself. Where there is much love between friends, a cold look is a matter of complaint." When least inclined to pray, we need to pray the more. When least conscious of Christ's nearness, we need to be most eager, like the old covenanter, to wrestle for access. If the King has not sent for you these many days, await Him in his court.

March

<table>
<tr><td>

15

</td><td>

And when it was day, he called unto him his disciples: and of them he chose twelve, whom also he named apostles.

Luke 6: 13

</td></tr>
</table>

THREE circles surrounded our Lord. The outer circle consisted of people who came to be healed in spirit or in body. They looked upon Him as the great miracle-worker, but had no more thought of Him than as a healer. Our Lord never rebuked them, nor did He send them away unhealed. In this He was the forerunner of the healing ministries of the church today.

The second circle consisted of His disciples. This second circle includes the largest segment of the Christian church today. These are people who go part way with the Lord, but not all the way. They listen to His Beatitudes and other principles. They accept His forgiveness of sin, and listen to His answers to the questions of life.

There is, however, a third circle. Out of the disciples He chose some to be apostles. These were disciples who began by learning, but after a while they were sent forth to teach. During the first years of our apprenticeship, we are learners. But then we as disciples become apostles, chosen to go out as His instruments to achieve His eternal purposes. Election is not primarily to salvation but to service; we are not elect that we may be sheltered from the destroying angel, but that we may go forth to teach men the law and love of God, and bring the world into captivity to the obedience of Christ.

<table>
<tr><td>

16

</td><td>

Notwithstanding, lest we should offend them, go thou to the sea and cast an hook, and take up the fish that first cometh up; and when thou hast opened his mouth, thou shalt find a piece of money; that take, and give unto them for me and thee.

Matthew 17: 27

</td></tr>
</table>

PETER, to whom Jesus spoke these words, had been fairly well-to-do. He had his house, boats, and nets. Whenever the tax-gatherer came to them in those days, Peter's wife had always the necessary coin waiting for him. There was no lack in the fisherman's house. But when Jesus said, "Come after Me," Peter had to leave all, and there was an immediate cutting off of the former sources of supply, so that when the tax-gatherer came there was nothing to meet his demand.

Our Lord argued that He personally was under no obligation to meet the call of the tax-gatherer. As a child, to use His own words, He was free; but He immediately identified Himself, as He always does, with His harassed disciple. We can never leave anything for Christ, without His recognition, and His being ready to defray whatever cost may accrue from obedience; and so, knowing that Peter could no longer help himself, our Lord brought the needed coin from the depth of the lake.

Then they shall understand the lovingkindness of the Lord.
Psalm 107: 43

17

THE HARVEST of a Quiet Eye is the fascinating title of a fascinating book. When the heart is quiet in God, the eye looks out on the scenes of nature and life around it, and detects everywhere, even where to ordinary men every appearance seems in the contrary direction, the loving kindness of the Lord. As life advances, and one climbs the hill, one is able to review the path by which life has been directed and controlled. We observe with the wisdom which we have obtained by long experience, and we understand God's reasons for many rebuffs, denials, and bitter disappointments. I believe that we shall one day turn to Him, and say, when we know all, "Thou couldst not have done otherwise. We would not have wished otherwise."

Consider the successive vignettes of this psalm. Love broods over the weary caravan that faints in the desert; visits the prison house with its captives; watches by our beds of pain; notices each lurch of the tempest-driven vessel; brings the weary hosts from the wilderness into the fruitful soil.

Love is quick to appreciate love. It is natural to a loving heart to find love everywhere. We view all things in hues borrowed from the heart. "He that loveth knoweth God, for God is love; he that loveth

March

not hath not seen him, neither known him." Ask therefore for a baptism unto the love of God—this will make you quick to perceive and understand his lovingkindness, where others miss it. Be patient also to await the end of the Lord. And when still the vision tarries, dare to believe that one day, when you know as you are known, you shall understand the loving kindness that underlay your darkest experiences.

18

First be reconciled to thy brother, and then come and offer thy gift.

Matthew 5: 24

WHAT does your brother have against you? It may be that you have done him a positive wrong, taking his possessions from him (Exod. 22: 17), or you may have failed to help him when he stood in need (Exod. 23: 4,5). It may be, even, that when he had come back from a long and distant journey, you regarded him without love, as the elder brother did in the parable of the Prodigal Son. You failed to warn him of his peril and assure him of your welcome. Perhaps you have cost him many bitter tears, much painful suffering, wounds in the house where he had every right to expect gentle kindness and mercy. What memories are these that come trooping back to us at the bidding of recollection, recovering them from the depths of memory? These must be the sins that cannot be forgotten, though they may be forgiven. We will remember these in heaven, I'm afraid. God may forgive us; those whom we have sinned against may forgive us; but we shall never forgive ourselves.

We are bidden to get right with man, as the first step in getting right with God. "Go thy way, *first* be reconciled to thy brother." Humility is necessary in every approach to God, and nothing will be so humbling as to confess our faults to our brethren. Truth is necessary in all right dealings with God, as nothing will so promote truth in our inward parts as to be transparent and simple in our dealings with our fellows. Sincerity in confession of sin is an essential beginning of peace with God, but how can we be sure that our confession is sincere unless it costs us something more than words? Finally, in His forgiveness we shall discover an emblem and expression of God's forgiveness. *"First* be reconciled with thy brother." Not only with the brother of human flesh, but the greater Brother in glory (Gen. 50: 17–21).

Go ye therefore, and teach all nations, baptizing them in the name of the Father, and of the Son, and of the Holy Ghost.
Matthew 28: 19

19

THESE words were spoken on a certain mountain in Galilee, which Jesus had made a meeting place for His disciples and Himself. It is supposed that some five hundred brethren met in this place, according to Paul. Matthew lays stress on the eleven apostles, but his words do not exclude the presence of others. It was, therefore, to the general assembly of the disciples that our Lord unveiled this command, good through the end of the world (according to v. 20). This embraces you and me, the Christian centuries that have passed since.

But there are conditions which we must comply with: (1) *Obedience.* "If a man keep my words . . . I will manifest myself unto him." "Make disciples of all nations, teach them to observe all things, and lo, I am with you." This is the path for our lives, clearly marked out by the Providence of God, either in levels of ordinary existence, or on some special mission. It is the right path, the path for you. (2) *Purity.* "The pure in heart seek God." It is only as we wash our robes that we stand before the throne and see the face of God. Therefore, a little child, or a maiden like Mary, or a man like St. Augustine, who has put off the works of darkness and put on the armor of light, is most likely to see. (3) *A quiet heart.* I do not say a quiet life. That is impossible, but a quiet heart, free from care, feverish passion, violent excitement, overbearing ambition, pride or vanity. It is when the storms of the inner life are still, in the early morning, when the boat rocks on the glassy surface of the lake, that you best see the reflection of Nature. (4) *Devoutness of spirit.* Andrew Bonar's life is well worth perusing if for no other purpose than

March

to see how he walked with God. He said that fellowship with God was not a means to an end, but the end of life. He resolved, in the strength of the Holy Spirit, not to speak to man till he had spoken with God. This practice will help us fulfill this mission.

20	*Teaching them to observe all things whatsoever I have commanded you: and, lo, I am with you alway, even unto the end of the world. Amen.*

Matthew 28: 20

THESE words are even more familiar in the language of the King James Version, but there is an added beauty and meaning in them when we translate the Greek into literal English, "I am with you all the days." How fresh! How vital! How inspiring! Spoken more than nineteen hundred years ago, they seem as though a friend spoke them into our hearts just yesterday.

We shrink back from the mysteries of life—we are painfully conscious of our crippling weakness—we dread pain, less for ourselves than for those who are closely twined into our lives. We need wisdom, strength, guidance, a shepherd's care, a brother's love, a Savior's intercession. But all is here, if only we can appreciate and receive the benediction of the wonderful *perpetual presence of Christ*.

It was literally true. Modern writers have attempted to convince us that this meant only that Jesus' teachings, example, and ideal of manhood would be with us throughout history. His memory would never die—Christianity would never be superseded—the gospels would be fountains of life from which nations could draw their noblest inspirations. All this is true, but not all the truth. If they meant nothing more than this, they would not have conveyed much hope to those to whom they were first addressed. No, bless God, He is with us—even unto the end of the world!

Ye are the salt of the earth. . . .

Matthew 5: 13

21

NO WONDER that the common people hung on Christ's words. He was a Master of the art of illustration, because he sought His emblems, not from remote corners of creation, or its sophisticated processes, but from the common incidents of ordinary human experience: salt and light; birds and lilies; gates and roads; trees and their fruit; houses and their foundations. But there was more than art. He knew the hidden secrets of creation, and could tell the heavenly pattern upon which everything was fashioned.

And how full of encouragement He was! He was so willing to give men credit for their best; and in doing so, he summoned to view qualities, of the existence of which their possessors had never dreamed, or encouraged them to continue in paths on which they had ventured with hesitating steps. It was not a small encouragement to these humble peasants and fishermen to be told that they were capable of checking the evil that was eating out the vitals of society around them, as salt stays the progress of corruption. Have we ever realized sufficiently or used, this antiseptic power with which all good men are invested?

Though he was rich, yet for your sakes he became poor. . . .

2 Corinthians 8: 9

22

THERE is nothing that men dread more than poverty. They will break every commandment in the Decalogue rather than be poor. But it is God's chosen lot. He had one opportunity only of living our life, and He chose to be born of parents too poor to present more than two doves at His presentation in the temple. All His life was spent among the poor. His chosen apostles and friends were, with few exceptions, poor. He lived on charity, rode in triumph on

March

a borrowed steed, ate His last meal in a borrowed room, and lay in a borrowed grave. Why is poverty so dear to God?

It is in harmony with the spirit of the Gospel.—The world-spirit seeks for itself the abundance of possessions. Its children vie with each other in luxury and display. The Spirit of Christ, on the other hand, chooses obscurity, lowliness, humility; and with these poverty is close akin.

It compels to simpler faith in God.—The rich man may trust Him; but; the poor man must. There is so much temptation to the wealthy to interpose their wealth between themselves and the pressure of daily need; but the poor man has no fortress in which to hide, except the two strong arms of God. He waits on Him for his daily bread, and gathers the manna falling straight from the sky.

It gives more opportunities of service.—The rich are waited on, and pay for servants to wait on those they love. The poor, on the contrary, are called to minister to one another, at every meal, and in all the daily round of life. In this way they become like Him who was, and is, as one that serveth, and who became poor, that through His poverty we might be rich.

23

He that standeth steadfast in his heart . . . doeth well.
1 Corinthians 7: 37

PERHAPS steadfastness is our greatest need: especially so as we gird up our loins for a new stretch of pilgrimage. We do not need nobler ideals. They flash over our souls. We read of Browning kissing, on each anniversary of his wedding, the steps by which his bride went to the marriage altar; and we vow to lift our wedded life higher. We read of Henry Martyn mourning that he had devoted too much time to public work, and too little to private communion with God; and we vow to pray more. We recall the motto written on Green the historian's grave at Mentone, "He died learning"; and we vow that each day shall see some lesson learned from the great store of Truth. We read those noble words of W. C. Burns, "Oh, to have a martyr's heart, if not a martyr's crown"; and we vow to give ourselves absolutely to witness and suffer for Jesus. But, alas! our ideals fade within a few hours, and the withered petals are all that remain. We need the steadfast spirit.

But this God can give us by His Holy Spirit. He can renew our will from day to day, and infuse into us His own unaltering, unalterable purpose. He can make possible, obedience to the apostolic injunction, "Be ye steadfast, unmoveable, always abounding in the work of the Lord." Hear what comfortable words the Apostle Peter says: "The God of all grace, who called you unto his eternal glory in Christ, after that ye have suffered a little while, shall himself restore, stablish, and settle you." Then we will move resolutely and unfalteringly onward; like Columbus, undaunted by discouragement, we will cross unknown seas, till the scent of the land we seek is wafted across the brief intervening distance.

. . . Present your bodies a living sacrifice, holy, acceptable unto God, which is your reasonable service.
Romans 12: 1

24

TO *present* takes us back to Romans 6. We might almost say that the intervening chapters, after the manner of the apostle, are one prolonged digression or parenthesis, and that he classes all the great doctrines he has been discussing as among the mercies of God, and as reasons for our entire consecration. Every disclosure of God's grace toward us is an argument for our complete surrender to His will and power.

We are called on to present *our bodies* as instruments of righteousness, because all true discipline of the inner life immediately affects the body in all its members; and, conversely, the consecration of the body reacts upon and affects the temper of the soul.

Such consecration must be *living;* that is, it must enter into all our life, being holy, well-pleasing to God, and rational. It is not only *reasonable* when we consider the relation we sustain to Him, but it should call forth all our intelligence and reasoning faculties. When we look at God's will from a distance, and before consecration, it seems impossible. It is only when we begin to obey, that we can say: "Thou sweet beloved will of God."

March

<table>
<tr><td>

25

</td><td>

All things are lawful for me, but all things are not expedient: all things are lawful for me; but I will not be brought under the power of any.

1 Corinthians 6: 12

All things are lawful for me, but all things are not expedient: All things are lawful for me, but all things edify not.

1 Corinthians 10: 23

</td></tr>
</table>

THE difficulty about amusements, where to go and where not to go, is not a new one. It agitated the Christians at Corinth centuries ago as it agitates us; and led to one of the questions which the apostle Paul answered in his first epistle. We must have recreation, times when jaded nerves recuperate themselves, and tired brains turn from their absorbing thoughts to lighter themes. We will perform the serious work of life more successfully if we have seasons of rest. Then the perpetual question arises, how far is all this amusement lawful and expedient? What should be our attitude as Christians toward amusement? First, we must never be enslaved by any form of pleasure. Second, we must have an eye to others. Whatever is in harmony with the tender, holy, unselfish, and blessed nature of Jesus, is an amusement which we may gladly become involved in. If it does not leave a bad taste in our mouths, or a feeling of guilt, if it is wholesome and health-giving, it will add to our effectiveness as children of God.

<table>
<tr><td>

26

</td><td>

Blessed be the God and Father of our Lord Jesus Christ, who hath blessed us with all spiritual blessings in heavenly places in Christ.

Ephesians 1: 3

</td></tr>
</table>

HUMAN speech could never tell the infinite variety of blessings which are required for the life of the saints. Grace to endure what God sends or permits, as well as to do what He commands. So destitute are we of natural qualities and powers that we need to receive all things that pertain to life and godliness. Everything that Christ asks of us must be received from Him before it can be yielded to Him. It is therefore a source of deep peace to learn that God has stored in Jesus every spiritual blessing. As all color lies hidden in sunlight, waiting to be drawn off by the flowers, so does help for every time of need reside in Christ.

But since these spiritual blessings are in the heavenly places, we must live upon that plane. This is where so many make their mistake. They know that all the land is theirs, but they do not put their foot down upon it. We cannot inherit the treasures of the everlasting hills, while we are satisfied with the heavy air of the valleys. Our daily life must be spent in fellowship with the living Jesus; our thought and heart must not only ascend to Him, but continually dwell with Him; we must experimentally sit in the heavenly places before we can claim or possess the things which God has prepared for them who love Him.

The angels that did not keep their own position but left their proper dwelling have been kept by him in eternal chains ... until the judgment of the great day.

Jude 6

27

GOD'S keeping power operates negatively as well as positively. Notice what happens to those angels who kept not their first estate. Whatever else it means, it must mean that they had the potential for high possibilities of service for which they were fitted—yet they forfeited it, and the very power by which they might have served became the chain by which they were enwrapped. Do not presume on the divine keeping power, for there is always the dread possibility of neutralizing it. Keep yourselves therefore in the love of God. Have you the light? Follow the gleam. Are you in the midcurrent? Don't get turned off into a side stream. Are you being used? Keep under your body and bring it into subjection, lest having preached to others you may yourself become rejected.

There is One who is able to keep us from falling, not only from within, but from without. We are of value to Christ for His saving and redemptive purposes. We are greater than worlds or suns, greater than time or space, greater than the universe in which we are found. We are "kept for Jesus Christ"; let us not be unmindful or ungrateful, for through the ages, this prayer continues to rise

March

from the heart of our Redeemer: "I pray, not that thou shouldest take them out of the world, but that thou shouldest keep them from the evil."

28	*To the intent that now unto the principalities and powers in heavenly places might be known by the church the manifold wisdom of God.*
	Ephesians 3: 10

MULTITUDES of holy beings are there. We know little of them. The vague term "principalities and powers in the heavenly places" veils as much as it reveals. But we will know them one day, and be known by them. And we will make them know the manifold wisdom and the eternal purpose of God. Here is the ministry that shall engage our redeemed energies in the land of the unsetting sun, where the flight of time is not marked, because time will be no more. Heaven is not set out with couches and beds of ease, for our luxurious enjoyment. His servants see His face and serve. And their aim is ever to pass on to others some deeper knowledge of the being and attributes of God. This is our role as we serve Him here.

29	*And to know the love of Christ, which passeth knowledge, that ye might be filled with all the fulness of God.*
	Ephesians 3: 19

GOD'S love in Christ passes knowledge. We may *apprehend* it, but we can never *comprehend* it. We may enjoy it without realizing its infinite extent; as a child may shelter in a cave from the incoming tide without being able to compute the dizzy cliffs that rise sheer above it toward heaven. A single gentian sent us by a friend gives some idea of the glory of the Alpine flowers; but how little can we imagine the effect of the myriads that make blue patches on the mountain slopes! Every time we manifest love to others we learn a little more of the love of Christ; but though we give eternity to our inquiries, His love will always pass our knowledge. The *eros* will ever be beyond us. There will always be as much horizon before as behind us. And when we have been gazing on the face of Jesus for millennia, its beauty will be as fresh and fascinating and fathomless as when we first saw it from the gate of Paradise.

Which in other ages was not made known unto the sons of men, as it is now revealed unto his holy apostles and prophets by the Spirit.

Ephesians 3: 5

30

HE IS the Spirit of Revelation. There are deep things of God, mysteries, hidden things, of which the apostle Paul often speaks. The eyes of the natural man cannot discern, nor his ear detect, nor his heart conceive them. Deeper than the azure heights above us, or the fathomless depths beneath, they defy the wise and prudent of the world. But they are revealed to babes—not in the land of light and glory, but here and now, through the grace of the Holy Spirit. "God hath revealed them unto us by the Spirit."

This is what Jesus promised, that when He cometh, the Spirit of Truth, was come, He would lead us into all the truth, and take the things of Christ and reveal them unto us. Let us be apt pupils of so transcendent a teacher. Be willing to do, and you shall know.

If any man speak, let him speak as the oracles of God; if any man minister, let him do it as of the ability which God giveth: That God in all things may be glorified through Jesus Christ, to whom be praise and dominion forever and ever. Amen.

1 Peter 4: 11

31

THE SERVANT who prepares my food, or saves me the necessity of doing the many duties of my home, thus setting me free to write, or preach, or minister to men, will, in God's reckoning, be credited

March

with no inconsiderable share of the results of anything which may have been achieved through my labors. The great deed that blesses the race seems to be wrought by one, but it is really the result of the contributed quotas of scores and hundreds of unnamed and unnoticed workers, and these, insofar as they entered into the spirit of his labors, shall share the reward. Those who sow and those who reap shall rejoice together.

This is the way to do a good day's work. Begin it with God; do all in the name of the Lord Jesus and for the glory of God; count nothing common or unclean in itself—it can only be so when the motive of your life is low. Do not be content with eye service, but as servants of God do everything from the heart, and for His "well done." Ask Him to kindle and maintain in your heart the loftiest motives; and be as men who watch for the coming of the Master of the house.

The Life of Faith

April

... The promise of eternal inheritance.
Hebrews 9: 15

OUR spiritual inheritance is a free gift, and yet we have a right to it. We do not ask for it—we were born into its blessed privilege. The child of royal parents may claim his broad ancestral estates simply by right of birth: and it is on that pledge that the saints hold heaven. By God's great mercy we have been born again.

What a heritage! "An inheritance incorruptible and undefiled, and that fadeth not away" (1 Pet. 1: 4). *Incorruptible!* Decay cannot affect it. Moth and rust cannot consume it, nor thieves break through to steal. No spendthrift hand can scatter or overspend its treasures. *Undefiled!* Not a stain on its pure robes; not a freckle on its leaves; not a taint of pollution on its atmosphere. Nothing enters into the city that defiles, or works abomination, or makes a lie. *That fadeth not away!* To use the Greek word, it is amaranthine. Some of the fairest hopes that ever blessed human vision; the most delightful friendships; the most perfect dreams of delight, have faded and withered before our eyes. This inheritance never can fade or wither.

It is kept for us, and we are kept for it. It is reserved in heaven for you.

"Who by the power of God are guarded through faith" (1 Pet. 1: 5). The idea is that we are being brought through an enemy's country under a strong escort—as the men, women and children from Egypt traveled with the protection of the pillar of cloud and fire, till they were safe from their Egyptian pursuers. We are not in heaven yet; but we are as safe as if we were.

April

<table>
<tr><td>2</td><td>Satisfy us in the morning with thy steadfast love, that we may rejoice and be glad all our days.
Psalm 90: 14, RSV</td></tr>
</table>

IT WAS towards the close of the desert wanderings that Moses wrote this sublime psalm, all the imagery of which is borrowed from the wilderness. The watch around the campfire at night; the rush of the mountain flood; the grass that sprouts so quickly after the rain, and is as quickly scorched; the sign of the wearied pilgrim (v. 9). As the old man looks back on life, he gives it as his experience that the heart which is satisfied with God's love in the morning, never fails to rejoice and be glad all its days.

There is no better hour for fellowship with God than the first hour of the day. If we would dare to wait before Him for satisfaction *then,* the filling of that hour would overflow into all the following hours. A bright Christian lad, giving his brief testimony for Jesus recently, told his secret when he said that at his conversion he trusted the Lord with his morning hour; and the way he spoke of it indicated the radiancy of the light that shone for him then.

Perhaps the morning of life was rather in Moses' thought. If so, the old man has prepared a prayer in which successive generations of bright children may join. Young one, do you want a glad and rejoicing life? Do you want to live by the wells that never dry up or freeze? See God in Jesus Christ our Lord, and the day will never dawn when you will regret having made that choice.

<table>
<tr><td>3</td><td>For by grace are ye saved through faith . . . not of works, lest any man should boast.
Ephesians 2: 8,9</td></tr>
</table>

THE PURPOSES of God have been hidden deep in unfathomable mines. From the first He knew that man would fall from his high estate; but He ordained that His purpose should still be executed by making man His son, His heir, the sharer of His glorious life. Yes, and further: He resolved that His dealings with redeemed men should bring out into clearer relief His own manifold wisdom.

So He created all things through Jesus Christ. The entire fabric of creation was based upon the Person and workmanship of our blessed Lord. He was the medium and organ through whom the creative purpose moved; just as He became that through which the redemptive purpose passed into execution.

For long ages the purposes of God were obscured. Men could not tell their drift, until the Spirit of Pentecost made them understand something of the marvelous design. The mystery, which in other generations was not made known unto the sons of men, was revealed to the holy apostles and prophets in the Spirit. And now all babes who are Spirit-taught, know things which the great and good of previous ages failed to discern.

I will fear no evil.

Psalm 23: 4

4

DO I not have God? In many ways and places, He spoke to, and helped his saints. Will He not come to me, and cast around me the soft mantle of His protecting love? And if I love Him, do I need any beside?

Did He not walk with Enoch, and then take him home, before the deluge came? Did He not shut Noah in, with His own hand, that there should be no danger from the overflowing flood? Did He not assure Abram He was his shield and exceeding great reward, quieting his fears against any possible combination of foes? Did He not preserve his servant Moses from the fury of Pharaoh and the murmurings of Israel? Was not Elijah hidden in the secret of his pavilion from the wrath of Ahab? Did He not send His angel to shut the lions' mouths that they might not hurt Daniel? Were not the coals of the burning fiery furnace as sweet and soft as forest glades to the feet of the three young confessors? Has God ever forsaken those who trusted Him? Has He ever given them over to the will of their enemies?

April

Wherefore, then, should *I* fear in the day of evil? I may be standing on the deck, while the ship is surrounded by icebergs and jagged rocks; the fog drapes everything, as the way slowly opens through this archipelago of peril: but God is at the helm—why should I fear? Days of evil to others cannot be so to me, for the presence of God transmutes the evil to good. "Wherefore should I fear in the days of evil?" (Ps. 44: 5).

I will say of the Lord, He is my refuge and my fortress: my God; in him will I trust.

Psalm 91: 2

THE STRUCTURE of this psalm is often obscured. It begins with the announcement on the part of the chorus of the general truth that to dwell in the inner place of fellowship is to abide under the protection of Divine Power.

Twice the psalmist speaks. In the second verse we hear him saying: "I will say of the Lord, he is my refuge and my fortress, My God in whom I trust." In the ninth verse he breaks in again: "For thou, O Lord, art my refuge." And each profession on his part is followed by the outburst of the chorus with an enunciation of all the blessings which most certainly will result.

In the last three verses God Himself is introduced, assuring His child of all that He is prepared to do and be. Have you ever said definitely, "O Lord, you are my refuge"? Fleeing from all other, have you sheltered in Him from the windy storm and tempest, from the harrow by day, and pestilence by night, from man and devil? You must declare it. Do not only think it, but say it. Keep saying it because it *is* true, rather than because you *feel* it to be true. Not only in the midst of sympathizing friends, but in hours of loneliness, desertion, and opposition.

In a farm, in which I am interested, we have an incubator, the artificial heat of which hatches hundreds of little chickens; but there always seems a great lack in their lives—no mother's call or wing. They invariably remind me of those who have not sheltered under the wing of God.

April

. . . O my God, be not far from me.

Psalm 38: 21

6

WHAT a change within the soul one short hour spent in God's presence will prevail to make! The psalmist was surrounded by ungodly nations and resisted by deceitful and unjust men. He mourns because of the oppression of the enemy; he questions whether God has cast him off. Then led by those twin angels, Light and Truth, commissioned and sent forth for that purpose from the presence of God, he enters in thought and spirit within the precincts of the Divine Tabernacle, and stands before the Altar. Immediately the clouds break. Putting his puny hand upon the great God, he appropriates all He is and has, as though it were his own, and takes again, in a very ecstasy of realizing faith, his harp, too long silent, and breaks into rapturous melody.

Have you not sometimes groped in the dark, till those two angels have come to lead you also to the altar where the High Priest stands? Then what a change! Your circumstances have not altered, but you have conceived a new idea of what God can be to you. You have said, This God is my God for ever and ever. You have said, O God, *my* God! You have laid your hand on God's wealth and called it all your own. You have admonished your soul for being disquieted and depressed while such a heritage is yours. You have spoken of God, first as the God of your strength; second, as the gladness of your joy; third, as the health of your face.

We, according to his promise, look for new heavens and a new earth, wherein dwelleth righteousness.

2 Peter 3: 13

7

OH, BLESSED hope! Is it not wonderful that so many chapters of the New Testament burst with the glad anticipation of the Master's quick return!

We should never lose this spirit of eager longing and waiting. It

April

has the promise of the life that now is, as of that which is to come. It lifts us above the darkness of the present age; it links the present with the great future; it comforts us in bereavement with the hope of speedy reunion; it quickens us to watchfulness and consecration by the thought of the shortening of our opportunities; it leads us to purify ourselves as He is pure, to trim our lamps and prepare our hearts.

Notice how often the New Testament writers combine the *service* of the living and true God, thus distinguishing Him from the dumb, dead stones of heathen idolatries, with this *waiting* for His Son from heaven. "To wait for his Son from heaven . . ." (1 Thess. 1: 10). It has been alleged that the hope of the Second Advent is a dreamy, mystical sentiment, which disqualifies one for the active fulfillment of the duties of life. Nothing could be further from the truth. Those who cherish that anticipation, who awake in the morning, saying, "Perhaps it will be today"; who go to their sleep whispering to their hearts, "Perhaps I shall be changed into His likeness in a moment as I sleep, and wake in my resurrection body"—these are among the most devoted, strenuous, and successful workers of the church. They are not recognized by the media; but God knows and honors them.

8	*O God . . . let not the flood sweep over me. . . .*
	Psalm 69: 13,15

MATTERS sometimes become desperate. For days the waters have been out on the low-lying lands, and slowly rising against the embankment, in the shelter of which some house is situated. Now, however, they have undermined and swept it away. With a crash it has fallen into the yellow foaming waters. A moment's agitation, and then not a trace of it. There is nothing now to keep back the flood, and it comes into the home, rising stealthily up the walls. In the life of the soul such a crisis sometimes comes. You have dreaded something, and the cold chill of fear has cast a shudder over you; but surely it could never come to *you!* There is that protection, that barrier, of position, money, wealthy friends. But one by one these are swept aside, and the waters come ever nearer, till there is nothing between them and your soul. They come in unto the soul.

It is well for a man to be able then to turn to God with the "Save me, O God!" of the psalmist (69: 1, RSV). God must have the entire trust of the soul. He takes away all that lies between Him and us, that we may hang on Him, and lie naked and open to Him in our utter helplessness. From the midst of your sorrows, from the deep sin in which you are sinking, from the deep waters that overflow you, cry to God. He knows your foolishness; your sins are not hid from Him. He will stretch out his right hand and catch you, saying, "O thou of little faith, wherefore didst thou doubt?" Then our crying and tears will be turned to joyous shouts. We will praise the name of God with a song, and magnify Him with thanksgiving; for the Lord heareth the needy, and despiseth not his prisoners (Ps. 69: 33).

So we know and believe the love God has for us. God is love.
1 John 4: 16, RSV

9

LIFE IS one long education in various phases and aspects of love. First as a child, then as a friend, then as a lover, as wife or husband, as father or mother. We are perpetually being allowed to sit in some higher form for the progress of this divine study. For to love is to live. To be loved is to drink of the sweetest cordial that can be prepared from the vintages of earth. And all is intended to help us to understand better the nature of God, who is love. As each new experience enters our life, we should consider a fresh facet or angle to break up and reveal to us the glory of God's love. We should say to ourselves, "Now I understand, and know more accurately than before how God feels, and what His love is."

The apostle says we have known the love of God.—Indeed, it is so. Through years of life, each of which has been filled with the varied experiences, but filled also to the brim with proofs of God's

April

tender lovingkindness, we have had innumerable proofs of His love, for "e'en the cloud that spreads above, and veileth Love, itself is Love."

The apostle says we must believe God's love.—Standing on the sure foundation of what we have proved God to be in the past, we may look on the present and future with perfect faith. We have known Him too well to doubt Him now. We have known, and now we believe. He has made no mistakes. He is making none. He has done the best, and is doing it. We do not understand His dealings, but we know Him who is behind the mystery of Providence, and can hear Him saying: "It is all right, only trust Me. Fear not! it is I."

 10   *And the King of glory shall come in.*

Psalm 24: 7

THIS IS what we all want. We must have the King of glory *within*. To have Him without, even though He be on the Throne, will not suffice. He must come in to abide, to reign, to rule, to keep the everlasting doors through which He has passed. This has been our difficulty, that those doors have so often been forced. We want one who is strong and mighty to keep them strongly barred against our mortal foe.

This psalm was first realized in the entrance of the ark into Mount Zion, when God went up with a merry noise. It is supposed that the first part of the verse was a challenge from the warders of the ancient gates, while the second was a reply from the escorting band that accompanied the sacred emblem. It was a moment of vast triumph when the ark of the King of glory passed to the ancient city of the Jebusites.

A still greater fulfillment took place when Jesus, having overcome the sharpness of death, victor over sin and the grave, mighty in battle, vanquished principalities and powers, and entered the city of God. Then to and fro these challenges and answers flew between the angels who awaited Him, and those who accompanied.

But the most vital fulfillment is when the heart opens to receive

Him, and He enters, to go out no more, and to hold it against all comers. Oh, beaten and baffled saint, it is impossible for you to fail when Jesus, all-victorious, guards your heart! He is strong and mighty. Do you need strength? It is in the strong Son of God. Do you want might? He is all-mighty. Do you desire deliverance from your foes? He is mighty in battle.

By faith he sojourned in the land. . . .
Hebrews 11: 9

11

SORROW and pain had taught the psalmist some deep lessons touching the life of men around him—they seemed to be shadows pursuing shadows. "I am a stranger with thee, and a sojourner" (Ps. 39: 12). They walked in a vain show and were disquieted in vain. At their best, that is, when most firmly rooted, they were only a breath, curling from lip or nostril into the chill morning air, and then gone forever. The outward life and activity of man seemed to him as the shadow which darkens for a moment a whole mountain side, and as you look, it is chased away by the succeeding rays of sunshine.

Amid all these vanities, the child of God is a pilgrim to the Unseen. He passes through Vanity Fair, with his eyes steadily fixed on the Eternal City, whose Builder and Maker is God. Abraham first described himself as a stranger and sojourner, when he stood up from before his dead, and craved a burying-place from the sons of Heth. All his children, those who inherit a like faith, must say the same. Faith cannot find a home on this side of the stars. It has caught a glimpse of the Infinite, and it can never be content with anything less.

But we are sojourners "with God." He is our constant companion. What Greatheart was to the women and feeble ones, God is to each of His saints. We may be strangers; but we are not solitary. We may be compelled to relax our grasp from the hands of beloved ones; but we are never alone—the Father is with us. Good company, safe escort, is it not? In the strength of it, we may obey with-

April

out reluctance or fear the old motto—*Habita, ut migraturus:* Live as those about to emigrate. "There is nothing greater than God; nothing less than I. He is rich; I am very poor, but I want for nothing."

---

12   *I cry to God Most High, to God who fulfils his purpose for me.*

Psalm 57: 2, RSV

WHAT a *comfortable assurance!* We often despair of ourselves. We awake to see that much on which we have prided ourselves, instead of being gold, silver, and precious stones, was mere wood, hay, and stubble. We discover, as Saul of Tarsus did, that the structure of righteousness which we have been raising is but as dross in the holy eye of God. We find ourselves falling through a bottomless pit of self-despair. Finally, we turn to the Lord Jesus, and say, What we cannot do for ourselves, and what no one can do for us, Thou must undertake. And there steals upon us the comfortable assurance that we have only to be faithful and true to His least prompting, and "He will fulfill His purpose for me."

What an *argument!* First, we plead for the mercy of God, the patience that endures forever, never surprised, never surrendering its cherished purpose, never renouncing heart and hope, but always enduring amid rebuffs of neglect and the proud rebellion of self-will. Because His love is without measure or end, we believe that He will yet be conqueror. He will have His way. We despair of ourselves. We hope infinitely in His mercy.

Secondly, we plead that we are the work of His own hands (Ps. 138: 8). Has He done so much, and will He not finish? Has He implanted a hunger that He will not satisfy? Has He led to the point of Pisgah vision, and will He not give the land? A mother might forsake her child, but God cannot forsake those whom He has made the subject of His thought and care. He cannot have created within us longings and desires that reach to the Infinite, merely to tantalize. "If it were not so, I would have told you." Yes, He will fulfill His purpose for us, some day, somewhere.

April

For the grace of God that bringeth salvation hath appeared to all men.

Titus 2: 11

13

THE EMPHASIS must surely rest on *appeared*. Kindness and love towards man were always in the heart of God, but they were not clearly revealed. "The kindness and love of God our Savior toward man appeared" (Tit. 3: 4). They might have been perceived in the order of nature and human life; but there are stormy winds as well as balmy breezes in the one—and in the other deaths as well as births; knells of hope as well as marriage peals. But in Jesus the true heart of God toward man was manifested. It is thus in human life.

At first God blessed us anonymously.—In Cowper's memoirs we read how Theodora, his cousin, pursued him throughout his sad life with her gifts; but they always came without indication of their source. As the poet unwrapped each new treasure, he would say, "Dear Anonymous has come again; God bless him." So, through years of thoughtless childhood, and afterwards in opening youth, we were the recipients of myriads of gifts contrived with the most exquisite skill to give us pleasure; but we did not trace them to their source. They were from God.

Since then His grace and lovingkindness have appeared.—We have had eyes to see, and hearts to understand. The Anonymous Benefactor is now recognized as our Father and Friend. We no longer praise our earthly loves for our cornfields and vineyards, but our Heavenly Spouse (Hos. 2). In the breaking of the bread we have recognized the Son of God, and we know now who it was who walked with us along the path of life, and why our hearts burned.

Blessed be the Lord, who daily bears us up; God is our salvation.

Psalm 68: 19, RSV

14

NEVER tired or out of patience, that mighty God, of whose advent the psalmist is so full, daily bends beneath our burdens, and

April

sets Himself to help us through crushing difficulties. They are unbearable to us, but to Him only a very little thing. If He taketh up the isles as a very little thing, surely your heaviest burden must be less.

But our mistake is that we do not realize that God is bearing our burdens. We think that we must cope with them; we let ourselves worry, as though we were the loneliest, most deserted, most pitiable beings in existence, when all the while God is going beside, ready to bear our burdens. The burden of our sins; of our anxieties about ourselves, and about others; of our frailties and infirmities: the responsibility of keeping us; the pressure of our daily need—all these rest daily on our God.

Oh, do not carry your burdens for a single moment longer; pass them over to Him who has already taken your eternal interests to His heart. Only be patient, and wait on Him, and do not run to and fro seeking for help from man, or making men your consolers and confidants. Those who do this have their reward. But as for you, anoint your head and wash your face, so as not to excite the pity of others. "Cast thy burden on the Lord, and He will sustain thee." But when it has been cast, leave it with Him. Refuse to yield to anxious worry, and instead burst out into a song of thankful confidence. Bless Him! Praise Him! Be glad, and rejoice! When the heart is lightened of its load, it will soar.

15

For ... God made promise to Abraham ... saying, Surely blessing I will bless thee, and multiplying I will multiply thee.
Hebrews 6: 13,14

IT WAS a miracle that this childless couple should have a child, and become the parents of a great nation, so that the stars of the heavenly vault and the sand-grains on the ocean-shore should not be more numerous. And it was enough to stagger any man to be told of it. "He staggered not at the promise of God through unbelief" (Rom. 4: 20). But Abraham staggered not. How was this?

It was not because he ignored the difficulties that obstructed its realization.—He might have done so. Whenever the natural obstacles arose in his mind, he might have ignored them. But this, according to the RV rendering of the previous verse, was not Abraham's policy. He quietly and deliberately considered the enormous difficulties that lay in the path of the divine purpose, and in spite of them "he staggered not."

His unstaggering faith arose from his great thoughts of Him who had promised.—He kept saying to himself, *He is able, He is able.* God would not have promised what He could not perform. Abraham knew that the God of nature was Lord of the nature He had made. He knew that no word of the Almighty could be destitute of power. "The father of the faithful" fed his faith by cherishing lofty and profound thoughts of God's infinite resources. There rang in his heart the assurance, *I am El Shaddai.*

It is remarkable that, throughout Abraham's life, God was continually giving him new glimpses into His own glorious nature. With every temptation, call to obedience, or demand for sacrifice, a new and deeper revelation was entwined. This fed Abraham's faith and gave it unstaggering strength. Child of God, feed your faith on Promise. For every look at your difficulties, take ten at what your God is.

The Lord God is a sun and shield: the Lord will give grace and glory. . . .
Psalm 84: 11

16

HOW God suits Himself to our need! In darkness, He is a Sun; in the sultry noon, a Shield; in our earthly pilgrimage, He gives grace; when the morning of heaven breaks, He will give glory. He suits Himself to every varying circumstance in our lives. He becomes what the extremity of the moment requires. And as the psalmist well says, He withholds no good thing from them that walk uprightly. Learn the art of extracting from God the special form of help of which you stand in need.

The sun is the source of light and life. With impartial beneficence he scatters his beams on palace and cottage, mountain summit and lowland vale. He is ever pouring out his beams. It is our part only

April

to stand in them, or to open casement or door. God is shining, dear heart. Get out of yourself, and sun your shivering frame in His untiring love.

A shield may be the shadow of a great rock in the scorching desert, or the canopy of a gourd's growth. Put God between yourself and the sirocco of temptation. Is the noon with its burning heat too much for you? Hide in the Lord God. The heat will not smite you by day, nor the frost by night.

Do you need *grace?* He is full of it. His grace is sufficient. With both hands He will give and give again; only practice the habit of taking. Grace is the bud of which *glory* is the flower. If He has given this, He will not withhold that. If you knew the gift of God, you would be sure that Glory in germ is within you, waiting only for the summer of Eternity to develop in perfect beauty. "We have had our access by faith into this *grace* wherein we stand, and we rejoice in hope of the *glory* of God."

17	*As ye have received of us how ye ought to walk and to please God, so ye would abound more and more.* 1 Thessalonians 4: 1

WHEN WE were first brought to Jesus, we received Him into our hearts by faith. Throwing open the door, we bade Him be welcome; and He came in never to depart again. Though He was as invisible as the wind, and silent as light, He came. And there was a perfume as of myrrh, aloes, and cassia; like that which fills the ivory palaces of eternity.

Now the apostle says that all our future Christian life is to be lived on the same principle. The holy life is not an *attainment,* but an *attitude.* Holiness is not an acquirement to boast about, but an openness of soul toward the Lord Jesus, as of a window unshuttered and uncurtained to the light. The believer is never independent of Jesus; at every moment he is receiving out of His fullness, and grace upon grace. He does not receive Christlike qualities and attributes as things apart from the Lord Jesus; but receiving Him, he obtains them. The holy man is he who has learned the art of receiving Jesus;

the holier, who has a greater capacity, through humility and faith; the holiest, he who can receive most of the life of the Son of God.

Our daily life is here compared to a walk. We cannot choose it. There is no alternative but to take what God has marked out for you; though you may choose your atmosphere, or, to use a more modern expression, your environment. Every step may be taken in Christ; rooted in Him as a tree in rich soil; builded up as a house on a rock; inhaling His very breath as the life of life. And whatever the need may be which the circumstances of the path suggest, there is always an abundant supply in the Lord Jesus, in whom all treasures are hid. He teaches us that we may *know;* He indwells that we may *be.*

They saw the deeds of the Lord, his wondrous works in the deep.
Psalm 107: 24, RSV

18

THERE are wonderful harmonies in nature. Voices call to one another across vast spaces. The depths below the firmament call to the heights above. The deep of the ocean calls to the deep of the azure sky. "Deep calleth unto deep" (Ps. 42: 7). Listen, O my soul, to the mighty voices sounding ever through the universe of God.

The deep of Divine Redemption calls to the deep of human need. —It sometimes seems as though the opposite were true, and as though the cry originated in man; but it is not so. God is always first; and as He looks into hearts stricken and desperate, conscious of unfathomable yearnings, and infinite capacity, He calls aloud, and the depth of His heart appeals to the depth of the heart of man. Would that it might ever answer back!

The deep of Christ's wealth calls to the deep of the saint's poverty. —He looks down upon our meager and poverty-stricken experience with an infinite yearning. He cannot endure that we should go through life naked and miserable, poor and blind, when He has gold, and precious stones, and white raiment. "Hearken, O daughter, and consider. Forsake thy father's house. Come unto me, and receive from my fulness. Open thy mouth wide, and I will fill it."

April

The deep of the Holy Spirit's intercession calls to the deep of the church's prayer.—He awakens in us groanings that cannot be uttered, and burdens us with the will of God.

Whatever depths there are in God, they appeal to corresponding depths in us. And whatever be the depths of our sorrow, desire, or necessity, there are resources in God from which full supplies may be obtained. You have the pitcher of faith, and the well is deep.

19	*There was a man in Jerusalem . . . Simeon . . . waiting for the consolation of Israel.*
	Luke 2: 25

THERE is an evident parallel intended between the first and second Advent, and especially in the manner of looking for it. At the first Advent there were many who were definitely looking for and hastening to that day. Simeon was waiting for the consolation of Israel; and Anna spoke of the infant Lord to those who were expecting redemption in Israel. To look for the consolation and to look for the redemption were the two articles in that early creed. And presently this quiet, patient waiting broke out into the rapturous song of the *Nunc Dimittis*.

But all Jews were not looking for that blessed Hope, the appearance of the Grace of God. When our Lord came, the leading teacher of Judaism was Philo, and he not only had no messianic hopes of his own, but discouraged them in other people. He conceded that there might be a return of Jewish national life; but he had no expectation of it being under the leadership of the Christ.

It has been truly remarked that this eager looking for the Advent has always been the mark of the living church. "Ye turned," said the apostle, "unto God from idols . . . to wait for his Son from heaven." And again he said, "A crown of righteousness which the Lord, the righteous Judge, shall give unto me in that day; and not to me only, but to all them that love his appearing."

As it was with the first Advent it shall be with the second. The Son of God will come at a time and in a manner for which men are

April

not prepared; and only the elect, who may have been persecuted and despised by the world at large, will discern Him, and go forth to meet Him in the air.

For thou hast delivered my soul from death, mine eyes from tears, and my feet from falling.
Psalm 116: 8

20

IT HAS been a wonderful deliverance! The blood and righteousness of Christ have satisfied the demands of a holy law. Into our souls, dead in trespasses and sins, He has poured the power of an endless life. The very life of God Himself has become resident within us, through the grace of the one Man, Christ Jesus. We cannot be hurt by the second death. We have eaten of the flesh, and drunk of the blood of the Son of Man, and ours is the everlasting life. Death and the grave are forever behind us. Before us is the city, whose streets are never shadowed by death or crying.

And will not God finish what He has begun? Has He given us life, and will He not give us all that is necessary for right and holy living? Does not the one necessarily involve the other, as the gift of the body involves the bestowment of food and clothing? Have we been saved by Christ's death? Shall we not also be saved by His life? Will it not be for the glory of God that we should walk worthy of the high calling? Trust Him, child of God, whatever the traps and pitfalls, whatever the slipperiness and difficulty of keeping a foothold; believe that He is able to keep you from stumbling, and that His ability is only exceeded by His love. Let your Guide bind you by a strong rope to Himself as you start each morning in His company.

The answer to these reasonings, the fulfillment of our hopes, comes back to us from a verse in Romans 5, "If, when we were enemies, we were reconciled to God by the death of his Son, much more, being already reconciled, we shall be kept safe by sharing in his life."

April

21	*According as he hath chosen us in him before the foundation of the world, that we should be holy and without blame before him in love.*

Ephesians 1: 4

GOD'S election points to His love. Men have sometimes thought and spoken of God's "choosing" in such a way as to encourage exclusive and proud conceit—as though God's love were a high wall enclosing a favored few, so that their flower and fruit might be kept from every defiling, pilfering hand. To think this is to misconceive the entire purpose of God.

If a man boast of his election in an arrogant and exclusive spirit, he shows that he has missed its point and aim, and is certainly outside its scope. The eternal purpose of God reveals itself, not merely in the new-found rapture, but in the new-found love. The love of God proves the election of God. If you do not love, you may prate of election as you will, but you have neither part nor lot in it. But, if we are in Christ, by a living faith, we have been chosen to love, and love must be divinely possible—even easy. God's choice always carries with it an equivalent of power to be and do that for which He has chosen us.

22	*So is he that layeth up treasure for himself, and is not rich toward God.*

Luke 12: 21

THE CONTRAST here is striking. Men, for the most part, look to riches to supply them with all they need richly to enjoy; but the apostle says that it is beyond all comparison better to look away from dead coin to a living Person, who takes pleasure in giving liberally without upbraiding. "Nor trust in uncertain riches, but in the living God . . ." (1 Tim. 6: 17).

Here is a rebuke.—Suppose you had your cellars filled with gold coin, would you not think yourself secure against all possible need and care? Almost certainly you would. But you ought to be even more at rest, since you have neither silver nor gold, and only your Heavenly Father's hand.

Here is a contrast.—Riches are uncertain at the best. A man in these difficult days finds it easier to gain money than to hold it. He who is rich today may awake tomorrow to find that some sudden turn of the market has made him poor. But God is not uncertain. He is the same yesterday, today, and forever. His covenants are certainties.

Here is an appeal.—Trust in the living God with as much faith as others have in their lands and bank accounts, and be almost glad if God takes away from you what you have clung to so tenaciously, that you may drop securely into His everlasting arms. You smile at the story of the lady who was told by the captain that he had done all he could for the vessel, and they must now look to the Almighty; and who replied, "O captain, has it come to that?" But you may be more like her than you suppose!

Here is an assured destiny.—Those who trust in riches are pierced through with many sorrows, and are caught in the maelstrom, which drowns souls in perdition; they who trust in the Lord are as Mount Zion, which cannot be removed.

For a thousand years in thy sight are but as yesterday when it is past, and as a watch in the night.

Psalm 90: 4

23

THERE is no succession of time with God: no past, no future; He dwells in the eternal present, as I AM. As we may look down from a lofty mountain on a stream in the valley beneath, tracing it from its source to its fall into the ocean, and feeling that each part of it is equally distant from the spot where we stand, so must time appear to the Eternal; who was, and is, and is to come. "One day is with the Lord as a thousand years" (2 Pet. 6: 8).

One day is as a thousand years.—He could do in a single day, if He chose, what He has at other times taken a thousand years to accomplish. Do not say that He will require so long to do this or that—to restore or convert the Jews; to introduce the millennial

April

age; to undo the effects of the curse, and fill the years with blessing. Do not say that He must have as long to make the second heavens and earth as the first. Do not say that the overthrow of the empire of darkness, and the conversion of multitudes to God, can only be achieved by the processes which are now in vogue. All this could be changed in a moment, in the twinkling of an eye; and between sunrise and sunset God could effect the work of a thousand ordinary years.

A thousand years as one day.—Periods that seem infinite to our finite minds are not so to God. A thousand years in our reckoning is but a day in His. You say it is two thousand years ago since Jesus died, or at least that we are in the evening of the second thousand. But in God's reckoning, the cross, the grave, the resurrection, took place in the morning of yesterday. Take wider views of God's horizon; believe in His mighty march throughout the centuries; He takes up the isles as a very little thing, and the centuries are as the beats of the minute hand.

24	*He shall not be afraid of evil tidings: his heart is fixed, trusting in the Lord.*
	Psalm 112: 7

THERE cannot be evil tidings to the soul which has fixed its trust in the Lord. Every messenger that comes post-haste into its presence with dispatches brings tidings of what has been permitted or done by our Father; and nothing which is of His ordering or permitting can really injure us. Tidings! tidings! they are always pouring in, by letter, postcard, and telegram. They are presented in the pages of every newspaper, and cried by the newsboys in the streets. But the child of God opens each buff-colored envelope with untrembling hands, and scans the newspaper columns with confident eyes. No tidings can be evil to him; "his heart is fixed, trusting in the Lord" (Ps. 112: 7).

But does not the Christian suffer anguish and pain, as others do? Is he stoical and unimpassioned, dull in his emotions, unsympathetic in his affections? Not so; but he refuses to judge things by their appearances. He knows that all things must be working for good on his behalf: in the hieroglyphics he detects his Father's handwriting; in the mysterious figure standing on the shore, veiled in morning mist, he beholds the Lord who died for him. If tidings were to come to you today of disease, loss, bereavement, death, they could not be evil if your heart dares to maintain a fixed trust in God; for such trust robs death of its sting, and the grave of its victory. I cannot understand, but I can trust *Him*. Like the fabled philosopher's stone, faith turns all metals to gold.

And they ... rested the sabbath day according to the commandment.

Luke 23: 56

25

THERE is a rest for weary souls.—God speaks of it as His rest. He entered it, we are told, when He had finished His work, and beheld it to be very good; and ever since the door has been standing open for the travel-stained, weary children of men to enter it. To every other creation-day there were evening and morning, but not to this; it partakes of the nature of eternity in its timeless bliss.

Let us rejoice that this rest remaineth.—"There remaineth, therefore, a Sabbath rest for the people of God" (Heb. 4: 9). Of course, the Sabbath, which was and is a type of it, could not exhaust it. And Canaan, with its sweet plains and cessation of the wilderness wanderings, could not completely fulfill it; because centuries after it had been given through Joshua, in the Psalms God spoke of yet another day, as though His rest were still future.

The rest may be a present experience.—The word "remaineth" has diverted the thoughts of commentators who have supposed it referred to heaven. There is rest, sweet rest, there. But "remaineth" means "unexhausted, unrealized, by aught which has taken place." The rest is for us here and now. "We which have believed *do* enter into rest." Where is it? In the bosom of Christ: "Come unto me, and I will give you rest." It is in ploughing the furrow of daily duty—"Take my yoke ... and find rest."

This rest is compatible with great activity.—He who enters into

April

the divine rest is not reduced to quietism. On the seventh day the Creator rested from creation; but He works in providence. Jesus, on the seventh day, rested from Calvary; but He pleads in heaven. Cease from your own works, after a similar fashion; abandon your restless planning and striving; by the grace of the Holy Spirit better service will be produced.

26	*The Lord knoweth how to deliver the godly....*
	2 Peter 2: 9

THE following authentic story will best illustrate and enforce this text. I give it as it was given to me by a friend who had verified the circumstances during a visit to Blankenburg. A godly Lutheran pastor, Sander, of Elberfeld, had been compelled to rebuke an evil man for some gross sin, and had thereby attracted to himself the man's hatred; and the man vowed vengeance on the pastor. One night the pastor was called to visit a home that could only be reached by passing over a plank which bridged a rushing torrent. Nothing seemed easier to his enemy than to conceal himself on the bank till the man of God was returning from the opposite end of the plank, to meet him in the middle, throw him into the deep and dangerous stream, leaving it to be assumed that in the darkness he had simply lost his foothold. When, however, from his hiding-place he caught sight of the pastor's figure in the dim light, he was surprised to see he was not alone, but accompanied by another. There were two figures advancing toward him across the narrow plank, and he did not dare attempt his murderous deed. As they passed his hiding-place, the one whom he did not know cast such a glance toward him as convinced him of the sinfulness of the act he had contemplated, and began a work in his heart which led to his conversion.

When converted, he sought out the pastor, to confess to him the murderous intention which had so nearly mastered him, and said: "It would have been your death had you not been accompanied."

"What do you mean?" asked the other; "I was absolutely alone." "No," said he, "there were two." Then the pastor knew that God had sent His angel, as He sent him to bring Lot out of Sodom.

Till we all come in the unity of the faith, and of the knowledge of the Son of God, unto a perfect man, unto the measure of the stature of the fulness of Christ.
Ephesians 4: 13

27

OUR GROWTH in the body is to be worthy of the Head. In a caricature you will sometimes see a large head on a very diminutive and dwarfed body; but there will be no disparity between the Head and the Body when the divine workmanship is complete. We are diminutive and dwarfed now; but as we abide in Him we will grow and expand until each member of the mystical body shall fill out its complete proportion, and the ideal man shall stand forth before the gaze of the universe in the measure of the stature of the fullness of Christ.

But this can only happen when each joint shall supply to the whole its appropriate nutriment, and when we all give ourselves unweariedly to perfect one another in the unity of faith, and of the knowledge of the Son of God.

The God of my mercy shall prevent me. . . .
Psalm 59: 10

28

GOD always goes before us. The word "prevent" is not as familiar to our modern English as it was when the Bible was translated. Then it meant "that which comes or goes before." And the idea is that God goes before us, preparing our way, and laying up supplies of grace to anticipate our need. This is the meaning of the prayer: "Prevent us, O Lord, in all our doings."

Go into the nursery where the mother is preparing for the coming of her little baby. You have no difficulty in telling what the wants of the child will be by all the articles which her tender forethought is providing; and when presently the little one opens its eyes in this strange, new world, it finds that it has been "prevented" with the blessings of goodness.

Still more is this the case in the kingdom of redemption. God has stored all the blessings of goodness in Jesus. In eternal ages, in the incarnation, the cross, the ascension, He has prepared beforehand for every possible need of our spiritual life. Whenever you pray, remember that you are not to procure unthought-of help; but to avail yourself of the blessings of goodness with which God has anticipated your coming. "Thou preventest him with the blessings of goodness" (Ps. 21: 3).

29	*Mercy and truth are met together; righteousness and peace have kissed each other.*
	Psalm 85: 10

THIS HAS been fitly called "the bridal ceremony of the earth and sky." *Mercy* is the love that finds its reason in itself, its measure in helplessness and grace. But in God it is always blended with *Truth*. God must be faithful to His covenant relations, to His son, to Himself, and to the law which He has instituted. Any display of mercy must be consistent with truth. These are heavenly twins. Where you meet one you will be sure of the other. Jesus was full of grace and truth. The love He brings is consistent with the highest considerations; and by His death it is so arranged that God acts consistently with His holy law in loving and saving the meanest and weakest believer.

Righteousness has for her twin sister *Peace*. "The effect of righteousness shall be peace." The King of Righteousness is after that the King of Peace. If you want peace, you must be right with God; and if you would be right with God, you must come to Jesus and become united to Him, who is made unto us the righteousness of God. At the cross these two kissed. The righteousness of God was satisfied, and the peace of man secured.

What a wondrous cross is that on which the Prince of Glory died! The question was—How could God be just, and yet justify the ungodly? How could He uphold the majesty of the moral law, and yet take sinners to His heart? But the answer came clear and satisfying, when the Maker of man took on Himself our sin and gave justice its due. Now see that perfect blending of the divine attributes, and that God is "just, and the Justifier of him that believeth in Jesus." Oh, that truth might spring up as the response and echo of our hearts!

Rooted and built up in him, and established in the faith, as ye have been taught, abounding therein with thanksgiving.
Colossians 2: 7

30

THE ROOTS that moor a tree to the soil and gather nutriment for its growth are very slender and delicate. So the actions to which the Spirit prompts us on behalf of others may seem very trivial; but each one gives us greater constancy and strength and makes us quicker to understand God's love to us.

A solid foundation is all-important for the building which is to tower into the air, affording distant glimpses of the landscape; and those who desire to behold, as in a panorama, the love of God, must be content to perform many deeds of unselfish goodness in the depths of obscurity and self-forgetfulness. What we do for others for Christ's sake, and what we feel toward them, is a priceless education, preparing us to know His love. Perform loving deeds; will to do them, even if you at first shrink from them; do them from a sense of duty, if not of delight; presently you will come to delight in them, and you will say to yourself, "This is something like Jesus feels toward me." Love apprehends love.

But love never lives alone. It summons *all saints* to its aid. No one saint or school of devout thinkers can compass all God's love.

The Suffering Life

May

1

... an angel touched him, and said unto him, Arise and eat.
1 Kings 19: 5

WHAT an infinite comfort it is to realize that God knows how easily our nature may become jangled and out of tune! He can attribute our doubts and fears to their right source. He knows the bow is bent to the point of breaking, and the string strained to its utmost tension. He does not rebuke His servants when they cast themselves under juniper bushes, and ask to die, but provides them food and sleep. And when they send from their prisons, saying, "Art Thou He?" there is no word of rebuke, but tender encouragement and instruction.

Our Lord deals with us as we with children. The dearly loved child may have its passionate outbursts, but what mother would judge the child by that transient manifestation? She knows that it is a mood, perhaps traceable in part to physical conditions; she realizes that beyond the passing cloud there is the blue sky of disposition. She says to herself, "The mood will pass, but the disposition will remain. Let me wait patiently, and help the child to regain its true balance." It is not otherwise with us. This is the human side of the great doctrine of imputed righteousness. The apostle says that God looks on us arrayed in the righteousness of Christ. He sees what we shall be, when in the meridian of eternity we are perfectly conformed to the image of His Son.

We may go to God and say, "I have not been myself today, but Thou knowest what I would be. I come back to myself, to Thine ideal, to the Christ ideal, and I stand before Thee 'accepted in the beloved.'" Even when we seem most feeble and unstable, the Lord believes in our essential self, which lies beneath all these moods, in the very depths of our being, until He shall call it forth.

May

Thus saith the Lord . . . I have seen thy tears: behold I will heal thee. . . .
                                    2 Kings 20: 5

2

IT IS a sad, sad world, and perhaps must grow sadder yet. It may be that we have not yet reached the darkest hour. Oh, the tears of the oppressed; the tiny children; the terror-stricken fugitives from war-torn lands, and the drunken tyrant of the home! "Behold, the tears of such as were oppressed" (Eccles. 4: 1). Through all the centuries tears have flowed, enough to float a navy.

There need be no difficulty in accounting for them. Our race has elected the service of sin and self. Turning our back on God, for whom we were made, we have turned every one to our own way, and are inheriting the ancient curse of travail, tears, thorns, and death. It is quite true that many suffer innocently and vicariously, because we are members one of another; and by the mysterious arrangement of the Almighty the whole race is bound together by mysterious but indissoluble cords. In Adam all die, all suffer, all sorrow and weep, just as in Christ shall all be made alive. The pain must last, till the Stronger than the strong comes to divide the spoils, and set the captives free.

How comforting it is to realize that God sees our tears, knows our sorrows, puts our tears into His bottle, is afflicted in all our affliction, and bears us on His heart.

. . . It was the latter growth after the king's mowings.
                                    Amos 7: 1

3

AMOS speaks of the king's mowings. Our King has many scythes, and is perpetually mowing His lawns. The musical tinkle of the whetstone on the scythe portends the cutting down of myriads of green blades, daisies, and other flowers. Beautiful as they were in the morning, within an hour or two they lie in long, faded rows. Thus in human life we made a brave show, which passes away like

May

the beauty of grass, before the scythe of pain, the shears of dis-appointment, the sickle of death.

There is no method of obtaining a velvety lawn but by repeated mowings; and there is no way of getting tenderness, evenness, sympathy, but by the passing of God's scythes. How constantly the Word of God compares man to grass, and his glory to its flower! But when grass is mown, and all the tender shoots are bleeding, and desolation reigns where flowers were bursting, it is the most acceptable time for showers of rain falling soft and warm.

O soul, you have been mown. Time after time the King has come to you with His sharp scythe. You have sadly learned that all flesh is grass, and that the efforts of your self-life are vain. Where are the king-cups and butter-cups of your pride? They are laid low that you would bear better crops than ever; and that you may do so, lo, He comes down as spring rain! He comes *down;* thus you have the miracle of His condescension. He comes down *like rain;* there you have the manner of His gentle advent. He comes *on the mown grass* (Ps. 72: 6); there is His expectancy, showing that His reason in mowing, followed as it is by the gentle raindrops, lies in the direction of new beauty and use. Do not dread the scythe—it is sure to be followed by the shower.

4

. . . The taste of it was as the taste of fresh oil.
Numbers 11: 8

THERE is perennial freshness in God—in the works of nature, in His love, and in the renewal of the soul. Does the eye ever tire of the changing beauty of the clouds? Though we look out from child-hood to old age on the same landscape, there is always something fresh to captivate the roving eye. Think of the unfailing freshness in love—love of woman to man, of mother to child. Think of the fresh-ness of each returning day, of earth in her springtime robe, with the myriads of sweet children, whose laughter is as ringing and their eyes as bright as if the earth were young, instead of being old and weary. And if God can do this for the works of His hands, is there any limit in the freshness which He will communicate to His children? "I will be anointed with fresh oil" (Ps. 92: 10).

Each morning bend your heads, ye priests of the Most High, for the fresh anointing for the new ministries that await you. The former grace and strength will not be adequate; old texts must be rejuvenated and reminted; old vows must be respoken; the infilling of the Holy Spirit must be as vivid, and may be as definite, as at the first. See to it that you do not rise from your knees till you can say, "I have been, and am, anointed with the fresh oil" (Ps. 92: 10). And the anointing that you receive from Him shall abide on you, teaching you how to abide in Him. So you shall bring forth fruit in old age, and in life's winter be full of vitality and fervor.

Pastor Harm used to say: Pray diligently. I do not mean your common prayer alone; but pray diligently in your room daily for the Holy Spirit. How their faces shine, who receive this daily anointing!

Whoso hearkeneth unto me shall dwell safely, and shall be quiet from fear of evil.
                                        Proverbs 1: 33

| 5 |

WHOSO. This promise is to us all. To the man in the street, as much as for those of us who have been nurtured in Christian homes.

The evil is taken out of things for those whose hearts are full of God. Nothing which God allows to come to us is really evil, except sin. Put away sin from your heart, and let it be filled with Love and Faith, and behold all things will become new. They will lose their evil identity, because you will look at them with new eyes. Men talk against the March wind; but when they understand that it is blowing a cleansing stream of fever-germs, they regard it as a blessing. Men dread change, anything unwonted or unaccustomed; but when they find that, like the transplanted fruit tree, they will often attain a greater maturity than when left to one spot of soil, they welcome it. If you look at things apart from God, especially if you anticipate the future without Him, you have good cause for fear; but if you hearken to and obey Him, if you know and love Him,

May

if you abide in God and God in you, you will see that the evil is not in the things or events, but in yourself. Give yourself as alms to God, and lo, all things will become clean to you.

Death shall lose its terrors, and become the Father's servant, ushering you into his presence. *Pain* and *suffering* will but cast into relief the stars of Divine promise. *Poverty* will have no pangs, and storm no alarms. You shall become so habituated to find the rarest blessings associated with what men often dread most, that you will be quiet from all fear of evil, and able to look out, with serene and untroubled heart, on a sea of troubles. In fact, it is very doubtful if anything is really evil for those who love God.

6

. . . How long wilt thou hide thy face from me?

Psalm 13: 1

MEN IN sorrow do not always speak wisely; and they ask many questions which God does not answer. Here is one. God does not stand afar off and hide Himself in times of trouble (Ps. 10: 1). As the psalmist sings, in a happier mood, He is "a very present help in time of trouble" (Ps. 46: 1). But he permits trouble to pursue us, as though He were indifferent to its overwhelming pressure; that we may be brought to an end of ourselves, and led to discover the treasures of darkness, the unmeasurable gains of tribulation. No cross, no crown. No pain, no gain.

We may be sure that He who permits the suffering is with us in it. . . . It may be that we shall only see Him when the trial is passing; but we must dare to believe that He never leaves the crucible. Our eyes are blinded; and we cannot behold Him whom our soul loves. It is dark—the bandages blind us so that we cannot see the form of our High Priest. But He is there, deeply touched. Let us not rely on feeling, but on faith in His unswerving fidelity; and though we see Him not, let us talk to Him in whispers as though we could detect Him.

As we begin to speak to Jesus, as being literally present, though His presence is veiled, there comes an answering voice which shows

May

that He is in the shadow, keeping watch upon His own. Do not be afraid of the darkness. Behind the cloud, the sun is shining. Little child, your Father is as near when you journey through the dark tunnel as when under the open heaven! Go nearer, and you will feel Him!

He who conquers, I will make him a pillar in the temple of my God; never shall he go out of it, and I will write on him the name of my God. . . .
Revelation 3: 12, RSV

7

ALL WHO lived on the seaboard of Asia Minor were familiar with the vast and beautiful temples, in which Oriental lavishness and Greek art combined to create the utmost magnificence. Their ruins litter the deserted sites of former cities to this day. The Lord therefore used familiar imagery in this promise. A column hewn from its rocky bed, richly sculptured, and conveyed to the rising-temple-structure!

Stability.—"Never shall he go out of it . . ." God Himself shall establish, strengthen, and settle, the soul who trusts Him, and is willing to follow at all costs where He leads. He will make such a one to be as Jachin or Boaz, the two mighty pillars which Solomon erected in the Temple court, their names signifying establishment and strength. There is no spectacle more inspiring than to behold the steadfastness of the soul who wavers and swerves not, but stands to its post, though all nature rocks.

Responsibility.—The pillar bears up some part of the structure; and it is Christ's good pleasure to call us to share with Him the weight of ministering to His church. As you show yourself true and faithful, God will allow you to bear up the common life of His people by ministering comfort, direction, encouragement, to those who could not stand by themselves.

Beauty.—The medieval architects and masons took great pleasure in their designs. In many cases each pillar is sculptured as to its capital in its own fashion. There is infinite variety and beauty in the patterns. So Jesus is cutting deep into us the name of His Father and Himself, and making us bear new revelations to the world. Do not shrink from the deep cutting of His chisel.

May

8

Good and upright is the Lord. . . .

Psalm 25: 8

GOD IS the only one who is truly good. He makes "all things work together for good to them that love him." . . . Our faith is sometimes assailed, as David's was, by the anomalies we meet with in the world. The wicked prosper, while the waters of a full cup are wrung out to the people of God (Ps. 73: 3). The scribes and Pharisees greedily devour widows' houses, and prey on the helpless; earnest merit seeks for work and recognition in vain. It is a strange world, full of contradictions, perplexities, and insoluble questions; but through it all God's children must dare to affirm that He is only good. You do not feel it? Nevertheless, reason, Scripture, experience, demand that you should assert it. The fact is, we have lost the standpoint of vision.

The psalmist found these things too painful till he went into the sanctuary of God, and then he understood. Do not take earth as the center of the universe, but the sun. Do not look at God from circumstances, but at circumstances from God. Live continually with Him: then will mystery become unravelled, and dark problems solved. Above all, be pure in heart, free from the stain of sense, with one purpose (Ps. 73: 1). You will see the soul of good in what seems evil.

9

How long, O Lord?

Psalm 35: 17, RSV

TO US, also, as to long-suffering David, God's dealings seem sometimes interminable. We do not understand why the cloud hangs over us so long, why the pressure of trouble lasts year after year. We cry, "How long, O Lord?" in gusts of impatience; but take care not to hurry God unduly. We must not force Him to forego doing His best work in our lives. The following truth helped me; may it help you to be silent, still and long-suffering. A bar of iron, worth $1, when wrought into horseshoes, is worth $2; if made into needles, it is worth $70; if into penknife blades, it is worth $650; if into springs for watches, it is worth $50,000. What a beating the poor bar must undergo to be worth this; but the more it is manipulated, the more it is hammered and passed through the fire, and beaten, and pounded, and polished, the greater its value.

So with ourselves. Those who suffer most are capable of yielding most; and it is through pain that God is getting the most out of us for His glory and the blessing of others. It will be all right some day. We shall see it and be satisfied. Yes, great Father, we would like to be watchsprings. Take no heed of our cry if sometimes we forget ourselves and say, How long?

The Lord is nigh unto them that are of a broken heart.
Psalm 34: 18

10

WHAT broke your heart? Unkindness? Desertion? Unfaithfulness on the part of those you trusted? Or did you attempt to do something which was beyond your power, and in the effort, the heart-strings snapped? A bird with a broken wing, an animal with a broken leg, a woman with a broken heart, a man with a broken purpose in his life—these seem to drop out of the main current of life into shadow. They go apart to suffer and droop. The busy rush of life goes on without them. But God draws nigh. The Great Lover of man is always at His best when the lights burn low and dim in the house of life. He always comes to us then. He shall sit as the Refiner.

Where do you see love perfected? Not between the father and his stalwart son who counts himself independent, or between the mother and the girl in whom love is awakening in its first faint flush: but where the crippled child lies in the sick bed, pale and wan, unable to help herself. There the noblest fruits of love ripen and yield refreshment. The father comes close to the little sufferer, as soon as he gets home at night, and the mother is nigh all the time to sympathize

May

and comfort and minister. So brokenness attracts God. It is dark; you think yourself deserted; but it is not so. God is there—He is nigh; call to Him—a whisper will bring a response.

11

Be pleased, O Lord, to deliver me: O Lord, make haste to help me.

Psalm 40: 13

MAKE haste!" Our frail patience gives out full often. We think that God is never coming. So many days I have waited for Him, and as yet there has not been one symptom of His approach. Why are His chariots so tardy? Lazarus is dying; a few hours more, and life will have ebbed away. Provisions are failing and water is scarce, and still the enemy is entrenched in proud security. The world scoffs; but the Lord does not come down the mountain slope, bringing salvation. Where is the Pentecost of which He speaks? Where is His Second Advent?

But God is making haste. On the wings of every hour, quicker than light leaps from world to world, He is on His way. Delays are not denials, but are necessary to the perfecting of His arrangements. "Lo, I come quickly!" is still true, though more than nineteen hundred years have passed.

We do not wish the destruction of our enemies, but their salvation. We long that God should be magnified, and souls saved. We yearn for the setting up of the Kingdom of God, which is peace on earth, and blessing. And for this end we desire that God should accelerate His coming. O God, make no tarrying! Your enemies boast themselves; our spirits faint for fear; men are sinking into perdition. Make haste!

Your God will not be a moment overdue. When the fourth watch breaks, He will intervene. Not too soon for education; not too late for deliverance. But dare to believe that He is never absent. He is near all the while, bending over you and all men, with tender pity, only waiting till He can see, with infallible wisdom, the best instant to intervene.

12

Can God furnish a table in the wilderness?
                                    Psalm 78: 19

OH, FATAL question! It shut Israel out of the Land of Promise, and it will do as much for you. Israel had seen the wonderful works of God, cleaving the sea, lighting the night, and giving water from rocks. Yet they questioned God's ability to give bread, and to spread a table in the wilderness. Surely it was a slur on His gracious providence to suppose that He had begun what He could not complete, and had done so much but could not do all.

But we are in danger of making the same mistake. Though behind us lies the gift of the cross, the miracles of Resurrection and Ascension, the care exercised by God over our early years, the goodness and mercy of our after lives, we are disposed to say, "Can God?" Can God keep me from yielding to that besetting sin? Can God find me a job, or provide food for my children? Can God get me out of this terrible trouble in which I am entangled? We look at the difficulties, the many who have succumbed, the surges that are rolling high, the poor devil-possessed child, and we say, *If* You can do anything, help us!

There is no *If* with God; there is no limit to His almightiness but our unbelief. The words are wrongly placed. Never say again, Can God? but *God can*. Never, If You Can; but If I can believe. Never, If You can You wilt; but If You will You can; and You will, since You made and redeemed me, and You cannot forsake the work of Your own hands. Argue from all the past to the present and future. Find arguments for faith in the days that have gone.

The floods have lifted up, O Lord, the floods have lifted up their voice; the floods lift up their waves.
                                    Psalm 93: 3

13

THERE is no commentary on this psalm like that supplied by the break of the waves. Sometimes the voice of the floods is deafening;

May

you cannot hear yourself speak; at other times all night through the porthole aboard ship, you hear their musical break beneath. The lifted up voice of the sea gives many notes in the great organ of nature, sometimes the deep bass, at other times the silvery treble. One says to one's self, "What are the wild waves saying?"

They may be inciting one another to a work of destruction and devastation, roaring in their rage, fretting for supremacy. Why should they endure the presence of man in their wild waste? He is an intruder. The sea gulls are welcome; they are at home as in their native element, but man has no right.

So do the waves of trouble roar wildly around the bark of our life. There are times when surge on surge rolls in upon the soul, and breaks with boom and roar; but always there floats upon the soul the refrain of this sublime canticle, "Above the voices of many waters the Lord on high is mighty." He sits as King, higher than the spray is tossed, deeper than the fathomless depths, mightier than the strongest billow. Let Him but say, "Peace be still!" and the greatest storm that ever swept the waves with wild fury sinks into the tranquil sleep of childhood. Or, if we sink beneath the wave, we will but fall into the hollow of God's hand, where the oceans are cradled.

14 *He was laid in iron.*

Psalm 105: 18, RV

THE MARGIN of the RV suggests another rendering: "His soul entered into the iron." May we not yet again turn the sentence round, and say that, the iron entered into his soul? When we first meet him, Joseph is a tender, yielding lad, with dreams of rule, but no conspicuous power. Yet he emerges from his captivity well qualified to take the helm of Egypt, just then sore driven and tossed by tempest. How can this striking transformation be accounted for, except that he had taken iron into his moral nature through his painful experiences?

The physician often prescribes an iron tonic for anemic patients:

and what iron is to the outer man, that also the captivity of circumstances, deferred hope, and anguish of soul are to the inner. You have been fickle and uncertain of late; dreaming of power, but powerless; yearning for the only good, but greedy of trifles; you must have a course of iron. God wants iron dukes, and iron souls. And there is a process also by which He can turn iron to steel. It means high temperature, sudden transitions, and blasts of heavenly air.

Life is very mysterious. Indeed, it would be inexplicable unless we believed that God was preparing us for scenes and ministries that lie beyond the vail of sense in the eternal world, where highly tempered spirits will be required for special service.

Then they cried to the Lord in their trouble, and he delivered them from their distress.
Psalm 107: 19, RSV

15

THE PSALMIST has found the quickest argument before his God. There is nothing that so quickly makes the bell ring in heaven as the touch of a troubled hand. When a man is full of the interests of life, of prosperity, and self-content; when the voices of applause resound on every side; when his house is full of children, and his barn of sheaves, his prayer halts, and God seems far away. But let trouble come—let the waters, swollen by many confluent streams, begin to rise within his soul, so that lover and friend are far away, and he overwhelmed with terror, then God bends His ear and heart.

O child of sorrow, do not assume that you are cast away! It is true that your Lord cried from His cross, "Why hast thou forsaken me?" but even He, though laden with the sins of the world, the Father held near His heart. And He has not left you, neither can He.

Try and think of trouble as storing your heart with seeds of joy; as acting upon you as the fire upon the primeval earth, scattering jewels through its crust; or as the glaciers that brought the rich soil into the valleys; or as the husbandman who buries the seeds of spring in the autumn fields. A veiled angel, nothing else!

May

16

Behold, I have refined thee, but not with silver; I have chosen thee in the furnace of affliction.

Isaiah 48: 10

SILVER is tried by fire, and the heart by pain. "We went through fire." But in the fire you will not be burned; only your dross shall be removed. "I will . . . purge away thy dross" (Isa. 1: 25). The smell of burning shall not pass upon you, for the form of the Son of God shall be at your side.

The main end of our life is not to *do,* but to *become.* For this we are being molded and disciplined each hour. You cannot understand why year after year the stern ordeal is perpetuated; you think the time is wasted; you are doing nothing. Yes, but you are situated in the set of circumstances that gives you the best opportunity for disclosing, and therefore acquiring, the qualities in which your character is naturally deficient. And the Refiner *sits* patiently beside the crucible, intent on the process, tempering the heat, and eager that the dross should pass off, and his own face become perfectly reflected in the surface.

17

Blessed are they that mourn: for they shall be comforted.

Matthew 5: 4

WHO DOES not know that our most sorrowful days have been amongst our best? . . . The soul which is always blithe misses the deepest life. It has its reward, and it is satisfied to its measure, though that measure is a very scanty one. But the heart is dwarfed, and the nature, which is capable of the highest heights, the deepest depths, is undeveloped; and life presently burns down to its socket without having known the resonance of the deepest chords of joy. "Blessed are they that mourn."

Stars shine brightest in the long dark nights of winter. The gentians show their fairest bloom amidst almost inaccessible heights of snow and ice. God's promises seem to wait for the pressure of

May

pain to trample out their richest juice as in a wine-press. Sorrow brings us nearest to the Man of Sorrows, and is the surest passport to His loving sympathy. Only those who have sorrowed know how tender His comfort can be. It is only as the door shuts upon the joys of the earth, that the window is opened to the blessedness of the unseen and eternal. Let sadness cover your face, Jesus will enter the heart, and make it glad, for the days in which you have been afflicted, and the years in which you have seen evil.

Is your face sad? Are you passing through bitter and trying experiences? Be of good cheer. Out of the sorrows that make the face sad will come ultimate joy. "By the sadness of the countenance the heart is made glad" (Eccl. 7: 8). This affliction is working out a far more exceeding and eternal weight of glory. And the day is not distant when God will wipe tears from off all faces.

The Lord lifteth up the meek; he casteth the wicked down to the ground.

Psalm 147: 6

18

GOD IS the God who lifts up His children. Contrasted to His treatment of the wicked, whom he casts down, the psalmist extols the uplifts of God. They come neither from east nor west, but from above. God is the supreme arbiter of human destiny. The horns of the wicked are cut off, and those of the righteous are lifted up, by the interpositions of His providence: for God is judge.

Are you depressed today? Look up to Him, and ask that you may be uplifted into fellowship with the risen, glorified Lord. The Ascension of our Lord is the measure and example of our own. . . . Seek for the wings of the dove, that with flitting wing you may make your way to the ark, where the hand awaits to take you in. . . . Claim that the mighty power which wrought in Christ when God raised Him from the dead, and made Him sit in the heavenlies far above all power and principality, may do as much for you.

This is also true in a temporal sense. Promotions in any direction, to positions of credit, influence, or consideration, are the gift and work of God. To be lifted up to a chief place in His church,

May

to the stewardship of large wealth, to the exercise of commanding influence, is due to the divine interposition. You do not hold it at the whim of man, but as the direct bestowment of your Father. Do not fear to lose it because you are true to Him. He expects you to be true to Him. He has put you where you are for no other purpose than that you should realize His purposes among men. "A man can receive nothing, except it have been given him from heaven." But if you received it, why do you glory?

19	*Behold, I have refined thee, but not with silver; I have chosen thee in the furnace of affliction.*

Isaiah 48: 10

WE ALL love the sunshine, but the Arabs have a proverb that "all sunshine makes the desert"; and it is a matter for common observation that the graces of Christian living are more often apparent in the case of those who have passed through great tribulation. God desires to get as rich crops as possible from the soil of our natures. There are certain plants of the Christian life, such as meekness, gentleness, kindness, humility, which cannot come to perfection if the sun of prosperity always shines.

Remember how we often shrank from the lessons set before us at school, and looked out of the windows, longing for the hour of release. But now how thankful we are for the tutors and teachers, appointed by our parents, who kept us steadily at our tasks. We feel almost kindly to the schoolmaster or mistress whom we formerly disliked. And, similarly, one day we will be glad for those hard lessons acquired on the altar of pain. "We have had fathers of our flesh to chasten us, and we gave them reverence: shall we not much rather be in subjection unto the Father of spirits, who chastens for our profit, and live?"

The tears of those who suffer according to the will of God are spiritual lenses and windows of understanding. As the weights of the clock or the ballast in the vessel are necessary for their proper operation, so is trouble in the soul-life. The sweetest scents are only obtained by tremendous pressure; the fairest flowers grow amid Alpine snow-solitudes; the rarest gems have suffered longest from the lapidary's wheel; the noblest statues have borne most blows of the chisel. All, however, is under law. Nothing happens that has not been *appointed* with consummate care and foresight. "No man should be moved by these afflictions: for . . . we are appointed thereunto" (1 Thess. 3: 3).

Let Israel hope in the Lord from henceforth and for ever.
Psalm 131: 3

20

A STOIC like Marcus Aurelius might have written the first two verses of this psalm, and then stopped short. He could not have said, "Hope thou in the Lord from henceforth, even for evermore." For him there might be the negative, the refusal to be perturbed by vain desire and intolerable care—but there was no such knowledge of God in His ability to fill the void of the soul, as to enable him to turn upward in hope. The stoic reckons himself dead to the thousand misfortunes of life; but he has no knowledge of the thousand compensations of God. He shuts all the doors and windows of the lower ranges of the heart, but fails to open the upper to the blue sky and the sunlit air.

Be sure if you are weaned from the breast of human comfort you turn with invincible comfort to the heart of God. Do not simply deny yourself, but receive from Christ all and more than all that you forego. Forsake what you will, but appropriate spiritual equivalents for all that you renounce. Hope in God, for the heart of a man has never yet conceived of all that He can become to those who give up all for Him. All human love and comfort are not comparable to the love and beauty of the Redeemer.

Hope in God forevermore. As the years pass they will but deepen and intensify the sense of His trustworthiness. Time can never utter all the depths that await us in God, the tenderness of His sympathy, the closeness of His heart against ours, the delicacy with which His hand wipes away our tears! Thus as the outer man decays, the inward man will be renewed day by day, and affliction will seem light

May

and momentary compared with the far more exceeding and eternal weight of glory!

21

Be thou in the fear of the Lord all the day long.
Proverbs 23: 17

I ASKED a working man the other day how he fared. His wife, the partner of many years, has died, and there is no one to welcome him on his return from work and prepare for him. His fellow-workmen, younger men, delight in tormenting him and increasing his burdens, because they hate his simple godliness. A physical weakness grows upon him distressingly. But he said that he was very happy, because he lived in God. All the way along it was Jesus—Jesus when he woke in the morning; Jesus when he went to bed at night; Jesus when he wrote a letter; Jesus when he went to the butcher's shop to buy his little piece of meat for Sunday—said he, "He made the beasts; He must know what is good to eat." And when I asked how he managed to maintain this life, he said, "I always ask Him to rouse me up early enough to have a good time in fellowship with the Master." From the way he spoke, he reminded me of the priest's portion of the shoulder and breast as symbolizing the strength and love of the Lord Jesus.

If we are in the love of God we will be in His fear; for though perfect love casts out fear that hath torment, it introduces the fear that dares not cause needless pain to the Infinite Lover of souls. We fear to tear open His wounds again, to expose His heart to the spear-thrust, or to miss aught of His gracious pains to make us what He wants us to become.

"If ye keep my commandments," the Master said, "ye shall abide in my love." To abide in His fear is equivalent to abiding in His love. They are two sides of the same coin. Only they love who fear. The woman feared Solomon's sword, because the babe was her own (1 Kings 3: 16–28).

May

Therefore I tell you, do not be anxious about your life. . . .
Matthew 6: 25, RSV

THUS IT has always been among men, and perhaps more so today than ever, when the pressure of life is heavier and the constraint of circumstances more overpowering. Are there not hours in which the clouds gather densely over the Ark of God, and the stoutest hearts tremble? Is it easy for even the Christian soul to look on a family of little ones, sleeping soundly, and know that they will certainly awake hungry for food, of which the cupboard is bare, and have no tinge of anxiety?

It is at such times that the apostle Paul bids us pray. "Make your requests known unto God." We do not have to agonize before Him, as though, like the priests of Baal, who cried and cut themselves, we can move Him by our anguish. Calmly, quietly, simply . . . take your burden into His presence and lay it down there. He is your Father. He who made the body, and gave it to you, will see to the supply of its needs. Your health, your children, the condition of His church, are dear to Him who notices a falling sparrow, and who numbers the hairs of your head.

23

Whom shall he teach knowledge? and whom shall he make to understand doctrine? them that are weaned from the milk, and drawn from the breasts.
Isaiah 28: 9

THE WEANING is God's part. At the destined moment, God will not hesitate to wean us from sources of supply which He permitted to us in the time of our comparative immaturity. He loves us too well to perpetuate ministries of creature help and comfort which are interfering with our attaining to the full stature of Christ. When the time comes for us to be weaned, God will wean us, but everything depends upon the way in which we take His discipline. We may at once acquiesce, and in this case we pass through the transition stage, at as little cost of suffering as may be. On the other hand,

May

we may petulantly resist. Then will come weeks and perhaps months of murmuring and complaint that will extend and wear us out. All the while we will be missing the deepest lesson God can teach—a lesson of loving, trusting acquiescence to His will, for in addition to the advantage of passing from a lower to a higher stage of Christian experience, this weaning is intended to bring out a more perfect trust. We thus doubly thwart the divine intention when we murmur and complain.

After awhile, exhausted, beaten, strengthless, helpless, we give up our insistence on our own way, our rebellion against His. We yield our will to His and fall back on the everlasting arms of Him who comforts us as a mother her first-born.

24	*When he is tried, he shall receive the crown of life. . . .* James 1: 12

DO NOT be surprised if you are passing through trials. The righteous Lord is exercising you toward righteousness, that your face may ever behold His in unswerving communion. As the trainer of a young athlete will place him, now in one position, and again in another, to call certain muscles into play, to strengthen them by use, and to make the whole organization supple and subservient to the impulses of the soul, so God tries us—to call into operation, and test by use, each faculty of our being.

There is a great difference between the temptings of Satan and the tryings of the Lord. The former are intended to make us fall; the great adversary takes pleasure in showing how weak and sinful we are, and in casting us down to destruction. The latter, that we may be led out toward faith, patience, courage, meekness, and other worldliness. "Tribulation *worketh* patience, and patience experience, and experience hope." Whatever spiritual power is latent within us, we may be unaware of its value or helpfulness till it is called into exercise by trial. But when once it has been called into action, it becomes the invaluable possession of all after time.

May

Thou, which hast showed me great and sore troubles, shalt quicken me again.

Psalm 71: 20

25

GOD *shows* us the troubles. We stand beside Him, and the mighty billows break around, but are shivered into myriads of drops. As we ride beside Him in the chariot of salvation, He points out to us the forms of dreaded evils, the ravines, the glaciers, the awful steeps; but it is as though we were cradled in some soft golden cloud which fringes the edge of the precipice, and glides along splintered cliffs where the chamois could not find footing. Look at this, says our Guide. These are the troubles that overwhelm souls, and drain their life! Behold them, but you will not suffer them! I show you them that you may know how to comfort and help those who have been overwhelmed. Sometimes, as this part of our education is being carried forward, we have to descend into "the lower parts of the earth," pass through subterranean passages, lie buried among the dead. But never for a moment is the cord of fellowship and union between God and us strained to breaking; and from the depths God will bring us up again.

Never doubt God. Never say that He has forsaken or forgotten. Never think that He is unsympathetic. He will quicken again. There is always a smooth piece in every skein, however tangled. The longest day at last rings out the evensong. The winter-snow lies long, but it goes at last. Be steadfast; your labor is not in vain. God turns again, and comforts. And when He does, the heart which had forgotten its psalmody breaks out in jubilant song, as does the psalmist's.

May the Lord direct your hearts to the love of God and to the steadfastness of Christ.

2 Thessalonians 3: 5, RSV

26

WE ARE as children feeling our way step by step into the paradise of Divine Love. But the earlier experiences are hard. It is as though

May

we had to make our way through a dense and dark thicket. Every time we dare to affirm that, notwithstanding appearances, God is love; every time we show that love to others, even though our own heart is breaking; every time we say *no* to self and *yes* to the Holy Spirit, we make further progress into the paradise of God's love. Dare to believe in the love of God even when the darkness seems to cover it. Dare to believe that it is over all, through all, and in all.

Let us exercise Christ's steadfastness until the sorrows and trials of life have achieved their destined purpose. The crucible is white with heat; the crushing and pounding of the hammer seems likely to destroy the diamonds; the hours drag so slowly while the nails of the cross are carrying out their work; but be patient amid the stern discipline. Don't fret, don't murmur, don't resist. Let patience have her perfect work, that you may be perfect and complete, wanting in nothing.

27

If we suffer, we shall also reign with him. . . .
2 Timothy 2: 12

THE CHILD of God is often called to suffer, because nothing will convince onlookers of the reality and power of true Christianity as suffering will do, when it is borne with Christian resignation and fortitude. And how great the compensations are!

He can keep in such perfect peace. He can make lonely times, when no one is near the couch, to be so full of sweet fellowship and communion. He can put such strong, soft hands under the tired limbs, resting them. He can give refreshment to the spirit when the body is deprived of sleep.

Everyone cannot be trusted with suffering. All could not stand the fiery ordeal. They would speak rashly and complainingly. So the Master has to select with careful scrutiny the branches which can stand the knife, the jewels which can bear the grinder's wheel. It is *given* to some to preach, to others to work, but to others to suffer. "To you it hath been granted in the behalf of Christ . . . to suffer for his sake" (Phil. 1: 29). Accept it as a gift from His hand.

May

Look up and take each throb of pain, each hour of agony, as His gift. Dare to thank Him for it. Look inside the envelope of pain for the message it enfolds. It is a rough packing-case, but there is treasure in it.

And does not suffering enable you to minister to other sufferers? Through suffering yourself dictate letters of comfort, or pray for them, or devise little alleviations and surprises for those who have not what you have. Suffering is on Christ's behalf; it must, then, be intended as part of that great ministry for the world in which He, with His saints, is engaged. There is a sense in which all suffering, borne in the spirit of Calvary, helps men, not in the way of atonement or propitiation, of course, but by the exhibition of the power of God's grace in the sufferer.

For yet a little while, and he that shall come will come, and will not tarry.
Hebrews 10: 37

28

THE LATE Dr. Gordon loved to read it, *Yet a little while, how little, how little!* which is the literal rendering of the Greek. A little while! compared with the eternal years; with the far more exceeding and eternal weight of glory; with the compensations which await us in the Home of God. Though our life were one long agony, it would seem but as yesterday when it is past; a dream, or a sleepless watch in the night, when the morning breaks.

There is a limitation to our suffering. "After that ye have suffered a little while" (1 Pet. 5: 10). It is only for a little while; but every moment has been fixed by the immutable purpose and love of God. The hour of darkness is timed with an exact measurement. You will not suffer one moment more than is absolutely necessary for your perfecting of God's glory; and for every moment there is an ample supply of grace.

But remember also that in Christ God has called you to His Eternal Glory. You heard that call years ago, and have been following it through days and nights of difficulty and trial. But the gifts and calling of God are without repentance, and He is waiting to fulfill

May

His eternal purpose. What a banquet that will be when God will satisfy the expectations of those whom He has called to partake of it!

And the suffering is being used in ways you little understand to perfect, establish, and strengthen you. It is from sick chambers and prisons that God brings forth His veteran hosts in the day of battle. Think not so much of affliction as of the love of Christ, and the blessedness of being like Him and with Him for ever.

29

Bless ye the Lord, all ye . . . which by night stand in the house of the Lord. Psalm 134: 1

THIS HYMN was composed for the night-watch of the Temple, for those that had gone to relieve the Levites who had been in charge during the day. It is to be noticed that these were specially summoned to bless the Lord and lift up their hands. For, after all, is it not they that stand in the house of God *by night* who are most in need of these exhortations? It seems to us that the sleepless sufferers among us are God's night-watch. When the busy workers are slumbering, they come on duty to bless the Lord, and to seek His blessing on the work of the past day, and the coming one.

It is comparatively easy to bless the Lord in the daytime, when sunshine lies like His smile on nature, and all the world is full of music, and our lives flow on quietly and peacefully. It does not take much grace to bless the Lord then. But when night has draped the earth and hushed the homes of men to solitude, and we stand amid the shadows that lurk around us in the sanctuary, facing the inexplicable mysteries of Providence, of history, of life and death; then the song falters on our lips, and chokes in our throats.

No sooner, however, do we dare to formulate the words of blessing, pursing our lips in the effort, daring to say, by the strong effort of will, what we may not say gladly and easily, there comes back to us, as to this ancient singer, the assurance that the Lord which made heaven and earth shall bless. Is it possible for Him to have made heaven and earth, and not to be able to bless the soul whom He has not only created, but redeemed! He cannot fail to bless those that bless. Indeed, their hearts, like sounding boards, but reflect to Him His own blessings.

. . . neither shall there be mourning nor crying nor pain any more. . . .
Revelation 21: 4, RSV

30

HOW CAN this be? Because its causes will have been ended. Satan will be bound, consigned to the abyss, and no longer able to afflict. There will be no more death, or Hades, for they will have been cast into the lake of fire. There will be no more sea, and so separation and loneliness will have been done away.

The body of this humiliation will be changed into the likeness of the body of His glory; and the inhabitant of the world shall no more say, I am sick.

We shall no more recall the pain of our present condition, than we can remember the aches and pains of childhood. The recollection of pain is always short-lived, but there it shall be as utterly obliterated as the traces of footsteps on the sands by the incoming tide, as the murmur of shells when the ocean waves thunder along the beach. The statues shall be complete, and the Almighty Sculptor shall cast away, never to take up again, the chisel with which He has achieved some of His noblest designs.

And God shall wipe away all tears from their eyes; and there shall be no more death, neither sorrow, nor crying, neither shall there be any more pain. . . .
Revelation 21: 4

31

THERE is much in Revelation which we mortals cannot understand: the sapphire throne, the glassy sea, the descending city of God, the bottomless pit—but amid these sublime and dazzling

May

heights there are sweet breaks of melody, like verdant, grassy plains. Here, at least, we can feast our weary souls. Such is this verse, musical in its rhythm, heart-tugging in its reminiscence of the anguish which is at an end forever—content to leave the positive marvels of heaven to unfold, if only it may assure us that at least the saddest elements in our earthly lives will be forever banished.

The pain of misunderstanding will be no more, since we will see eye to eye, and know as we are known. The pain of suspense will be no more, because we will behold the purposes of God in their ultimate and beneficent outworking. The pain of waning love will be no more, because in that happy land, as the children sing, love is kept by the Father's hand and cannot die.

The pain of bereavement will be no more, because death cannot intrude into that glad City of Life. No more pain—what a prospect!

The Witnessing Life

June

A true witness delivereth souls: but a deceitful witness speaketh lies.

Proverbs 14: 25

1

BE TRUE in your speech. Do not say one thing to a man's face, and another behind his back. Do not flatter where you inwardly despise and condemn. Do not exaggerate as you repeat your pet stories, for the sake of effect, and to win a smile. Let your speech mirror your convictions, so far as may be right and possible. Let your yea be yea, and your nay, nay. Do not puff the article you want to sell beyond its real value, or say a single word more of it than you can verify. In the old fable, the palace walls were paneled with mirrors, on which a mist arose when insincere and untruthful words were uttered within their precincts; realize that such mirrors are ever around you, and see that you never cause a stain or blur.

When thou saidst, Seek ye my face; my heart said unto thee, Thy face, Lord, will I seek.

Psalm 27: 8

2

THE BIBLE reminds us of a dictaphone. God has spoken into it, and as we read its pages, they transfer His living words to us. There are many things in the Bible, which, at first, we may not be able to understand, because, as the heaven is higher than the earth, so are God's thoughts higher than ours. Mr. Spurgeon used to say that when he ate fish, he did not attempt to swallow the bones, but put them aside on his plate! So when there is something beyond your

June

understanding, put it aside, and go on to enjoy that which is easy of spiritual meditation.

The Bible contains many thousands of promises. It is God's book of signed checks. When you have found a promise which meets your need, do not ask God to keep His promise, as though He were unwilling to do so, and needed to be pressed and importuned. Present it humbly in the name of the Lord Jesus! Be sure that, so far as you know, you are fulfilling any conditions that may be attached; then look up into the face of your Heavenly Father, and tell Him that you are depending on Him to do as He has said. It is for Him to choose the time and manner of His answer; but wait quietly, be patient, and you will find that not a moment too soon, and not a moment too late, God's response will be given.

3	*Lead me to the rock that is higher than I.*

Psalm 61: 2

WE DO NOT have to choose our pathway, or cut it through the thick undergrowth of a forest, or to scheme it through the trackless waste. It is all prepared, and we but have to walk in it, with God, one step at a time. Put your hand into God's, look up into His face, saying, "Lead me, Father, in the prepared way." The only serious matter is to discover the prepared path. We may do this by abiding fellowship with the Spirit. Remember how when Paul wanted to turn aside from the prepared path of his life, and to go first to the left to Ephesus and then to the right into Bithynia, in each case the Spirit of Jesus suffered him not. For the most part the trend of daily circumstance will indicate the prepared path; but whenever we come to a standstill, puzzled to know which path to take of three of four that converge at a given point, let us stand still and consider the matter, asking God to speak to us through our judgment, and to bar every path but the right.

When once the decision is made, let us never look back. Let us never dare to suppose that God could fail them that trust Him, or permit them to make a mistake. If difficulties arise, they do not prove us to be wrong; probably they are less by this path than they would have been by any other. Go forward! The way has been prepared.

That Christ may dwell in your hearts by faith; that ye, being rooted and grounded in love.
Ephesians 3: 17

4

WE ARE in Christ as the sphere of daily life and experience. It is the intention of God that we who believe should ever live in Christ Jesus, as the very element and atmosphere of our life; never traveling beyond the golden limits established by His love, life, or light: In Him as the root in the soil, or as the foundation in the rock. Always in His love, because never permitting in speech or act what is inconsistent with it. Always in His life, because ordering our activities by the laws of His being. Always in His light, because saturated by His bright purity, and illumined by His gentle wisdom. Oh, to be always one of the faith in Christ Jesus, and to be able to say with the psalmist, "I have no good beyond thee" (Ps. 16: 2).

5

For the word of the king is supreme. . . .
Ecclesiastes 8: 4, RSV

WHEN OUR King speaks it is done. He spoke in creation, and power went with His word to call all things out of nothing. He spoke in His earthly ministry, and power accompanied every word, in giving eyes to the blind and life to the dead. He spoke, and the paralyzed had power to talk. He spoke, and the winds dropped, while the tumultuous waves were hushed to rest. He spoke, and men knew their sins were forgiven, to be remembered against them no more for ever. He spoke, and the dying thief passed into Paradise.

June

Whatever He bids you do by His Word, be sure that He will enable you to do it by His power. He works in us to will and to work of His good pleasure; that is, He never directs us in any path of obedience or service without furnishing a sufficient supply of grace. Does He bid you give up some evil habit? The power to overcome it awaits you. Claim it. Does He bid you walk on the water? The power by which to walk only waits for you to claim it. Does He bid you perform some dull duty? There is such transforming power issuing from Him as to make duty a delight, if only you will put His power to work in your life. Whenever you are called to stand up to speak the word of your King, be sure to seek and obtain the power— *that* will prove your best credential. Take the power of the King with you: it is His signet-ring, by which men will be convinced that you have been entrusted with His Word.

In the morning sow thy seed, and in the evening withhold not thine hand. . . .

Ecclesiastes 11: 6

WE ARE ALL tempted to look too much to the winds and clouds. We study the faces of people, their moods and circumstances, and say, "It is not a favorable time to approach them about their souls. He does not look to be a likely case, or in a likely mood." But how do we know? If we are always waiting for favoring conditions, we resemble the farmer who is ever looking out for perfect weather, and lets the whole autumn pass without one handful of grain reaching the furrows; or who is always studying the clouds, seeking for a spell of hot summer weather; and presently the chance is gone, and the crop is lost.

In fact, we can never tell what God is doing in the secrets of the heart. He may have been prosecuting his deep and wise designs with the souls that appear most untoward and unprepossessing. He may have led them to such a point that they are most eagerly yearning for the hand to lead them into the light. The eunuch in his chariot might not, from a distance, have seemed specially ripe for the Christian evangelist; but, on coming near, he was discovered to be an

June

inquirer. Saul of Tarsus was the least likely man in all Palestine to be a Christian; but God had been at work in him. Let us dare then to trust God, not looking for winds or sunshine, but scattering everywhere the precious seed of the gospel.

Put ye on the Lord Jesus Christ.

Romans 13: 14a

7

DO NOT BE content with a negative religion. Be positive. Do not only put off—put on as well. Put off by putting on. It is not enough to doff the robes of night, you must don the armor of light. Cast away the works of the flesh, because you have become encased in that glistening panoply woven out of sunbeams and light. Do not only resist impurity—put on Christ as your purity.

If you put on Christ as your purity, you will have no difficulty in being free of the taint of impurity. Do not simply forbid wrath, anger, malice, but assume Christ's heart of compassion, His kindness, humility, meekness, longsuffering and forbearance. Indeed to cultivate these will make those impossible. You need make no provision for the flesh, not expecting to sin, not living in perpetual fear of its outbreak and solicitations, when once you have put on by faith and in the power of the Holy Spirit, the Lord Jesus Christ.

For he put on righteousness as a breastplate, and an helmet of salvation on his head. . . .

Isaiah 59: 17

8

EACH CHRISTIAN has to meet with the powers of darkness, in his own life and in his capacity as a soldier of the gospel of Christ. This is the aspect of the Christian life with which the apostle Paul was concerned in Ephesians 6. Paul's stress on the fact that the

June

powers of evil are the world-rulers, or the rulers of the darkness of this world, is significant of that wider conflict within the church, and each member of it is called upon to maintain that battle against those systems of superstition, cruelty, and pride which oppose the gospel of Jesus Christ.

It is well for us to recognize this supernatural element in the evil by which our work for God is confronted. We have to wrestle, not simply with stupidity, barbarity, or the intellectual acumen of flesh and blood, but with the spiritual hosts of wickedness which are in heavenly places (see Dan. 10).

There is no need, however, for us to be unduly afraid, for in His ascension all these principalities and powers were put under the feet of our Redeemer; as we abide in Him, we share His conquest; we are more than a match for the mightiest forces of hell; we walk upon high places.

But we are to be alert, putting on the whole armor of God, that we might not fail. If Christians are not careful as to their personal character, the devil can laugh them to scorn. By their inconsistencies they cut off their faith and disassociate themselves from the only source of victory that Satan dreads.

Let us walk honestly, as in the day; not in rioting and drunkenness, not in chambering and wantonness, not in strife and envying. But put ye on the Lord Jesus Christ and make not provision for the flesh, to fulfil the lusts thereof.
Romans 13: 13, 14

TO THIS passage Augustine contributed his entire conversion and emancipation. "Behold," he says, "I heard a voice from a neighboring house, as of a boy or a girl, I knew not whether, saying in a singing note, and often repeating, *Tolle lege, tolle lege,* take up and read. Whereupon, the course of my tears being suppressed, I got up and interpreting it to be nothing less than a divine admonition that I should open the book, and read the place that I first lit upon. Therefore, I returned in haste to the place where I had lain down the book of the apostle; when I arose . . . I caught it up, opened it, and read in silence the place in which I first cast mine eyes; 'not in chambering and wantonness, not in strife and envying. But put ye on the Lord Jesus Christ and make not provision for the flesh, to fulfill the lust thereof.' I could read no further, nor was there need. For with the end of this sentence, as if a light of confidence and security streamed into my heart, all the darkness of former hesitation was dispelled." May similar effects accrue to each one of us! As we ponder these words, may light stream into our hearts.

For us, as for Augustine, there is always, in the earlier stages of our Christian lives, some perplexity as to the method of treating the evil habits which have grown with our years and cling to us with grim tenacity. Shall we leave them behind us in the course of time? Will they relax their hold? Is there any way of providing for their gratification within fixed and defined limits? Is it to be a perpetual struggle between us and them, in which sometimes we and sometimes they will conquer? To all these questions, a sufficient answer is suggested by the apostle. He insists on the definite, sudden, and entire abandonment of the works of darkness, and the immediate, final, and irrevocable acceptance of the Armor of Light. If we will put on the Lord Jesus Christ, we will, in effect put away the old man.

Let us walk honestly, as in the day. . . .
Romans 13: 13a

10

IT IS nothing to us that the shadows appear to linger over us; for us at least the day has broken, for the daystar has arisen in our hearts, and we are called upon to live as children of light and of day. Our eternity has already begun. We have come out of the great tribulation to rest within the silken curtains of God's pavilion; we have washed our robes and made them white in the blood of the Lamb; we already walk the streets of the New Jerusalem. Only let us day by day allow our light to shine.

Let us live on the level of God's thought for us. Let us walk as in the day, as we shall do when the time of the restitution of all things has taken place, in those blessed years when the sun will no

June

more go down or the moon withdraw herself, and the Lord will be the Everlasting Light.

To do this, we must put on the Armor of Light (Rom. 13: 12). In an earlier epistle the apostle had already suggested the thought: Let us since we are of the day, be sober, putting on the breastplate of faith and love, and for a helmet, the hope of salvation. And in a later epistle, he carefully enumerates its successive pieces. But here he gathers up all into one comprehensive phrase: "The Armor of Lights!" It is just the Lord Jesus Christ. Put Him on—His gentleness, His meekness, and humility; His purity and truth; His obedience to the will of God and sensitivity to every cry of weakness or suffering; and what seems soft to the flesh will be armor of proof in the day of battle. None are so invincible and stalwart as those who are arrayed in the meekness and gentleness of Christ.

11	*And your feet shod with the preparation of the gospel of peace.*

Ephesians 6: 15

THE CHRISTIAN warrior must follow after peace. There is undoubtedly a reference in these words to Isaiah's vision of the messengers, who with beautiful feet, speed across the mountains to proclaim the good tidings of the gospel. But there is the further thought that those who carry the gospel of peace must tread gently and softly.

If the gospel of peace is our message, the peace of God should mantle our face with a holy calm; breathe through our lips like a benediction; and defuse itself like the dew of the Lord over the places of human rivalry and hatred. Ours should be the blessedness of the peacemakers. Our tread should be only in the paths of peace, except when the trumpet of God clearly calls us to war against the sins and wrongs around us. "If it be possible, as much as in *you* lieth, be at peace with all men. So then, let us follow after things which make for peace, and things whereby we may edify one another. The Lord's servant must not strive; but be gentle toward all, apt to teach, forbearing, in meekness correcting them that oppose

June

themselves." Be it ours, then, always to be on the altar to promote peace and love among men; not incensed or irritated by their rancorous dealings with ourselves; not catching fire at the flame of their wrath and indignation.

For as many of you as have been baptized into Christ have put on Christ.
Galatians 3: 27

12

IN JESUS there is supply for every need, armor against every attack, fullness for every deficiency. Avail yourself of Him; make use of Him; appropriate His sufficiency; go into every day, whatever its anticipated emergencies, temptations, and perils, as those who are encased in the very nature and character of Jesus, which they offer as their answer to every possible demand.

Put on the Lordship of Jesus. For this cause He died and lived again, that He might be Lord of both the living and the dead. Let His authority be supreme, His will and prompting our law.

Put on the humanity of Jesus. From the day when He went back to Nazareth, and was subject to His parents, to the day when He pleaded for His murderers on the cross, He presents a lovely example of holy and spotless manhood.

Put on the anointing of Jesus. He is the Christ of God. Never rest till God, who anointed Him as Head, has anointed you the member of His Body, and you are a Christian (an anointed one, in deed and in truth).

And herein do I exercise myself, to have always a conscience void of offense toward God, and toward men.
Acts 24: 16

13

WHAT A beautiful contrast there is between the laxity of too many of us and the scrupulous care of the apostle Paul! How watchfully

June

he exercised himself to have a conscience void of offense toward man as well as toward God! How sensitive to the least appearance of self-seeking, that he might cut off occasion from them which desired an occasion! How gladly he went without what was in itself lawful, to make sure that his ministry would not be blamed!

It becomes the Christian to put beyond the power of man or devil to point to some inaccuracy or inconsistency in his life, and to say, "This man belies his profession, and contradicts his own teaching." Rather let us suffer wrong and submit to overcharge, and give men even more than they can justly claim. Anything of loss or suffering may be cheerfully met, in order that night after night we may wash our hands in innocency and feel that we have not put a stumbling block in the path of any man. This is only possible as we abide by faith in Christ our Righteousness. And when we have done our best, we shall have nothing to boast of. We are always unprofitable servants, who have only done what they ought.

Whereof I was made a minister, according to the gift of the grace of God given unto me by the effectual working of his power.

Ephesians 3: 7

THE POWER of God is shown in the communication of spiritual gifts. The apostle took a lowly view of himself. He was but a minister, a deacon, a servant; like the Master, who, when none of His disciples would wash the feet of the rest, put an end to the hesitation as to who should do it, by doing it Himself. Only the greatest can stoop to these menial offices without loss of position or self respect.

But the position that the great apostle occupied was distinctly, in his judgment, the gift of the grace of God. And he never ceased magnifying the exceeding abundance of the grace which had not only saved him, but had given him an office in the church.

The grace of God which calls us into His blessed service is connected with the energy of His power; so whatever the work may be to which we are called, there is ever sufficient power awaiting within our reach for doing it. The grace of God permits us to be His fellow workers in the salvation of men; and the power of God moves parallel with the line of our activities, to do that which would baffle our unaided efforts. Whatever you are called to do by the grace of God, you may be enabled to do by the power of God; and you will acquire the marvelous faculty of making men see the meaning of mysteries long veiled from their view.

That He would grant you, according to the riches of his glory, to be strengthened with might by his Spirit, in the inner man.

Ephesians 3: 16

15

HE IS THE Source of spiritual strength. There is no limit to the spiritual power we may receive and exercise. It is said of the Gadites who came to David, while he was in prison, that the least was equal to a hundred, and the greatest to a thousand (1 Chron. 12: 14). This might be typically true of each of us. We might, like Micah, be "full of power by the Spirit of the Lord, and of judgment, and of might" (Mic. 3: 8).

There is one preliminary condition, however, which we must fulfill. We must be weak enough—willing to abjure the use of those sources of success on which others boast themselves; content that the thorn in the flesh, or the test of the stream, or the wrestle at the Jabbock, should reveal our utter helplessness—that the power of Christ should rest upon us. When we are weak, we shall be strong. When we are worms, God will make us new sharp threshing instruments. When we are among things that are not, God will use us to bring to nought things that are.

Enoch walked with God. . . .

Genesis 5: 22

16

OUR WALK is a synonym for our life. Life is a walk from the cradle to the grave. Our steps emerge from the jeweled gates of birth,

June

traverse rock and sand, beautiful meadow and difficult mountain steeps, and ultimately pass within the portal of death, which, though somber enough when seen from afar, is often found to be brightly lit with light from the world beyond.

In this sense the word occurs in all parts of Scripture. In the opening chapters of Genesis it is said of Enoch that he *walked* with God. And, in one of the last Epistles, we are bidden to walk even as Jesus *walked*. Between these extreme points, the pages of the Scripture are strewn with similar references. Indeed, the comparison of life to a pilgrimage is based on the same conception. The race of man goes afoot, as a vast host.

A walk is made up of steps. Though a man circles the globe, yet he must do it by one step at a time; and the character of the steps will determine the character of the walk. So life is made up, for the most part, of trifles, commonplaces, the reiteration of familiar and simple acts. What we are in these, that will be the color and value of our lives and the verdict of eternity. Life is not made by the rapturous but brief moments which we spend on the transfiguration Mount; but by the steps we take to and fro along the pathway of daily duty, and of sometimes monotonous routine.

17	*I, therefore, the prisoner of the Lord, beseech you that ye walk worthy of the vocation wherewith ye are called.*
	Ephesians 4: 1

THE SIMPLEST words are the deepest. Take, for instance, the word *call*. It is constantly on our lips. The mother calls her child. The businessman calls his friend. And God appropriates it in His dealing with men. He *calls* them. From the throne of His glory He speaks to every soul of man, once, twice, many times, as when He said, "Samuel, Samuel," or "Saul, Saul." In some solemn hour of decision, in a moment of awful crisis, by human voice or written word, or by the pleading and remonstrance of conscience, God's voice may be heard calling men to Himself to heaven and to a saintly life. On that call the apostle bases his argument for holiness. Act worthily of the love which summoned you, and of the goal to which you have been called. Stand still and ask yourself before you speak, or act, or decide—is this worthy of that great ideal which God has conceived for me, when He called me from the rest of men to be His priest, His son, His saint? If not, avoid it like the plague!

Till we all come in the unity of the faith, and of the knowl-edge of the Son of God, unto a perfect man, unto the mea-sure of the stature of the fulness of Christ.
Ephesians 4: 13

18

FROM THE hands of the ascended Savior, gifts are distributed to His church. He gave some apostles; some prophets; some evange-lists; some pastors and teachers. But to every member of the church, the weakest and the obscurest, some special grace was given, accord-ing to the measure of the gift of Christ. Every joint in the body has some function to perform to all the rest, and to the growth and per-fectness of the whole.

Alas! too many of the saints are unaware of the possession of gift or gifts, and they leave them buried, or they are out of joint, and so unable to do their specific work. The special function of the officers of the church—the apostles, prophets, pastors—is to stir the saints to discover their gifts; and, if need be, to put them into articulated union with the Lord, so that they may take up the work of min-istering to the rest of the body. This thought is somewhat obscured in the older version, but made abundantly clear in the Revised Version: "To equip the saints for the work of ministry, for building up the body of Christ" (4: 12). We may seem to do nothing else than minister to the particles or members just against us, but this reacts on the whole. And presently—it may be nearer than we sup-pose—the body will have reached its full growth, will have attained to the measure of the stature of the fullness of Christ, and will be worthy of its Head. All the saints with Jesus will make together a full-grown perfect man, which shall realize in completeness the divine ideal.

June

19

This I say therefore, and testify in the Lord, that ye hence-
forth walk not as other Gentiles walk, in the vanity of their
mind. . . . Walk as children of light.

Ephesians 4: 17; 5: 8b

WALK IN the light. God is light; and we live in daily, hourly communion with Him, in such a frame of mind that His name is frequently on our hearts, or murmured softly by our lips, or spoken
when temptation is near. Thus we may be said to be walking in the
light. And it is just in proportion as our steps tread the crystal
pathway of light, that our understanding becomes enlightened. In
God's light we see light. When the heart is pure, the eye is single.

The contrary to this is also true. When we are alienated from the
life of God, our understanding is darkened to the truth of God. The
seat of infidelity is in the heart. Once let a soul be shut out from the
life of God through the hardening of the heart; once let it give itself
up to evil, and to make a trade with uncleanness for cleanness; then
the light of the knowledge of the glory of God beats against a shut-
tered window asking for admittance in vain. Let us not walk "in the
vanity of their mind."

20

And walk in love, as Christ also hath loved us, and hath
given himself for us an offering and a sacrifice to God for
a sweetsmelling savor.

Ephesians 5: 2

WE ARE TO imitate God's love in Christ. The love that gives, that
counts no cost too great, and in sacrificing itself for others, offers
all to God—and does all this for his sake. Such was the love of Jesus
—sweet to God, as the scent of fields of new-mown grass in June;
and this must be our model.

Not to those who love us, but who hate; not to those who are
pleasant and agreeable, but who repel; not because our natural
feelings are excited, but because we will to minister, even to the
point of the cross, must our love go out. And every time we thus
sacrifice ourselves to another for the sake of God, we enter into some
of the meaning of this sacrifice of Calvary, and there is wafted up
to God the odor of a sweet smell.

June

For ye were sometimes darkness, but now are ye light in the Lord; walk as children of light.

Ephesians 5: 8

21

IF YOU would know God, you must resemble God. If you would learn God's secrets, you must walk with God. If you would know the doctrine, ye must be willing to do His will.

But there is something even better than walking in the light; it is to become children of the light. What an exquisite conception! Dewdrops sparkling in the light of dawn; stardust glittering on the vault of night; hummingbirds flashing in the tropic sun; children dancing in light-hearted glee—none of these are so truly sons of light as they who have been begotten by the Father of Light; who carry within them the Light that lights up hearts, and who in goodness, righteousness, and truth, prove what is well pleasing unto the Lord. Let us live as such.

See then that ye walk circumspectly, not as fools, but as wise.

Ephesians 5: 15

22

WE ARE TO walk carefully. We are to pick our way amid the pitfalls of the world. We are to gird up our flowing robes with care, lest they be soiled by the filth of the street. Beware of any sidepaths that might lead our steps away from the narrow track. Watch and pray. Especially be careful to turn every moment of time into an opportunity of making progress in the divine life. We are to take heed to the moments and the hours will take heed to themselves.

All these injunctions, however, will baffle us and leave us stranded on the shore, when the impulse of their stimulus ebbs unless we blend with them the thought that God is willing to walk with us— no, *in* us; for He says, "I will dwell in them, and walk in them." Abide in God, and God will abide in you, and walk in you, till you walk with Him in white being found worthy.

June

<table>
<tr><td>23</td><td>Stand therefore, having your loins girt about with truth, and having on the breastplate of righteousness.
Ephesians 6: 14</td></tr>
</table>

THE CHRISTIAN warrior must be true. The loins are significant of strength; and girded loins represent the opposite of self-indulgence, or carelessness. Hence the need for the girded loins; and our Lord solemnly insists on it as a prime necessity for His servants. "Let your loins be girded about, and your lamps burning."

We must gird ourselves with truth. We must be true to the laws of our nature, never overstepping the limits of moderation, never using for self-indulgence the powers which were intended only for the maintenance of the fires of life; never yielding to the worst self which lurks in us all, beneath our civilized front. We must be true to God who made and redeemed us; true to our best selves, our noblest ideals; true to those with whom we live, and who are certainly affected for good or evil by our self-restraint or the reverse.

<table>
<tr><td>24</td><td>And righteousness shall be the girdle of his loins, and faithfulness the girdle of his reins.
Isaiah 11: 5</td></tr>
</table>

THE CHRISTIAN warrior must be righteous. "Put on the breastplate of righteousness." This righteousness is not primarily that which is reckoned to us, as soon as we believe in Jesus, but rather that personal righteousness which is wrought in us by the Holy Spirit, and in virtue of which our characters are conformed to that of Jesus Christ the Righteous. The apostle refers to it when he reminds Titus that the grace of God instructs us to deny ungodliness and worldly lusts, and to live soberly, *righteously*, godly in this present world. It is the temper we should cultivate and manifest in all our dealings with men. The breastplate is worn upon the heart, the seat of our affections and emotions. In these especially we must be right.

It is very necessary to remember this. Of what use is it to speak of Jesus to those who are rankling under the sense of our injustice, or are sensible of some glaring inconsistency in our character? The effect of our most eloquent entreaties is neutralized by our deeds, which speak even louder. The Christian warrior must be *righteous*.

And take the helmet of salvation, and the sword of the Spirit, which is the word of God.
Ephesians 6: 17

25

THE CHRISTIAN warrior must know God's salvation in his own experience. He must be saved from the guilt and penalty of sin before he can proclaim the plentitude of God's forgiveness to the chief of sinners. He must know the gospel as the follower of God unto salvation from the dominion of sin in his own heart. He must be anticipating the consummation of God's purpose in the redemption of the body. As the helmet glistens in the sunshine, so must the crown of the Christian's experience point upward to heaven and onward to the glory yet to be revealed. He must speak that which he knows, and declare what he has seen and heard. It is when we are experiencing the power of God's salvation that we can declare it to others, with a freedom and a power that needs no further collaboration. And it is when men see the salvation of God exemplified in our own lives and characters, that they will be prepared to accept it as indeed the Word of God.

Above all, taking the shield of faith, wherewith ye shall be able to quench all the fiery darts of the wicked.
Ephesians 6: 16

26

THE CHRISTIAN warrior must be vigorous in faith. As each fiery dart, tipped with the flames of hate, comes speeding to the soldier of the cross, deafened by the din and blinded by the smoke of battle,

June

he must catch and quench it on the golden shield of faith, that it reach not his head or his heart.

Sometimes a slander will be circulated, for which you have given no occasion; or a venomous speech or article will be hurled at you; or some horrible suggestion will be thrust between the joints of the armor—or some deadly reminder of the sins of the past, which you can never recall without burning remorse. At such times we are tempted to give back, to renounce our work, to withdraw from the battle. And those will certainly yield to the temptation who are not inspired by the faith that can hand these things over to the compassionate and mighty Savior, who knows all, but loves better than He knows, and who interposes to cover our heads in the day of battle.

But faith like this is only possible to him whose hands are clean and heart pure; who is living in daily fellowship with Jesus, and whose soul is nurtured by daily feeding on the Word of God.

|27| *Finally, brethren, whatsoever things are true, whatsoever things are honest, whatsoever things are just . . . think on these things.*

Philippians 4: 8

A FRIEND of mine, educated in one of our great English schools, says that the most formative words of his life were addressed to him by his headmaster, as he said good-by: "Be true," he said, "always be true." My friend records that those words have often come back to him at critical moments of his life, indicating his path, as with finger of light.

Every man, in his heart of hearts, has some knowledge of what is eternally right and good. You see it in the little child who blushes and conceals himself when he has told a lie; it may be a dim flicker, but it is there. The radiance that streams through the open door of heaven may have become very faint by the time it reaches the spot on the dark area where you stand, but unless you willfully turn your back on it, it falls around your feet and on your heart. Truth, so far as it concerns us, is that attitude of soul which thinks and acts its inconsistencies with its highest ideals and the marvel is, that as we act consistently with our ideals, they tend to become always nobler and purer, and to approximate more nearly those higher standards which exist in the nature of God. If a man be true to his better self, he will become the pupil of the Spirit of Truth, and catch a glimpse of further horizons, so that ultimately he will come out into the great light of eternity, as it shines from the face of Christ.

By faith Moses, when he was come to years, refused to be called the son of Pharaoh's daughter.

Hebrews 11: 24

28

MOSES fed daily on the promises of God, pleading them in prayer, and leaning his whole weight upon them. And he often knew what it was to leave behind him the familiar and tried, for the strange and new; at the bidding of God, he stepped out, though there seemed nothing to tread upon, launching himself and three millions of people absolutely on the care of God, assured that God's faithfulness could not fail.

Are you willing to die to your own strength; to forsake your own plans for God's; to seek out and do His will absolutely; to take up the attitude of entire and absolute surrender to His purposes; to feed daily on the promises of God; to step out in faith, reckoning, without emotion of any kind, on the faithfulness of God, only fully persuaded that He will perform all that He has promised? Then surely through you God will, here or hereafter, work as in the times of old, of which our fathers have told us.

Wherefore lay apart all filthiness and superfluity of naughtiness, and receive with meekness the engrafted word, which is able to save your souls.

James 1: 21

29

IT IS impossible to estimate the value of good and sunny dispositions, which go through life with a song, looking always on the

June

bright side of things and yielding to the blows and disappointments with an unfailing grace. It is often associated with a sound constitution and abounding health, and there is undoubtedly a close connection between the two; but it is not dependent on these, for, as the great Dr. Arnold testified of his sister, who was for years a confirmed invalid, but whose chamber was the sunniest room in the house, keen suffering and pain have often only set forth to greater advantage the wellspring of sweetness and good nature which has poured forth like strains of sweet music amid the clatter of a dusty, noisy thoroughfare.

But how may those afflicted with ill temper be delivered? The Apostle Peter says, "Laying aside all malice, and all guile, and hypocrisies, and envies, and all evil-speakings, as new born babes, desire the sincere milk of the word that ye may grow thereby" (1 Pet. 2: 1,2). The *laying aside* is a remarkable expression, for it means that the thing may be done by one sudden, definite act. We are not to wait till these evil things die down in our hearts, but are to make up our minds, once and forever, to lay them aside; evenso a beggar lays aside his rags when new clothes are offered him. It is a definite act of the will. Will you make it now?

30

He that saith that he abideth in him ought himself also so to walk, even as he walked.

1 John 2: 6

WHAT SCOPE for love this verse suggests. Envy and jealousy need have no place. God has prepared the path for each of us, according to His infinite wisdom and love. One way is adapted for one, and another for another. Peter is girded and carried where he does not want to go; John tarries until the Master comes for him in the peaceful decease of old age. "What is that to thee? Follow thou Me," says the Lord. Each, then, can take a loving interest in the life plan of another, sure that nothing can interfere with the evolution of his own, save his laziness or sin. Prepare us, O God, for all that you have prepared for us. We will not be ambitious for great things, but to walk, day by day, humbly with Thee, and so fulfill our course. In this way we will become Your workmanship.

July

Lord, who shall abide in thy tabernacle? who shall dwell in thy holy hill? He that walketh uprightly, and worketh righteousness, and speaketh the truth in his heart.
Psalm 15: 1, 2

| 1 |

BE TRUE in your actions. If you are an artist, portray nature as you find her, never using your colors for mere effect or display. If you are a mechanic or manufacturer, do not make articles merely for show or sale, but because they accomplish the purpose they profess: boots to keep the feet dry, clothes to wear, furniture to last. The world is full of shoddy and sham, of mediocre workmanship in our houses, of articles that do not perform as they are advertised, of tinsel that resembles gold, of paste jewels that resemble the real thing, of veneer that looks like aged wood. Do not deal in counterfeits, lest you contract the habit of falsehood and inaccuracy. See that your hands and eyes and heart are in rhythm with your highest conceptions of what is honest, lovely, and of good report. Bear witness, as Jesus did, to the Reality of Things. Did Paul ever make a tent which deceived the purchaser? Live your life as he did.

I will take heed to my ways, that I sin not with my tongue: I will keep my mouth with a bridle. . . .
Psalm 39: 1

| 2 |

WHAT WE say influences others, but it has a reflex influence on ourselves. When we speak unadvisedly and impurely, we sow seeds of ill harvests not in others only, but in ourselves, and the very utterance injures us. When, on the other hand, we refuse to give expression to a wrong or unkind thought, we choke and strangle it.

July

Will each reader and hearer of these words carefully bear this in mind? If you express what is uncharitable or wrong, you gratify the evil nature that is in you, and you strengthen it. If, on the contrary, you refuse to express it, you strike a death-blow at the cursed thing itself. When you keep your mouth you keep your life, because you weaken that which is gnawing insidiously at the root of your life. If there is fire in a room, be sure not to open a door or window; for air is its fuel and food. And if a fire is burning within you, be sure not to give it vent. What goes forth from you defiles you. Would you see good days? Refrain your lips from evil.

Perhaps you find yourself unable to bridle your tongue. You are only discovering the truth of those terrible words: "The tongue is a fire, the world of iniquity among our members, which defileth the whole body, and setteth on fire the wheel of nature, and is set on fire of hell. . . . The tongue can no man tame; it is a restless evil, full of deadly poison." If man cannot tame it, the Savior can. Cry to Him then, saying, "Set a watch, O Lord, before my mouth; keep the door of my lips." The fire of God's love will burn out the fire of hell. Hand the bridle, or rudder, as the Apostle James calls it, over to Him.

3	*For God, who commanded the light to shine out of darkness, hath shined in our hearts, to give the light of the knowledge of the glory of God in the face of Jesus Christ.* 2 Corinthians 4: 6

THIS MAY be referred to the work of God in the heart. He who commanded light to shine out of darkness has shined in our hearts, to give the light of the knowledge of the glory of God. A little glimmering ray at first, God's light in the soul grows ever from less to more, revealing Himself and manifesting ourselves, so that we are growingly attracted from the self-life to circle around Him.

But probably it is true also of the graciousness of the believer's life. At first it shows itself in little acts of blessing on children and the poor; but the range of influence is always apt to increase, till what was a glimmer of helpfulness becomes as the sun shining in strength. The Sunday school teacher becomes the preacher; the visitor among the poor becomes the philanthropist; the witness to the gospel in the factory is called to witness in the great theater of the world. See to it that there is a steady obedience to God's least promptings and warnings. Follow on to know the Lord, and to be conformed to His all-wise purpose.

Once again, notice the comparison in its exquisite beauty. Light is so gentle, noiseless, and tender. There is no sound; its voice is not heard. So is the influence of the holy soul. Its life becomes the light of men. As with the angel over the plain of Bethlehem, it sheds a light around those whom it will presently address. Like the Gulf Stream, which changes our climate from northern rigor to the temperate zone, so a holy life gently and irresistibly influences and blesses the world. The world is no worse than it is, not because of the holy words spoken on the Lord's Day, but for the holy lives of obscure saints.

Hear my prayer, O God. . . . Behold, God is mine helper.
Psalm 54: 2, 4

4

THERE ARE only seven stanzas in this psalm. It is one of the briefer of David's compositions. Written when the Ziphites told of David's hiding-place and compelled him to shift his quarters, perhaps it attests by its brevity some hasty moment snatched from the hurry and bustle of the necessary flight. It is said that Mr. Gladstone made his memorable Latin version of "Rock of Ages" during an interval of a House of Commons debate. It is worthy of remark that, however hurried David might have been, and however great the responsibility resting upon him, he found time to turn to God for help. He had learned the secret of abiding in the Divine Presence.

There must be no division of interests, if God is to be all. You must consider yourself as a stone before a carver, whereof he is to make a statue—presenting yourself before Him that He may make his perfect image in you and do as He will with your life. You must realize that He has permitted this interruption of your peace, this intrusion of Ziphite hate. You must look beyond the hand that

July

smites, to the Father who permits. Then the soul will rock itself to rest; and before you have been five minutes with God you will be able to say as David, "He hath delivered me" (Ps. 54: 7). Be of good cheer; rest on his Name; He will deliver you out of *all* trouble.

5	*Mine age is departed, and is removed from me as a shepherd's tent. . . .*

Isaiah 38: 12a

THE TENT of our lives is not always perfect to begin with. Some of us start out on our pilgrimage with a crazy house which is always in need of attention and repair. Life is much more difficult under such conditions. Paul's thorn in the flesh made it less likely that he could achieve as much as other men; it was by God's grace that he actually achieved more. All honor to the men who have triumphed over the limitations and deficiencies and have become more than conquerors through Him who loves them.

Few things in our language are more touching than the comparison made by the Northumbrian chieftain on the eve of the introduction of Christianity, between man's life and the flight of a sparrow through a lighted hall, coming out of the darkness of the storm, and after a brief flight, going forth into it again. Life, lived in the light of this comparison, is fleeting. We must live it to the full while we have it.

6	*For the Lord is good; his mercy is everlasting; and his truth endureth to all generations.*

Psalm 100: 5

THERE IS the strongest obligation that we should often stand foursquare before the mirror of truth; which is Christ—Christ the Light that lighteth every man; Christ in conscience; Christ in the Word. There is no more stringent test than this. With unfailing accuracy we will discover our true selves, as we come face to face with Him, who is girt with righteousness as the girdle of His reins, and faithfulness as the girdle of His loins (Isa. 11: 5). Let there be any inconsistency, and it will at once and unerringly be revealed. No distortion of the inner life can escape detection or condemnation before the judgment seat, whose decisions are ratified by each soul's secret convictions of justice. Would that we were all in the habit of submitting to that fateful scrutiny—not the greater matters only, but all the smallest details of our lives!

Then let us, in the name and by the power of Jesus, put away all that has been shown to be inconsistent with His character and claims, and let us submit in everything to His control. It will cost us something. We may have difficulty with our judgment warped and injured by self-preference. We may have to contend with our will, reluctant to sign the death warrant of some favorite habit. We may feel powerless to carry into effect what we know, in our loftiest moments, to be our only safe and blessed policy. But happy are we, if we dare to catch up the trailing robes of self-indulgence, and restrain them under the umbrella of inexorable truth and purity.

By the rivers of Babylon, there we sat down, yea, we wept, when we remembered Zion.

Psalm 137: 1

$$\boxed{7}$$

WE ARE exiled beside the rivers of time, as Israel was in Babylon, and we mingle our tears with its waters as we reflect on the brevity and transience of our days. "When the earthly house of this tabernacle is broken up, we have a building of God, a house not made with hands, eternal in the heavens" (2 Cor. 5: 1). It has been truly said that we are not flesh and blood, but are made *partakers of flesh and blood.* Each one of us is an immortal spirit created in the likeness of God, and for a little while we are brought under the conditions of mortality, and an education for our eternal condition. During our brief sojourn here, we reside in a body as our tent. It is the house of our pilgrimage. That tent is frail. Only a veil hangs between us and the great constellations of eternity, between us and

July

the world of realities, between us and the face of God. A breath may wave it, an insect's sting may pierce it, a thorn may rend it. But this is the house of our pilgrimage.

8

The wicked is snared by the transgression of his lips; but the just shall come out of trouble.

Proverbs 12: 13

IT HAS been well remarked that God has set many snares in the very constitution and order of the world for the detection and punishment of evildoers. Among others, is the liar's own tongue. Watch a criminal trial, and you will find abundant illustrations of this in the detection of a false witness, who makes statement after statement, which are not only inconsistent with truth, but with each other. Presently he comes to a point, where he falls into one of his own lies, which he had forgotten, and flops floundering like a wild beast in a snare. It is impossible for a liar to imitate the severe and inflexible majesty of truth. In his endeavor to appear true, he will fall into a trap of his own setting.

But while the wicked goes into a snare, "the righteous shall come out of trouble." It is not said that he will always escape it. Our Master clearly foretold that all lives which were molded on the example of His own would pass through similar experiences. For them also the bitter hatred of the world, the title Beelzebub, and at last the cross. "But the just shall come out of trouble." It is not possible that we should be kept by it.

9

Blessed is the man that feareth the Lord.

Psalm 112: 1

THE SPECIAL phase of blessedness here, is that of the home life (Ps. 128). The Jews have always been distinguished for this. A recent writer, describing the Jews of the middle ages, says: "The sanctity of the home was an affectionate tradition, linking them with a golden chain to their fathers before them; and amidst the degradation heaped on them, they were emancipated in at least one spot on earth, and learned from their domestic peace to look with pitiful rather than vindictive eyes upon their persecutors."

Our religious life, when it is genuine, will always cast a halo of blessedness on the home. Not lightly does Wordsworth blend "the kindred points of heaven and home," for the man who fears God brings heaven into his home. We must not be sullen or self-absorbed there. We must divest ourselves of business cares and anxieties; of irritation and fretfulness; of the brooding clouds that have gathered on our faces; we must carefully maintain the courtesies of home, and be our sweetest, gladdest, loveliest selves.

What a charming cluster of images we see in Psalm 128. The wife as a vine twining round the carved trellis work of the inner court of the Oriental home—as though the woman gives the rich wine of life, which is love, as well as shadowing fertility and graceful beauty; while children as olive plants are sources of perennial joy. Would you have such a home? Its keystone is the fear of grieving the Spirit of God.

The heart of her husband trusts in her, and he will have no lack of gain.

Proverbs 31: 11, RSV

| 10 |

THIS alphabetical poem to godly womanhood is one of the gems of the Old Testament. It should be read from the Revised Version, that its significant and beautiful touches may be appreciated. Clearly the Hebrew woman was held in high honor, and had as much freedom of action as she enjoys in Christian countries. Herein the contrast was very marked, as against the women of other oriental nations. But in the whole delineation there is hardly any trait more beautiful than this—absolute trustworthiness. You can see the pair together: the husband comes in from sitting among the elders, his heart weighted with affairs of state, and he seeks her confidence and advice. He has no fear of her betraying his secrets. He can safely trust her.

This surely is the most sacred joy a woman can have. To be con-

July

sulted, to be trusted, to share the common toils and responsibilities. Who would not work willingly with her hands, and rise while yet night, and engage in ceaseless toils, if only she had the inspiration that trust brings!

Can Christ, in like manner, safely trust us? (John 2: 24, RV). Can He trust us with His secrets, His interests, His money? Abraham was one whom God could safely trust, and He did trust him as His friend: "Shall I hide from Abraham, . . . for I have known him?" It is required of us also that we be absolutely trustworthy.

11

I am my beloved's, and his desire is toward me.
Song of Solomon 7: 10

THIS IS the thankful recognition of the Bride. She knows that she belongs to, that she is loved by, the Bridegroom in that His desire is turned toward her with ineffable longing.

Dear soul, do you realize the desire of your Beloved toward you? You love Him; but He loves you ever so much more. You desire Him; but His desire toward you is as much greater than yours towards Him, as sunlight is more brilliant than moonlight.

How have we responded to His great desire? I'm afraid our response has sometimes been very uncertain and unsatisfactory. Sometimes we have felt a pure flame of answering affection; but it has soon been obscured with clouds of smoke, or has died down for want of oil.

The Lord desires more of our time, that we should withdraw ourselves from the busy rush of the world and the absorbing interests of life, to allow Him to commune with us. He desires more of our affection, that He may teach us how to respond to His love. He desires to teach us how to share His riches, as His joint-heirs; how to sit with Him in heavenly places; how to work in the energy of His Spirit. Let us yield ourselves to His desires, and allow Him to effect in and for us all He desires for us, so that we may give Him delight. "As the bridegroom rejoiceth over the bride, so shall thy God rejoice over thee." If, as Zephaniah says, He is silent in His love, because His

July

love is too strong for speech, we may yield ourselves to it without misgiving.

*And what agreement hath the temple of God with idols?
for ye are the temple of the living God; as God hath said,
I will dwell in them, and walk in them. . . .*
                                            2 Corinthians 6: 16

12

THIS SENTENCE should be deeply pondered; every word in it is significant. Evidently Paul intends that we should know its deep and solemn meaning. This doctrine must be one of the standards of our holy faith. However, this knowledge should not be merely that of the intellect, but it should be born out of the deep pondering of the heart.

The holy Temple—Built up of the dust of the earth, our bodies are rarer than the most glorious structures that ever the sun shone upon, because they are meant to be the shrine and home of God. Jesus spoke of the Temple of His Body; and if He was so zealous for his Father's House that He drove out the greedy money-changers, and refused to allow a vessel to be carried through the courts, should we not be equally careful? We are the custodians of the divine residence; let us be very careful that there is nothing there to offend or trouble the celestial Inmate.

The Divine Inmate—Too often He is grieved, and driven to occupy the most secret shrine, concealed and hidden beneath the heavy veil of our inconsistency and unbelief. He is not driven *out* by our sins, but driven *in*. Whenever, on the contrary, we put away our sin, and walk in the light as He is in the light; whenever the veil is rent and the whole heart thrown open to Him—He comes in power to occupy every part of our being, so that there is no part dark, and the very body becomes transfigured.

The great price—We are bought as any slave standing in the marketplace for sale! Ransomed from the direst slavemaster to the dearest Lord! The price—not corruptible things, as silver and gold—but precious blood! Our life is henceforth not our own, but His.

July

13

For where your treasure is, there will your heart be also.
Luke 12: 34

OUR SAVIOR told of a man who, in plowing his field, heard his plowshare chink against buried treasure, and the man hastened to sell all that he had to buy the field. In speaking thus, He pictured Himself as well as us. He found us before we found Him. The treasure is His people, to purchase whom He gave up all that He had, even to His throne (Matt. 13: 44). "But you are a chosen race, a royal priesthood, a holy nation, God's own people, that you may declare the wonderful deeds of him who called you out of darkness into his marvelous light" (1 Pet. 2: 9, RSV).

Where his treasure is, there is a man's heart. If it is in ships on the treacherous sea, he tosses restlessly on his bed, concerned for its safety. If it is in fabrics, he guards against moth; if it is in metal, against rust and thieves. Is Christ less careful with His own? Does He not guard with equal care against all that would deteriorate our value in His esteem? Need we fear the thief? Will not our Lord keep us that the evil one shall not touch us (Matt. 6: 19,20)?

God's treasure is His forever. "They shall be mine, says the Lord of hosts, my special possession . . ." (Mal. 3: 17, RSV). He will hold His own, as men cling to a treasure.

Let us note the conditions: to obey His voice and keep His covenant; then on eagles' wings He will bring us to Himself. Compliance with these is blessed in its results. God regards us with the ecstasy of a love that rejoices over us with singing; and counts on us as a mother on her child, a miser on his gold.

14

There is forgiveness with thee, that thou mayest be feared.
Psalm 130: 4

YES, thank God, there is forgiveness, because at *His* right hand He lives for evermore who put away sin by the sacrifice of Himself. Forgiveness at any moment for the sins of a life; repeated forgiveness for the sins of every hour; forgiveness instantaneously upon confession. He pardons and absolves all those who truly repent and unfeignedly believe in Him of whom the gospel speaks. And when God once speaks forgiveness, it can never be unspoken. Fear and doubt and misgiving may question, but cannot revoke it. Based on the Blood of the Covenant, on promises ratified by the most solemn assurances, there is irrevocable forgiveness with God. Weary, sinning, ashamed soul, the fountain of God's forgiveness springs perennially from his heart; as clear and full as when that fountain was first opened for sin and uncleanness. Take it and go your way. Even if there be no rush of emotion, or sense of pardon, yet dare to believe that your cries and tears and confessions have been heard and answered.

Just because God is so ready to forgive, there is wrought within our hearts an ever-deepening dread of giving Him pain. There is forgiveness with Him, that He may be feared (1 Kings 8: 40). There is a greater fear in the heart of the true child of God of grieving his Father than there is in the unregenerate of the penalty of transgression. The element of fear comes back into our nature, refined and purified through the fires of love. There is no fear in love; and yet love fears with a perpetual dread of giving needless pain. Because God is a consuming fire of tender love, let us serve Him with godly fear.

I have chosen you . . . that ye should go and bring forth fruit.
John 15: 16

15

IF WE do the little duties of life faithfully, punctually, thoughtfully, reverently—not for the praise of man, but for the "Well done" of Christ—not for the payment we may receive, but because God has given us a little piece of work to do in His great world—not because we must, but because we choose—not as the slaves of circumstances, but as Christ's freed ones—then far down beneath the surge of common life the foundations of a character are laid, more

July

beautiful and enduring than coral, which shall presently rear itself before the eyes of men and angels, and become an emerald islet, green with perennial beauty, and vocal with the songs of Paradise.

We ought, therefore, to be very careful how we fulfill the common tasks of daily life. We are making the character in which we have to spend eternity. We are either building into ourselves wood, hay and stubble which will have to be burnt out at great cost; or the gold, silver and precious stones, that shall be things of beauty and joy forever.

16	*Who is this that cometh up from the wilderness, leaning upon her beloved?*

Song of Solomon 8: 5

STANDING on the mountainous plateau with which Judea passes into the desert, the daughters of Jerusalem behold the Spouse, coming slowly up from the wilderness, leaning hard upon her Beloved; and in this we have an emblem of the church, and of each faithful soul. The wilderness can well be taken as an emblem of the experience of believers, who are allowed to hunger and thirst, exposed to the sun of temptation, and pacing wearily over the lowlands of a somewhat arduous and monotonous existence.

But the wilderness life is not destined to be our perpetual experience. We are bidden to come up from it. Life is meant to be an unceasing ascent from strength to strength until we stand in Zion before God. Is your path trying and perilous? Does it seem as though you will never gain the heights that rear themselves before your gaze? Do you feel prepared, like Hagar, to yield to despair and death? See, there is One who goes beside you. Turn to regard Him. His hands are as though they had been pierced. He is your Beloved; lean on Him. He gives you His arm to rest upon, and He will sustain you when heart and flesh fail. The wilderness will bring out a tenderness, an all-sufficiency, a readiness of resource, on His part, which you would never have guessed unless your critical circumstances had become impossible to bear. Be sure of this, lean hard, and believe.

Therefore, that disciple whom Jesus loved saith unto Peter,
It is the Lord. Now when Simon Peter heard that it was
the Lord, he . . . cast himself into the sea.
                                     John 21: 7

17

JOHN discerned Him first, as it was meet. To others it was a stranger who paced the sand and looked across the steel-gray water. To him who loved, and knew that he was loved, there was something in the gesture, inquiry, and tone which unmistakably indicated the presence of Jesus. A quick remark, in a whispered undertone to Peter, was enough to cast that impetuous follower headlong into the water, and in a few moments with rapid stroke, the strong swimmer was making for the Master's feet. The Man of love discerned, the man of action pressed through the intervening space to be the first to attend that unexpected interview.

Be always on the outlook, fellow disciple, for your Lord, especially in the early morning, when the world is fresh. . . . While the pulses are unstirred by the fever of the world's passion, and the atmosphere of the soul is untainted by the soil of the world's sin, you will hear the voice of your heart saying, "It is the Lord." You will know Him by the considerateness of His care, by His pity as a father to His children, by His knowledge of mysteries hidden from all else; and when you know Him to be present, gird your coat about you in the modesty of true humbleness, plunge through the dividing waves, and never rest until you have found your way to His feet.

18

Jesus saith unto them, Come and dine. . . .
                                     John 21: 12

IT IS wonderful what Jesus is to those who meet Him in the morning. They may be tired after the night-watch, weary from lack of success, out of heart and out of hope, but they never approach Him without finding a fire kindled by His hand, fish and bread prepared, and a welcome to breakfast. Never let that chance of the morning interview pass on unused. Never let Him stand there in vain; never

July

let love see Him without the strength of mighty purpose bearing you to His embrace.

And it is not only thus that you should meet Him. Perhaps you have been involved in your daily toil, tearing yourself from work you considered more sacred. The night may have settled upon you, disappointment, heart-weariness, and failure; *then* with a tread no mortal ear could detect, He shall glide in, and He will be standing there amid the scenes of common toil. He is familiar with carpenters' shops. He knows well how to handle a boat. His delights are in the habitable parts of the earth—the marketplace where trades are plied and handcrafts wrought. The quick heart may still whisper gently to itself, "It is the Lord," and the soul will have broken through the restraint of the chill waters of reserve, and will be locked in a companionship which even the presence of others cannot break.

When thou shalt be old, thou shalt stretch forth thy hands and another shall gird thee, and carry thee whither thou wouldest not.

John 21: 18

WHAT revelations of ourselves Jesus gives us when we stand together in the presence of our brethren. He shows us ourselves—no, we see ourselves reflected in the light of His life. We stand manifested before His judgment seat, and discern what He has discerned in us.

Has He not led you through the chambers of memory, and shown you how much of all your work has emanated from self? He leads you back to your youth and shows you how much the world praise was the result of the forceful energy of your eager soul—so much was wood, hay, and stubble, which you accounted gold, silver, and precious stones; so much was void which you thought resulted from consecration; so much was carnal instead of being spiritual and eternal. I hear Him saying to me, "Thou girdest thyself and walkest whither thou wouldst." Yes, that was our mistake. We were always girding ourselves up to new resolves, endeavors, sacrifices, and exploits. We were fond of taking our own way. So many steps taken in vain! So much walking to no effect!

Then the Lord foreshadows the future: "another shall gird thee. . . ." This might make us fear if we interpret it as indicating the coming of a stranger, or Satan himself, but if the "other" is a veiled allusion to Himself, or to the Holy Spirit, by whom men of old were borne along, we are content. Come, Holy Comforter, bear us whither You will, though the flesh cry out, and the cross loom in front, and after it the grave in which we rest at last. Beyond it all lies the upper chamber, the scenes of Pentecost, the church built on the foundation of the apostles and prophets, the new Jerusalem.

Wherein in time past ye walked according to the course of this world, according to the prince of the power of the air, the spirit that now worketh in the children of disobedience.
Ephesians 2: 2

20

THE APOSTLE does not scruple to unveil the past, "the walk of the old life," of those of whom he addressed. "Look," he cried, "to the rock whence ye were hewn, and to the hole of the pit whence ye were digged. You were once dead in trespasses and sin." But, though in our unconverted state we were utterly dead to the claims of God and the life of the spiritual world, yet we were very much alive to the promptings of that malign trinity of evil, which is ever set upon the ruin of the souls of men. "Ye were dead . . . ye walked."

As the doctrine of the divine Trinity is never expressly formulated in the Scripture, though it may be derived from many an obvious reference, so there is no difficulty in showing that the world, the flesh, and the devil are in essence one in their endeavor against our souls. Here, for instance, in successive phrases, the apostle speaks of "the course of this world"; "the prince of the power of the air, the spirit that worketh in the sons of disobedience"; and of "the lusts of the flesh and of the mind" (v. 3).

It is thus that we walked once. But God loved us, lifted us out of these dark and dangerous paths, and put us on the ascension track; may He keep us from choosing or treading these old paths again. Hedge up those ways with thorns, dear Lord, and make fences against us that we may not find them.

July

<table>
<tr><td>

21

</td><td>

The doors were shut, but Jesus came and stood among them, and said, "Peace be with you."

John 20: 26b, RSV

</td></tr>
</table>

WHEN JESUS meets the disciple, He has much to say. We need the anointed ear, as well as the quick eye. He asks for love, for the noblest love of which the heart is capable, the love of respect, devotion, consecration. Such love we should give to God. He asks, that He may give us an opportunity to express it. He asks, because He loves to hear us express it. He asks with a special significance, when we have acted in any wise inconsistently with its great demand.

As He asked of Peter, so He asks us, "Lovest thou Me?" Let us never dilute the attachment that should bind us to Him. I noticed that He asked of Peter the great divine love, worthy of God, and Peter proposed in return to give Him a weaker, more sentimental affection. Let us avoid Peter's mistake, and when Jesus asks the best from us, let us not put Him off with second best; when He asks the supreme, let us not give Him the inferior; let us not drag Him down to our level, but let us confess ourselves willing to rise to His. Let us bring Him such love as we have and lay it at His feet, and as it fails to fill out the measure of His demand, entreat Him to take it in His hand, and for silver to bring gold, for iron, brass—and for stones, jewels (see John 21: 15).

<table>
<tr><td>

22

</td><td>

For God is the King of all the earth. . . .

Psalm 47: 7

</td></tr>
</table>

BEFORE a man can say that God is his King, he must have very definitely consecrated himself to God. The relation of too many believers to Christ falls short of this supreme act of the soul; and in consequence their lives lack directness, power, victory over temptation. Some of you have been sorely tried by overmastering temptations before which your resolutions have been swept as children's sand-heaps by the tide. Have you from the very depth of your being ever said to God, "Thou art my King" (Ps. 44: 4)? The kingship of Jesus is always associated with victory; and just as soon as His supremacy is acknowledged, He will begin to command deliverance and victory.

Behold, your King comes to you, having salvation. Lift up your heads, O ye gates, and the King of Glory shall come in; but He is also the merciful Savior. God has exalted Him with his right hand to be a Prince and a Savior. It is always Prince first. If you shall confess with your mouth Jesus as Lord, you will be saved.

Whenever temptation is near; when the foe seems about to take the citadel by assault; when heart and flesh quail before the noise of battle—then look up to the living Christ, and say, "Thou *art* my King, O Son of God: command victory!" There is no devil in hell but would flee before that cry, and God could not be neglectful of such an appeal. It is thus that Jacob Behmen begins one of his letters: "May the Overcomer, Jesus Christ, through Himself, overcome in us all *his* enemies."

. . . give attendance . . . to doctrine.
1 Timothy 4: 13

23

THERE SEEMS to be a great prejudice against doctrinal preaching in these degenerate days, wherein men seek an attractive edifice, with little regard to foundation-laying. But the Apostle Paul lays great stress on doctrine (his letters to Timothy provide a solid doctrinal statement for that young Christian), and he says it is as essential to Christlikeness as the mold is to the fashioning of metal into the predestined design.

Doctrine is to the words of Scripture what those great generalizations, which we know as laws, are to the facts of nature. The comet obeys the attraction of the sun, the apple falls to the ground, the grain of dust follows a certain curve in its drift through the air, and men class them together under the great common law of gravitation. Similarly, we find in Scripture different declarations about God that may be classed under certain majestic common statements, and

July

we call these statements doctrine. Doctrines, therefore, are the laws of the spiritual realm, gathered from a comparison of many scattered texts; and as we ponder them reverently and prayerfully, we are thinking over again the deep thoughts of God. In meditation and obedience we surrender ourselves to them, or, in the words of the apostle, "We are delivered unto them"; and as we obey them from the heart, we take on their shape, which is the image of Jesus Christ.

24	*The eyes of your understanding being enlightened; that ye may know what is the hope of his calling, and what the riches of the glory of his inheritance in the saints.*
	Ephesians 1: 18

WHAT AN extraordinary combination! It is a mystery that God should find his inheritance and portion in the love of men and women like ourselves. But that he should find the riches of glory in them! This passes thought. It may, however, be explained by a farming secret I learned lately. The other day, traveling in Scotland, I was introduced to some farmers whose soil was naturally of the poorest description; yet in answer to my inquiries, I found that they were able to raise crops of considerable weight and value. This seemed to me very extraordinary. Out of nothing, comes nothing is the usual rule. But they unraveled the mystery by telling me that they put in, in enriching compost, all they took out in the days of golden harvest.

Is not this the secret of any grace or wealth there is in Christian lives? Whatever our Lord gets out of us, He must first put in. All the crops of golden grain, all the fruits of Christian grace, are His from us because He has by His blood and tears, by the sunshine of His love, and the rain of His grace, enriched natures which in themselves were arid as the desert and barren as the sand. Augustine therefore said truly, "Give what thou commandest, and then command what Thou wilt."

Give all you have to God. As He bought, so let Him possess everything. He will occupy and keep you. He will bring fruit out of your rockiest nature. He will put into you the grace that you must give back to Him in fruit. He will win for Himself a great name, as He turns your desert places into gardens, and makes your wilderness blossom as a rose.

. . . the church of God, which he hath purchased with his own blood.

Acts 20: 28

25

IT IS NOT enough that Christ should deliver us from the condemnation and penalty of sin. He has also redeemed us to Himself, to be a people for His own possession, so that we should become His bondservants and slaves. Ah! what a claim is this, that He should be able to put His hand on each of our members and say, "This is Mine; I purchased it for Myself, and to use it at any prompting but Mine is sacrilege."

You cannot overcome sin by a negation, you must have something positive with which to combat its solicitations. Sin asks that our members should be presented to it as weapons for its unholy use; but it cannot produce a single sufficient argument or ground for its claims. Then Christ comes and claims that we should place our members at His disposal, and produces His Father's warrant that all His blood-bought ones should be considered His in a unique and special sense: "Thine they were, but thou gavest them me." As He produces this warrant there is no excuse for dallying or delay: we gladly present our members as servants to righteousness unto sanctification.

For we are his workmanship, created in Christ Jesus unto good works, which God hath before ordained that we should walk in them.

Ephesians 2: 10

26

BEFORE THE vision of Isaiah, the evangelistic prophet, arose the conception of a highway that should intersect the desert. It was the way of holiness; the unclean could not pass over it. No lion or beast of prey could haunt it; none but the redeemed would tread it. As soon as they touched it, gladness and joy would greet them like twin radiant angels; sorrow and sighing, that had pursued them hitherto, would drop away disappointed like dark angels of the pit.

That causeway was prepared for the ransomed before the founda-

July

tion of the world; but it was fully opened and revealed by the work of Christ and the grace of the Holy Spirit. Directly we yield ourselves to these blessed influences, we begin to tread it. We find that each step has been prepared for us, so that we have but to put down our feet. As long as we keep it we are safe from alarm and molestation. Our hearts beat out the glad marching music to which our feet answer blithely. Sorrow and sighing flee away.

27	*That he would grant you, according to the riches of his glory, to be strengthened with might by his Spirit in the inner man.*

Ephesians 3: 16

BENEATH the play of our outward life, and beneath the workings of our busy brains, there lies a deeper self, which the apostle calls "the inner man." There is an objective and there is a subjective self. The former occupies itself with collecting impressions and thoughts from the world around, and in action or speech; but the latter, veiled from observation, muses, carries on long trains of thought, holds fellowship with itself and God, and the unseen. It is this part of our nature which perceives truth—not by trains of argument, but by the flash of intuitive perception—and which receives those throbbing pulsations of Divine power that wait around us seeking for admission. This inner man is in us all; but many of us live in the outer courts of our nature, occupied with the mere externals of our life and the world. We give these inner chambers over to neglect and dust, seldom entering them, hardly cognizant of their existence, save when in hours of unusual solemnity they assert themselves and compel attention.

It is in this inner man that the Holy Spirit finds His home in His home and seat. Here He elaborates His purposes, formulates and issues His decrees, and stirs to heroic action. And, when all its avenues are open to Him, He so infills with His power, and indwells with Divine energy, that the inner man is strengthened with might, according to the riches of His glory.

July

That ye put off concerning the former conversation the old man, which is corrupt according to the deceitful lusts.
Ephesians 4: 22

28

THE OLD MAN is the aggregate of habits and methods of life which marked us before conversion. The phrase describes the impression which we produced as men and women upon our fellows. But we were wont to be, and say, and do that form of character in life which was ours before the great change operated through faith in Christ.

It is called *the old man,* as if there were but one, because the habits and tastes, the thoughts and acts of men, before conversion, have much in common. There is not much to choose between them. It is the one evil nature; one likeness to all in Adam; one type of evil, though its forms are slightly modified in different temperaments and by special circumstances.

This old man is under the control of deceitful lusts, promising liberty and happiness and joy, but resembling the siren sisters, whose upper form was fair, but whose lower extremities were ugly while their sweet songs lured the unwary mariner only to ruin.

We must not defer this "putting off." The tense indicates the sudden resolve of the will, inspired and empowered by the Holy Spirit to be no longer under the dominion of these terrible passions. Once and forever let us divest ourselves of them; as the beggar his rags, or as Lazarus his grave clothes.

And that ye put on the new man, which after God is created in righteousness and true holiness.
Ephesians 4: 24

29

THIS IS the aggregate of blessed habits that mark the life of the converted—the white robe of purity, the belt of self-restraint, the silver of humility, the jewels of holy character. All through the epistles, we are bidden to put it on. "Put on the armor of light." "Put on, as God's elect, a heart of compassion." "Put on the Lord Jesus Christ."

July

It is *the* new man, because the habits and character of the children of God are very similar. There is a family likeness common to all. It is *after* God, because it is created in His likeness. It is the fashion of God in human nature, perfectly exemplified once in Jesus Christ, and now waiting to be imparted by the Holy Ghost. It is *righteous* toward man. It is *holy* toward God. It is *true,* perfectly transparent and sincere. Put on this holy thing created in Jesus, and therefore not to be woven by human effort or spun by outward obedience to rites but to be simply assumed.

Put it on by faith. Do not try to build up Christ's likeness by your repeated endeavors, just assume it by faith. Believe it is yours. Reckon that it is so. Go out believing that Christ's likeness is on you, and His beauty clothing you as a beautiful robe; and men shall increasingly realize that it is not you but Christ.

30	... *Christ also hath loved us, and hath given himself for us an offering and a sacrifice to God for a sweetsmelling savor.* Ephesians 5: 2

HOW SWEET the offering up of the Son was to the Father! The burnt-offering was an imperfect type of His entire devotion to the Father's will. When Jesus saw the inability of man to keep the holy law, and volunteered to magnify it, and make it honorable when He laid aside His glory, and stepped down from His throne saying, "I delight to do thy will, O my God"; when He became obedient even to the death of the cross—it was as sweet to God as the fragrance of a garden of flowers is to us.

Let us never forget the Godward aspect of the cross. The sacrificial fire fed on every part of the sacrifice, on the interior as well as the exterior; so did the Holy God delight to witness the spotless and entire devotion of the Son to the great work in which the entire Godhead was most deeply interested. The fragrant graces of Christ were made manifest on the cross, and are perpetuated in His intercession for us.

There is a sense also in which our consecration to God is fragrant and precious. When we see His claims, and yield to them; when we

July

submit to His will, and commit our lives wholly to His direction; when we offer and present ourselves to Him, a living sacrifice, keeping nothing back—His heart is gladdened, and His fire of complacency feeds on our act. Always count on this; you may feel no thrill, and see no light, but reckon on God, believe that He accepts what you give, and will crown your sacrifice with the fire of Pentecost. Who today will surrender to God and become an offering of a sweet savor?

For we wrestle not against flesh and blood, but against principalities, against powers, against the rulers of the darkness of this world, against spiritual wickedness in high places.

Ephesians 6: 12

31

NEVER IN this life can we escape from temptation. The holier we get, the more subtle and vehement will be the assaults of the dark legions, though they may wear white over their grey armor. The nearer we get to our Prince in thought and fellowship, the more we will be assaulted. It is from under the opened heaven that we are driven to the wilderness to be tempted. There is no such fighting as in the heavenly places themselves. Here we wrestle not against flesh and blood, but against the world-rulers of this darkness. But the issue cannot be doubtful. In the thought of God, and in the Ascension of our blessed Lord, they are beneath our feet and conquered; and He waits to realize His purpose in the weakest of His saints. "Having done all, *stand*"; God will fight for you, and you shall hold your peace.

The Day-by-Day Christian Life

August

The Lord will perfect that which concerneth me; thy mercy, O Lord, endureth forever. . . .

Psalm 138: 8

IT SEEMED to David that he was condemned to spend his days in a lion's den; on every side were blasphemy and reproach; his enemies breathed out flames, and their slanders cut like swords. But amid it all he steadily looked away to God, the Most High, who from His elevation would reach down to deliver, and would surely accomplish all that was necessary. It is a marvelous thing to consider that God is literally willing to perform *all* things in us, and for us, if only we will let Him. "I will cry unto God most high; unto God that performeth all things for me" (Ps. 57: 2). The problem is that most of us insist on performing all things in the energy of our own resolve, in the strength of our own power. We shut God out of our life: and while He is coming to our help, we have gone our own way, and offered the sacrifice to our own hurt.

Before, therefore, God will perform all things for us, as He did for His servant, we must learn, like him, to wait in His presence that He may teach us our absolute poverty and helplessness; that He may assure us of our need of absolute and unceasing dependence; that He may open our eyes to see the well-spring which Hagar saw on the desert sand. The fixed heart (v. 7), fixed only upon God, set upon waiting His time, receiving His help, and doing all things according to the inspiration and energy of His Spirit, is absolutely essential.

Awake the dawn, O child of God (8). Give thanks to God: sing His praises (9); let thy aspiration be for His exaltation (5, 11): let thy heart be fixed in its resolve to take deliverance from none other—and He will send forth His twin-angels, Mercy and Truth (3). They will come, even into the lion's den, and save thee from those who would swallow thee up (4).

August

Then shall we know, if we follow on to know the Lord: his going forth is prepared as the morning. . . .
Hosea 6: 3

2

THE SPOT of the earth's surface on which you live has taken leave of the sunshine, and is plunging ever farther and farther into the blackness of darkness; as the hour of midnight strikes you are as far removed as possible from the last gleams of the evening glow. But you are hastening toward the dawn, which awaits you in solemn pomp. Let the lonely night watcher understand that at each swing of the pendulum he is hurrying to meet the smile of the morn which awaits his coming, in preparation of golden clouds and bars of amber light, and delicate tints of green and amber.

The morning is *prepared;* it waits, it has been decked by the hand of the Creator to comfort and bless the returning hilltops and seas, and flowers, and homes of men. Dare to believe that so God is waiting for you—only follow on. Do not be dismayed by the darkness—follow on. Do not give up heart and hope, because the delay is long—follow on. God will break upon you in all the loveliness of His Being; you will see His glory in the face of Jesus; the dawn of a more tender and intimate fellowship is nigh; only follow on till the voice of the herald is heard crying: "Arise, shine, thy light is come, and the glory of the Lord is risen upon thee."

Therefore they shall be as the morning cloud, and as the early dew that passeth away. . . .
Hosea 13: 3

3

WE HEAR a sermon on the nobility and beauty of a life of self-sacrifice; we are told that the fullest field for its manifestation is in the home; we see how we may acquire this noble quality amid the daily grind and frustration of the home circle, and are quite anxious to get back to our home to put these principles into practice; but when we find ourselves face to face with the hard facts, the harsh reality, the thorns and briars, our resolution fails us, and we are as

August

crabbed, awkward, and morose as ever—it seems impossible to break through the reign of frost, and be the genial, tender, and self-forgetting person we want to be. Our goodness seems to be as the morning cloud.

We hear an address on the need for more prayer and Bible study. The quiet hour with God is so presented as to enthrall our interest and capture our desires. We hear the Master saying, Can ye not watch with Me one hour? and ardently respond, With all our hearts. On the following morning we spring from our beds an hour earlier than our usual practice; the next morning we manage only a half-hour; within a day or two we are just as sluggish and careless as ever. Our goodness is as the morning cloud.

What is the answer? Not our goodness but His allowed to be lived out in us. With such a surrender of our wills to His, we will no longer dissipate like the morning cloud and early dew.

[God] only is my rock and my salvation; he is my defense. . . .

Psalm 62: 2

DAVID IS in the wilderness, fleeing from Absalom. It seems to him that he is at the end of the earth. He prays, "Lead me to the rock that is higher than I." His soul seems wrapped in gloom; then, from afar, he sees the Rock of his salvation, and asks to be led to it, and established upon it.

Can you not see that rock? All the desert is baking like a furnace. The very pebbles burn the hand like cinders. Nothing can endure the scorching glare but the little green lizards that dart to and fro among the stones. Sunbeams strike like swords on the head of the luckless travelers who dare to brave their glittering edge. But yonder there is a rock, rising high above the shimmering sands, and casting a deep black shadow on one side. Little lichens hide in its crevices, streaks of vegetation are enameled on its steep surfaces, and at its foot there are even a few rock-plants growing as best they can in the arid soil. That is the higher rock—the rock higher than the traveler's stature. He makes for it; or if he is too faint and over-

August

whelmed, he is led to it, and beneath its gracious shadow finds instant rest. The shadow of a great rock in a weary land!

Jesus will be all this to you, dear heart. You must reach the end of the earth and of yourself; call out to Christ, and He will bring you, faint and ready to die, to Himself as the Shadow from the heat. The Man of men can be this for you, because He is higher than you are. Higher than I, because of His Divine origin; higher, because of His perfect obedience; higher, because of His supreme sufferings; higher, because of His ascension to the right hand of power. Yet His side is scarred and cleft.

5

. . . hear what the Lord will command concerning you.
Numbers 9: 8b

THIS IS the secret of a holy and blessed life. Most of our sorrows and disappointments have come to us because we have chosen our own path, and done according to our own will.

In obeying we must sometimes walk in the dark. When Noah began to walk with God, he did not know it would lead him into collision with his generation, with the suggestions of common sense and experience, and with much that he held dear in his life. But walking each day, he grew strong to trust in the bare word of his Almighty Guide, and grasped it as men in the dark cave will keep their hand on a tiny string or cord until they reach the first streak of daylight. Obey absolutely the voice that speaks in your heart; the way is dark, but it is the way.

In obeying we must learn to wait. For 120 years the longsuffering of God waited, and during the weary period Noah's true heart failed not. Then for seven days the patriarch waited behind the closed doors of the ark. It is not easy thus to bear the strain of waiting. To rush into the battle, to do something desperate, to strike for liberty—this is the choice of the flesh; but to live in hourly fear, to toil on without result, to see the years stealing away the bank on which our heart had erected its structures of hope—this is the hardest of all, unless our hope is anchored beyond life's ebb and swell.

August

6

As for man, his days are as grass; as the flower of the field, so he flourisheth. For the wind passeth over it, and it is gone; and the place thereof shall know it no more. But the mercy of the Lord is from everlasting to everlasting. . . .
Psalm 103: 15–17

NOTE THE contrast: man's frailty against the everlastingness of God's mercy. We are frail as the flower of the field. Each generation of man comes forth like the grass and flowers, which clothe the meadows in spring only to meet the remorseless scythe. But frail as is our physical life, our resolutions and intentions are still more so. One day our soul is covered by the laughing beauty of hope, and faith, and love, kindly thoughts, heavenly aspirations, gracious deeds—the next the whole crop lies smitten and withered.

But God's love does not alter with our alterings, or change with our changes. Does the mother's love fluctuate with the moods of her sick babe? God loves constantly, with an ardent, intense affection, which delivers from dross the heart that is yielded to Him, and secures at last its transformation into His own likeness. If you will let Him, God will yet love you right. Love will make even your tough nature a miracle of beauty. But the friction of the lapidary's wheel and the diamond dust may hurt you a little. Never mind, love is behind it all. There never was a time when He did not love you— His mercy is from everlasting; nor a time when He will love you less—it is to everlasting.

7

For by one offering he hath perfected for ever them that are sanctified.
Hebrews 10: 14

WE ARE not perfected yet.—There is a great chasm between our highest and our Master's lowest; between where we stop and He begins: between our light, which is twilight at best, and His meridian glory. When we compare ourselves with ourselves, or with our neighbors, our standard is altogether too low; we should compare ourselves with Him, the beloved Master. Job, who was reputed perfect, abhorred himself, and repented in dust and ashes when he had *seen* God, of whom he had formerly only heard.

But we shall be perfected one day.—"Every one when he is perfected shall be as his Master" (Luke 6: 40). That *when* has a hopeful ring. But to what period does the Master point? Not till sorrow, sanctified by God's grace, has done its work; not till the snow and frost, the light shower and the bitter wind, the earth and sun, have contributed their shares to the desired quota. Not till the perfect image of Jesus has emerged from the sculptured stone; not till the molten metal reflects each lineament of the glorified Lord.

When we are perfected we shall be as our Master.—"We shall be like him, for we shall see him as he is." It seems altogether too much to expect! To think that we will be changed into His image; we will bear His stamp; we will be as like Him as Gideon's brethren to Gideon, of whom the princes of Midian testified that they were like the children of a king. Yet it shall be so. The Lord Jesus became like unto us in our low estate, that we should become like Him in His glory. There must ever be the limitation of the creature as compared with Him by whom all things were made. But in our measure there will be the same perfect beauty—His beauty upon us—for a mountain lake may as perfectly reflect the wide blue heaven as an ocean.

Restore us, O God; let thy face shine, that we may be saved.
Psalm 80: 3, RSV

Oh, restore us again!
Psalm 60: 1, RV

YET thou hast cast us off and abased us, and hast not gone out with our armies" (Ps. 44: 9). Cast off! There is a sense in which that can never be. God will not cast off from salvation any soul of man that has sheltered under the covert of His Almighty wings. He may withdraw the tangible enjoyment and realization of His presence; but He cannot cast off forever, in the sense of consigning any fugitive to his foes or to the fate he dreads.

And yet there is a sense in which we are cast off, when we have been unbelieving and disobedient. Allowed to take our own way, that we may learn its bitterness; permitted to hunger and thirst,

August

that we may know how evil a thing it is to seek our supreme good anywhere else than in God; given over to the tender mercies of the gods we have chosen, that we may be taught their helplessness. It was thus that God cast off His people. He showed them hard things, and allowed them to reap as they had sown.

But now they cry for restoration. "O God, thou hast rejected us, broken our defenses; thou hast been angry; oh, restore us" (Ps. 60: 1, RSV). Put us back, they say, into the old place; be to us what You were, and make us to You as we were. Restore us again. He did it for Peter, putting him back to the front place in the Apostolic band; for Mark, allowing him, who had gone back in his first missionary journey, to write a Gospel; for Cranmer and many more, who in the first burst of fiery trial shrank back, but to whom He gave more grace. Believe in the restoring grace of Christ, who not only forgives, but puts back the penitent and believing soul where it was before it fell away. Indeed, it has been suggested that the prodigal fares better on his return than those who do not go astray. It is not really so. But there is much music and song when the lost is found and the dead lives.

Say unto wisdom, Thou art my sister; and call understanding thy kinswoman.

Proverbs 7: 4

THIS WISDOM might seem to be too unearthly and ethereal to engage our passionate devotion, unless we remember that she was incarnated in Jesus Christ, who, throughout this book, seems forthshadowed in the majestic conception of wisdom. And who shall deny that the most attractive and lovable traits merged in His matchless character as Son of Man and exalted Redeemer.

With what sensitive purity He bent His face to the ground and wrote on the dust, when her accusers brought to Him a woman taken in the act of sin! With what thoughtfulness He sent word to Peter that He was risen, and provided the meal for His weary and wave-drenched sailor friends on the shores of the lake! With what quick intuition He read Mary's desire to anoint Him for the burying!

August

It was this combination of what is sweet in woman and strong in man, which so deeply satisfied men like Bernard, Rutherford, Fénélon, and thousands more, who have been shut out from the delights of human love, but have found in Jesus the complement of their need, the satisfaction of their hunger and thirst. In Him, for them, was restored the vision of the sweet mother of early childhood; of the angel-sister who went to be with God; of the early love that was never destined to be realized.

Women find in Jesus strength on which to lean their weakness; and men find in Him the tender, thoughtful sympathy to which they can confidently entrust themselves. We are born for the infinite and Divine; earthly loves, at their best, are only patterns of things in the heavens. They are priceless; but let us look into them and through them, to behold the unseen and eternal that lie beneath.

He that hath pity upon the poor lendeth unto the Lord; and that which he hath given will he pay him again.
Proverbs 19: 17, RV

10

WHAT a revolution would be wrought among us if we really believed this! We are glad to lend to our friends in a temporary strait, especially when we know that our money is safe and will come back to us with a substantial increase. To have an IOU is quite sufficient. But in the light of this text we are taught to look on God as the great Borrower. He comes to us, asking that we will lend to Him. In every needy one who deserves our aid the request of the Almighty may be heard asking a loan.

What mistakes we make! We think we keep what we hold and invest well. But we really keep what we give away. The best investments are the heavenly shares and stocks, which are found in the needs and sorrows of the poor. Will you not, my reader, resolve that you will begin to lend to the Lord in the person of those who need your help, whether for their personal necessities or the work in which they are interested? You are called to be a steward of God's free gifts to you. You must be ready, as His steward, to deal out His wealth. He will pay you for doing it, by giving you your own present

August

maintenance; and one day He will say, "I was hungry, and you fed Me; thirsty, and you gave Me drink: inherit the place prepared for you."

Just ponder the magnificence of this promise: "His good deed will He pay him again." God will never be in your debt. He is exact and punctual in His repayment. No man ever dared to do His bidding in respect to any case of need, and found himself the poorer. "Give, and it shall be given to you; good measure, pressed down and running over shall they give into your bosom." Was not Ruth's love to Naomi well compensated?

11

Blessed . . . Blessed . . . Blessed. . . .

Matthew 5: 3–11

THE REALM of blessedness is all around. It may be entered at any minute, and we may dwell in it all the days of our life. Our enjoyment of blessedness is totally undetermined by outward circumstances. If you stand in some great department store and watch the faces of the women, you will be greatly instructed. There sits a richly dressed lady with society and fashion, dress and money at her command, but her manner and tone are utterly weary and dissatisfied; across the counter a girl waits on her, whose thin face and simple attire tell their own story, but her expression and bearing betoken the possession of an inner calm and strength, an inexhaustible store of patience and sweetness. Such contrasts meet us everywhere. The realm of blessedness dips down into humble and lowly lives on every side of us. Have we entered it?

Christ's beatitudes give us eight gates, any one of which will immediately conduct us within its confines. David gives us another: "Blessed is he that considereth the poor" (Ps. 41: 1). Even if you cannot help or relieve them to any appreciable extent, consider them; let them feel that you are thinking of and for them; do not hurry them when they recite their long, sad story; put them at their ease; treat them with Christian courtesy and consideration. Begin at once. There are plenty around you, who, if not poor in the things of this world, are poor in love and hope and the knowledge of God. Tell them of "the blessing of the Lord," which "maketh rich, and he addeth no sorrow with it." Silver and gold you may have none; but such as you have be sure and give. Learn to consider people. Try to look on things from their standpoint.

I am my beloved's, and my beloved is mine.
Song of Solomon 6: 3

12

IN THE earlier stages of Christian life, we think most of what we have in Christ; afterwards we love to dwell on His possession of us. We are His estate, for Him to cultivate and rear successive crops for His praise and glory. We are His jewels, to obtain which He renounced all, and on which He will expend infinite care, cutting our facets, and polishing us to shine brightly in His light. We are His house in which He can dwell, opening out unexpected apartments and passages. We are members of His body, through which He will fulfill His holy purpose. We are His bride, to win whom He came from afar. We are owned, possessed, inhabited, loved, with a peculiar personal affection. As Keble says: "Thou art thy Savior's darling: doubt no more."

Glory to God in the highest, and on earth peace.
Luke 2: 14

13

THESE two conditions are joined together, and none can separate them. Do you want peace? your highest aim must be the glory of God. Do you seek God's glory as your highest aim? then, the inevitable result will be the peace that passeth understanding.

Glory to God in the highest.—It was said of the soldiers of the

August

first Napoleon that they were content to die in the ditch if only he rode over them to victory. With their last breath they cried, "Long live the Emperor!" It seemed as though they had lost all thought and care of their own interests, so long as glory was given to his name. So should it be of us. Higher than our own comfort, or success, or popularity, should be the one thought of the glory of our God. Let Christ be honored, loved, exalted, at whatever cost to us.

On earth, peace.—It will come, because when the heart has only one aim to follow, it is delivered from dividing and distracting cares. It will come, because the glory of God is so lofty an aim that it lifts the soul into the atmosphere of the heavenly and eternal world, where peace reigns unbroken. It will come, because we are not greatly troubled by the reverses and variations of fortune that are incident to all work in this world, since the main object is always secure and beyond fear of failure. Though the waves ebb and flow, yet the tide is certainly coming up the shore, and will presently stand at high-water mark.

This peace is said in the RV to come only to men in whom God is well pleased. Live to please God, and He will breathe on you His peace. Seek His glory, and He will make your heart His home. Do His will, and thereby good shall come to you.

14

Neither shall they learn war any more.

Isaiah 2: 4

THE psalmist promises: "He maketh wars to cease" (46: 9).

God makes *the wars of the outward life* to cease, so that as life's afternoon comes the man who had fought his way through overwhelming odds—as a reformer, or inventor, or philanthropist—spends his years amid troops of friends and loving recognition.

God makes *the wars of the home* to cease! so that the disturbing elements pass out, or are transmuted by invincible patience and love.

God makes *the wars of the heart* to cease, so that Satan no longer annoys. The storm dies down, and the river which makes glad the city of God flows quietly through the soul. Sennacherib and his vast array lie as the leaves of autumn, silent in the last sleep.

If as yet God has not made your wars to cease, it is because He knows that you have still strength to fight on. Do not faint in the day of battle. Ponder those great words of Cromwell: "Call not your burden sad or heavy, for if your Heavenly Father sent it (or permitted it) He intended it to be neither." It is through the fight that you are winning experience, strength, the approval of your Captain, and the crown.

Casting all your care upon him; for he careth for you. | 15
1 Peter 5: 7

WE ALL know the story of the man wearily trudging along the road with the burden on his back, to whom a farmer offered a lift in his cart. To the latter's surprise the traveler sat beside him with his burden still strapped to his shoulder. "Why do you not put your burden down?" the farmer asked. "Thank you," was the reply, "I am so obliged at your carrying me that I will not trouble you with my burden also." And so he hugged it still. How many a child of God trusts Him with his soul, but not with his load! Yet if God has undertaken the greater, surely He may be trusted with the less. If He has borne your sins, He can surely carry your sorrows.

Your burden, as the margin reading of Psalm 55: 22 suggests, is "what he has given you." Whatever it be—the weight of a church, the pressure of a family, the burden of other souls—your Father hath given it to you. Give its pressure back to Him, while you retain the salutary lesson of hourly patience and faith. God imposes burdens, to see what we will do with them. We may carry them to our undoing, or we may cast them on Him.

Notice, that if we cast our burden, we must believe He takes it. We must definitely leave it with Him, and count as a positive sin the temptation to reconsider it. When you cast your burden, God will take it, and will do more. He will sustain *you*. He will catch up your burden and you, and bear you all the day long between His shoulders. "Cast your burden on the Lord, and he will sustain you; he will never permit the righteous to be moved" (Ps. 55: 22, RSV).

August

16

By faith Abraham . . . obeyed. . . .

Hebrews 11: 8

GOD PRECEDES His commands with such revelations of Himself that obedience comes easily to the believer. Before calling Abraham, He described Himself as El Shaddai, the Almighty. What might we accomplish if we availed ourselves of the almightiness of God? O to know the exceeding greatness of His power to usward who believe! Our problem is that we do not know God and therefore fail to perform the exploits He would require of us. "Thus saith the Lord, Let not the wise man glory in his wisdom, neither let the mighty man glory in his might, let not the rich man glory in his riches: but let him . . . glory in this, that he understandeth and knoweth me . . ." (Jer. 9: 23,24). Lie on your face and let God talk to you, and tell you the conditions on which He will make Himself known to you.

There must be wholeness in our surrender. No part of our natures may be curtained or barred off from God. Every chamber must be freely placed at His disposal, every relationship under His direction, every power devoted to His service. All we have and are must be entirely His.

17

[Jesus prayed]: Sanctify them through thy truth; thy word is truth.

John 17: 17

OUR GOD has set Himself the work of our sanctification. As the Greek indicates, He looks upon us as his inheritance, and He will not rest until He has brought every acre of territory under cultivation. It is not enough that briars and thistles should be exterminated; they must be replaced by the rare growth of Christian virtue, which is Christ.

The work of sanctification is quiet and silent.—It is wrought by the *God of Peace.* "The God of Peace Himself sanctify you wholly" (1 Thess. 5: 23, 24). The mightiest forces of nature are stilled; and

August

when God comes with power into the human spirit there is often no hurricane, tempest, fire, or earthquake, but the thrilling whisper of the still, small voice. Do not be afraid, as though God would treat you roughly. So long as peaceful, gentle methods will bring about His purpose, He will gladly employ them.

The work is also gradual.—We are not made *faultless,* but we are *preserved blameless;* i.e., we are kept from known sin, preserved from incurring perpetual self-reproach. "There is no condemnation." I saw the other day the love-letter of a little boy to his father. It was anything but faultless; but the father, at least, did not count it worthy of blame. He carried it next to his heart! So we are not to be faultless, as judged by God's perfect standard, till we are presented before the presence of His glory; but we may be blameless up to our acquaintance with the divine will.

The work is from within outwards.—Notice the order—spirit, soul, body. The Shekinah of His presence shines in the holy of holies, and thence pours over into the holy place, and so out into the outer court, until the very curtains of the body are irradiated with its light.

There was a man of the Pharisees, named Nicodemus, a ruler of the Jews: The same came to Jesus by night. . . . Jesus answered and said unto him . . . No man hath ascended up to heaven, but he that came down from heaven, even the Son of man which is in heaven.
John 3: 1, 2, 13

| 18 |

IN HIS conversation with Nicodemus, while the night-breeze played over the sleeping city, coming and going as it would, our Lord spoke of Himself as being already in heaven. His bodily presence was evidently in the chamber of that house in Jerusalem, robed in the simple peasant garb which His mother had spun for Him; but in spirit, He was much more really in heaven than there. So, according to the teaching of the Apostle Paul, the church, consisting of those who believe in Christ, is really less a citizen of earth than of those heavenly places which have been entered by her Lord. They are not heaven, but they are heavenlike. This is our position as Christians— and the blessings that are ours as we walk with Him.

August

19

Behold the Lamb of God, which taketh away the sin of the world!

John 1: 29

THIS IS the calling of Jesus Christ. He came, not as the Jews expected, to break the yoke of Caesar and reestablish the kingdom of David. He came to break the yoke of sin, and set up the sinless kingdom of God. The church has too often misunderstood the object of His advent, as though He meant simply to save from the consequences and results of sin. This were too limited a mission for the Son of God. To cancel the results and leave the bitter cause; to deliver from the penalty, but not from the power; to rescue His people from the grasp of a broken law, but confess Himself unable to deal with the bad virus of the blood—this were to fail. No, we are to take this announcement in its full and glorious meaning, written as it is on the very opening of our Savior's life.

What a blessed blending of blood flowed through His veins! Let your eye glance down His genealogy. Men and women, notorious for their evil character, lie in the direct line of His descent. This was permitted, that He might fully represent our fallen race; that no sinner, however bad, should be afraid to claim His help; and that it should be clearly shown how powerless sin was to tarnish or taint the holiness of His sinless nature. Made in the likeness of sinful flesh, He knew no sin. The germs of corruption could find no welcome in His heart.

Are you one of His people? Have you accepted His rule, and allied yourself with Him? For if so, He will save you. Though you may be possessed with seven devils, He will drive them out.

20

I am the good shepherd: the good shepherd giveth his life for the sheep.

John 10: 11

WE DO NOT live until we have been born again. The moment of regeneration is the first moment of life. All the years before are as though they had never been. But from the moment we receive the life of the eternal God into our being, we begin an endless progression.

The entrance of that life makes us lambs in the flock of the Good Shepherd.—We no longer resist, or fight, or boast of things of which we should be ashamed. We become pure, sweet, gentle, lowly, and submissive. We are willing to lay down our lives for others. We follow the way of the cross without murmur or complaint. Every time we eat of that bread and drink of the cup we witness to the world our desire to absorb more and more of the lamblike nature of the Son of God. Hence, it is said, the Lamb shall lead, shall shepherd, shall tend us as His flock. "For the Lamb which is in the midst of the throne shall feed them, and shall lead them into living fountains of waters: and God shall wipe away all tears from their eyes" (Rev. 7: 17).

The life which God has implanted yearns for satisfaction.—As a parched flock desires the crystal streams that ripple over the pebbles, so the flock of God in this life and the next cry out for God, for the living God. Nothing will satisfy God's lambs and sheep but God Himself. And this desire is satisfied in Jesus. In Him the eternal God comes near to us; we follow Him without fear.

And in that life there is eternal progression.—Jesus leads us from one fountain to another, from one well to the next; always deeper into the heart of heaven, always further towards the very center of all things, which is God. We shall always be satisfied; but our capacity will constantly enlarge, and it will become necessary to give us fuller manifestations, according to His own promise (John 17: 26, RV).

. . . That he might be just, and the justifier of him which believeth in Jesus.

Romans 3: 26

21

THIS VERSE is often quoted as though the word *yet* must be inserted to bring out its meaning. "Just, and *yet* the justifier." The marvel of a just God justifying sinful men is thus strongly accen-

August

tuated. Of course, this is a true thought and marvelous to contemplate. But it is not the precise idea of the apostle, when he says that the just God is the justifier of those who have faith in Jesus. Paul means that the very justice of God has come on our side, and that His love may have its unhindered way, not only consistently with His justice, but because of it.

This is the *heart* of the gospel. Jesus has stood as our representative. He has borne our sin, in its curse and penalty; has met the claims of a broken law, and satisfied the demands of infinite righteousness. To have done this in our name and on our behalf not only makes us free from any penalty which might otherwise have accrued, but gives us a claim—the claim of the righteous—on all those blessings which the righteous government of God has to bestow.

The moment we become one with Jesus by a living faith, we stand possessed of all that He has done and is. In Him, we have already suffered all that the holy law of God could demand as the just penalty of our sins. In Him we have laid in the grave, paying the uttermost price that could be exacted. In Him we have been liberated from the prison, and have passed into the presence and welcome of God. We may claim, therefore, that the law of God should militate *for* us, as once it *militated* against us. We are saved not only by the grace, but by the justice of God. He is faithful to His Son and just to the law, when He forgives us our sins.

22

... And we shall reign on the earth.

Revelation 5: 10

ALL God's dealings with us are on the same principle. *As* we received Christ Jesus the Lord, *so* we must walk in Him. Whether it be justification or sanctification; whether reconciliation or reigning in life that is under consideration—the same mighty principles underlie and control the divine gifts and our participation in them. "They which receive abundance of grace . . . shall reign in life by one, Jesus Christ" (Rom. 5: 17). We *receive* reconciliation as a gift at the beginning of our Christian life, and we have to *receive* all else by the same medium to the end. Forever and forever we have just to wait till God fills us, as the flower-cups that are now filled with sunshine and now with dew or rain.

You have already received the reconciliation (Rom. 5: 11).—Unable to earn it by your own endeavors, you were at last content to receive it as a free gift placed into your open hand; now you have to maintain the same position with respect to all the spiritual gifts that you need for the maintenance of a godly life, and to enable you to reign. Faith—simple, open-handed, heaven-regarding faith —is the one unchanging law of the holy life.

This reigning in life is not to be relegated to the unseen and future. —It is meant to be our present experience. He has made us kings to God, even the Father. We are called to the royalty of men, the abundance, the freedom, the consciousness of power and victory, which we usually associate with those who reign. To reign in the ordinary life of the home, the shop, the bank—such is our high calling in Christ Jesus. And it may be ours if we receive "abundance of grace" of the one Man, Jesus Christ.

. . . He hath chosen us in him before the foundation of the world, that we should be holy and without blame before him in love.

Ephesians 1: 4

| 23 |

FROM "before the foundation of the world"! Who can compute the contents of the vast unknown comprehended in that phrase? The beginning of creation was preceded by the anticipation of Redemption, and the love of God to all who were one with Christ. "God hath from the beginning chosen you to salvation through sanctification of the Spirit . . ." (2 Thess. 2: 13).

God's aim and purpose—salvation.—Not simply our deliverance from the penalty, but from the power of all besetting sin; He wants us to be delivered from the fear of our enemies, and to serve Him in holiness and righteousness all our days. This He is prepared to *give* to us; but we must claim it by faith.

August

God's choice.—Whom He did foreknow He also did predestinate. From all eternity He saw those who would be attracted to Jesus by a divine affinity, and these were included in His gift to the Son. "Thine they were, and thou gavest them me, and they have kept thy word." We must not presume on the eternal choice; but we may be very grateful that the downward slide from the Fall are met, in mid-flow, by the grace and choice of the Almighty.

God's method. Through sanctification of the Spirit.—The Holy Ghost sets us apart from sin, and consecrates us to God. "Know ye not that your body is the temple of the Holy Ghost, which is in you, which ye have of God, and ye are not your own? For ye are bought with a price." Our sanctification is not the property of our soul, but its possession by the Holy One; not an attribute, but a Person. *And belief of the truth.* Let the Word of God dwell in you richly. Hide it in your heart, that you may be kept from sin. We are sanctified by the truth insofar as we expose our hearts to its entrance and rule. We are cleansed by the washing of water through the Word.

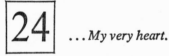

| 24 | *...My very heart.* |

Philemon 12, RV

THIS FRAGMENT of ancient letter-writing gives us a model of the way in which our commonest or most prosaic dealings, and our letters, even on business matters, may breathe the spirit of Christ. It also illustrates the relation in which we stand to Jesus Christ. What Onesimus was to Paul and Philemon combined, that we are to our Lord.

What was Onesimus to Paul?—His child, whom he had begotten in his bonds. He had probably been discovered by some of his companions in the purlieus of Rome, where criminals concealed themselves from justice, and abandoned characters gave vent to the wildest passions. Or, having heard that the apostle, whom he had so often met in his master's house, was residing in his own hired house in Rome, the runaway slave had found him out, when in the extremity of hunger. In either case he had now become dear to the

August

apostle's heart; had learned to minister to him in his bonds; had proved more than a servant—a brother beloved. O Lord who hast redeemed us from our sins, may we be all this to You!

What was Onesimus to Philemon?—He had been unprofitable; and we have been. He was sent back; and we have returned to the Shepherd and Bishop of our souls. He had been a servant, henceforth he should be a beloved brother; and we are no longer servants, but friends. He had grievously wronged his master; but his sin had been forgiven, and so covered by over-abounding grace, that it would bring him into a position of greater privilege and blessing than ever before. In this man's sin and restoration we see ourselves. Where our sin abounded, grace has much more abounded, through the tender pity of Him who placed our debts in His own account.

Wherefore I also, after I heard of your faith in the Lord Jesus, and love unto all the saints.
Ephesians 1: 15

25

LOVE AND faith are inseparable. When there is faith in the Lord Jesus, there will always be love toward all the saints. Because faith is the faculty of taking God into the heart. Faith is God-receptiveness. Faith appropriates the nature of God, as the expanded lungs the mountain air, or as the child the parent's gift. Faith, like a narrow channel, conveys God's ocean fullness into the areas of human need. Wherever, therefore, faith links the believer to the Lord Jesus, His nature, which is love, pure as mountain dew, begins to flow *in* to the waiting, expectant heart; and then to flow *out* thence toward all the saints.

The love of God knows no favorite sect. It singles out no special school; but, as the sun and wind of nature, breathes and shines alike on all. It is cosmopolitan and universal. You cannot imprison it within the walls of any one Christian community. It laughs at your restrictions, and with equal grace raises up witnesses and standard-bearers from all parts of the church. Thus, as we become more like God, our love overleaps the barrier of our little pond and passes out to greet all saints, and to expend itself on the great world of men.

August

26	*. . . Ye should show forth the praises of him who hath called you out of darkness into his marvelous light.* 1 Peter 2: 9

THERE ARE many dark things around us in which we detect light only when we behold them in the light which streams from the face of Jesus. In His light we see light in them. "In thy light shall we see light" (Ps. 36: 9). Yonder lies a bit of charcoal, black and opaque; and even when it has been changed by chemistry to crystals; it is dull and dense, so long as it is in the dark. Who could guess that such depths and fountains of light exist in that insignificant atom? But let it be brought into the rays of the morning sun, and as it flashes and glistens, in that light we see its light; fountains of light welling up; caverns of light, where the elves and fairies of childish story hide.

So it is of the Bible.—Its pages seem devoid of help and comfort, till we open them under the light of Jesus. Cleopas and the other learned this on the road to Emmaus.

So it is of nature.—The Greek, lover of nature though he was, never saw in her face the loveliness which has been the theme of Christian poetry and art. In the light of Christ's parables and allusions we see light.

So it is of human love.—There is a new preciousness, tenderness, thoughtfulness, blessedness, where the love and light of Jesus reign in home and heart. We see a loveliness and beauty in our dear ones that had eluded us till we beheld them in the love of Jesus.

27	*He that spareth his words hath knowledge.* Proverbs 17: 27, RV

THE AV and the RV margin suggest a better rendering, "He that hath knowledge spareth his words." It is a wise thing to say as little as possible to man, and as much as possible to God. The ultimate test of friendship has always seemed to me to be in the ability of true friends to be silent in each other's presence. In silence we best may open the heart to receive the infillings of the Divine Spirit. When people are always talking about God, they are likely to lose the first fresh sense of God's presence.

Ordinary conversation greatly weakens character. It is like the perpetual running of a tap which inevitably empties the cistern. It seems to me disastrous when the whole of a summer holiday is spent in contact with friends, however dear, who leave no time for the communing of the soul with itself, nature, and God. We cannot be perpetually in society, speaking to the nearest and dearest, without saying things which will afterwards cause us regret. We shall have spoken too much of ourselves, or too little of Christ, or too much about others; or we shall have allowed the things of the world and sense to bulk too largely. Besides, it is only in silence and thought that our deepest life matures, or the impressions of eternity are realized. If we are always talking, we give no opportunity for the ripening of the soul. Nothing makes the soul more fruitful than to leave it fallow. Who would pick a crop of fruit when first it began to appear on the trees? Live deep. Speak as little as you may. Be slow to speak, and swift to hear.

Commit your work to the Lord, and your plans will be established.

Proverbs 16: 3, RSV

28

THERE ARE four matters which we are to commit to God—ourselves, as the Messiah in Psalm 22; our burden; our way; and here our works. This is the genesis of Christian work. We become conscious of the uprising of a noble purpose. We are not sure at first whether it is of God or not, till we have taken time to subject it to the winnowing fan of His good Spirit. It is always wise to subject it to the fire of His criticism before it takes shape. Even then, however, all is not done. We must submit our plans before they are executed, our methods by which they are being executed, and the results of the execution, to the infinite wisdom of our Heavenly Father.

What a comfort it is to commit our works to God! That servant of God who is carrying the responsibilities of a vast missionary

August

enterprise! That preacher with his church and organizations! That promoter of philanthropic and helping agencies! Let them roll their works upon God, and be content to take the subordinate place of acting as his agents and executors. The heart will be light, and the hands free, if only we can learn the blessed secret of imposing the responsibility and anxiety of our efficiency, finance, and success on Jehovah. Commit your works, and see that they do not roll back upon you again. Put on the restraint of faith to make them keep their position. Reckon that God takes what you give; and when you have let your works go, be sure to cast yourself after them on His patient carefulness. Remember that He desires to work in us to will and to work of His good pleasure.

29	*. . . thy Father which seeth in secret shall reward thee openly.*

Matthew 6: 6

JESUS repeats these words tenderly and lovingly (vv. 4,6,18). Though compelled by circumstance to live in the public eye, His heart was always sighing for the secret place of fellowship with His Father, who waited for Him there.

The main purpose of these paragraphs was to point His disciples away from the excessive shallowness and superficiality of the age in which He spoke, and which necessarily detracted from the singleness, directness, and simplicity of the religious life. It is impossible to live our Christian lives before men, without unconsciously considering what impression we are producing, and how far their estimation of us is being enhanced. And insofar as we seek these things, the stream is contaminated with mud and silt, and becomes impure. We have just as much religious life as we show to God in secret—just that, no less, no more. Whatever is not open between you and God, with no record but His eye, is chaff which the wind drives away.

Here is a test for our charity, our prayers, and our fasting from sin and self-indulgence. If we do any of these to maintain or increase the consideration that men have for us, they count for nothing in the eye of God. But whatever is done for Him alone will secure His inevitable notice and reward. Dwell on that very definite assurance: *"Shall* recompense thee."* There is no doubt about it. For every petition breathed into His ear; for every sigh and tear; for every abstinence from sin and self—there will be a certain compensation according to the divine measure. Such seeds will have a prolific harvest. Seek then the secret place, where prying eyes cannot follow, and curious ears cannot overhear.

And being made perfect he became the source [author] of eternal salvation to all who obey him. . . .
Hebrews 5: 9, RSV

30

IN THE OLD Covenant the stress was laid on the outward rite of sacrifice; but in the New Covenant, for burnt-offerings and sacrifices for sin are substituted, first the entire devotion and consecration of the blessed Lord to His Father's will; and next, ours in Him.

It is very noticeable that by the offering of the cross, in which the Savior's yielded will culminated, we are said to have been sanctified, consecrated, or set apart *once for all* (Heb. 10: 10). The thought there is, evidently, that our Savior's death has implicated us for evermore; and that His church, whom He represented in that supreme act, is forever pledged to be dead unto the world and sin.

But still later we learn that He has perfected for ever them that are sanctified (Heb. 10: 14). The change of tense surely indicates that what was accomplished *for* us in the purpose of God when Jesus died, must be accomplished *in* us by the operation of the Holy Spirit. Every time, therefore, our will is brought into more perfect union with that of God, a further step is taken toward that glorious elevation which Jesus made ours in the death of the cross.

And if you would have an incentive to this, remember how Jesus promised that all who would do the will of God should be reckoned members of the holy family (Matt. 12: 46–50). Are you a member of that family? You may be, and sit only on the outer circle, for the constituent members are always altering their position toward the central Christ; now advancing toward the inner heart, now receding.

August

Oh, see to it that you are not only within the holy circle of God's will, but that you are near the golden center where Jesus is seated.

31	*Are you he who is to come, or shall we look for another?*
	Matthew 11: 3

IN REPLY to this question from John the Baptist, Jesus said, among other things, "Blessed is he, whosoever shall not be offended in me" (Matt. 11: 3). This is a reflection of Isaiah's prophecy, "He shall become . . . a rock of offense, a rock of stumbling" (8: 14). The Baptist was tempted to take offense with Christ, first, because of his long delay in asserting Himself as the promised Messiah; and secondly, because of his apparent indifference to his own welfare. "If He is what we were led to expect, why does He leave me in this prison, sending me no comfort, nor trying to free me from these bonds?"

Don't we have days like this ourselves? We ask, If He really loves us and is as powerful as He says He is, why doesn't He deliver us from this terrible situation? Why does He not hurl these prison walls to the ground? Why does He not vindicate and bring me out to the light of life and joy?

But the Lord made no attempt to emancipate His servant; and He may seem to be unmindful of our situation. All He did for John was to send him materials on which his faith should feed, and rise to a stronger, nobler growth. "Go back," He said in effect to John, "tell him what I can do; he is not mistaken—I have all power, I am the expected King; and if I do not come to his help in the way he expects, it is not through lack of power and willingness, but because of reasons of divine policy and government, to which I must be true. Tell him to trust Me, though I do not deliver him. Assure him of the blessedness which must result to those who are not offended at My apparent neglect. I will explain all to him some day." Thus He still speaks. He does not attempt to apologize, or to explain—He only asks our trust; and promises blessedness to those who do not stumble at life's mysteries.

The Spirit-filled Life

September

And the woman said to Elijah, "Now I know that you are a man of God, and that the word of the Lord in your mouth is truth."

1 Kings 17: 24, RSV

$$\boxed{1}$$

ELIJAH'S nature was powerful and passionate. He revealed the *passion of patriotism,* as when he was prepared even to witness the sufferings of his people, if these sufferings would secure their repentance; of *tenderness,* as when he bore the dead body of the widow's son to his room; of *righteousness,* as when he slew the prophets of Baal; of *love for nature,* as shown when he threw himself on the ground and asked to die; and *devotion to God's glory,* as when he cried, "I have been very jealous for the Lord God of hosts." All these passions dwelt within his breast, and he might have availed himself of any or all of them, had he so desired; but if he had, his life work would have faded as the mirage on glistening sand.

Undoubtedly, this charisma lies at the heart of some of our most popular revivalists today. Without their being conscious of it, perhaps, there is a magnetism about them which proves irresistible to their hearers; but this is far from being the most enduring influence. When their presence is withdrawn, those whom they have affected are apt to drop back again to lethargy and sin, as the paper and straw caught up by the rush of an express train rise and flutter for a few moments, only to drop back motionless on the railroad track. Some souls are born of the flesh and of the will of man, and others of God. It is the latter who abide. Let us learn to pray more, that we may be filled with the passionate love to our Lord Jesus and toward dying men. We dare not be cold and apathetic in this moving, teeming universe, electric with living energy.

September

2

And I will give her her vineyards from thence, and the val-
ley of Achor for a door of hope: and she shall sing there,
as in the days of her youth. . . .

Hosea 2: 15

THE VALLEY of Achor stands for defeat. Following their vast victories, the army of Israel expected an easy triumph, but God had a
lesson for them.

Is there a single life without its valley of Achor? Is there one of
us who has not gone up against a temptation which appeared quite
insignificant at a distance, but proved to be more than a match for
all our resolutions? Has not the sense of our inability to withstand
certain forms of temptation been borne in upon us by bitter experience? Can good come out of such evil, and sweetness from such
bitter disaster?

The book of Joshua tells how defeat can bring about good. The
disaster led to the searching out of Achan and the cutting away of
the gangrene which was eating at the heart of Israel. It led to humiliation, self-examination, prayer and faith, and so at last back again
to victory. As Israel passed the sad monument of Achan and his
family, it seemed to the inspired imagination of Hosea as though a
door of hope had suddenly swung open in the side of the cliffs, and
they passed on into assured victory. Is this perhaps the way our de-
feats will bear fruit in our lives?

3

O Ephraim, what shall I do unto thee? O Judah, what shall
I do unto thee? . . .

Hosea 6: 4

THE DIVINE question, What shall I do unto thee? is answered in
the proclamation of the New Covenant. What shall I do? I will give
My Son. What shall I do? I will give My Spirit. I will come and
indwell. I will expend blood for their cleansing and fire for their
sanctification. This is the difference between the old covenant, under
which God's people lived in the days of Hosea, and the new covenant
which was introduced to take its place, and remedy its confessed

failure. For if that first covenant had been faultless, then a second would not have been necessary. But there was a disannulling of the former, because of its weakness and unprofitableness, for it made nothing perfect.

The difference may be stated in a word. Under the first, Israel after the flesh sought to realize its fair ideals and fulfill its resolutions, in the energy of its own will and power. Under the second, God enters the heart, in Jesus, and through the Holy Spirit, to effect within us His own ideal, and to make permanently our own those visions of beauty that, like the new Jerusalem, come down to us from God out of heaven. It is because we choose to live under the old, rather than exercise the privileges we have under the new, that our goodness, like Israel's, has resembled the morning cloud, and the dew which passes away. He must do it to us—we cannot do it ourselves!

It is like the precious oil upon the head.
Psalm 133: 2, RV

4

BROTHERLY love binding together kindred hearts is here compared to oil, the chosen symbol of the Holy Spirit, because it is only through His grace that it is possible to love. The love of the brethren is the earthly manifestation of love to God. We have just as much to Him as we have to them; and such love, whether to them or Him, can only be shed abroad in our hearts by the Holy Spirit given unto us. Is love wanting? Seek a baptism of the Holy Spirit. Pentecost meant the most wonderful manifestation of love which the world had ever seen.

The Holy Spirit, as oil, was poured upon the head of our great Aaron as He arose from the waters of baptism, and again when He ascended into the presence of His Father; and it has been descending ever since upon us who are as the skirts of His garments. To the Jew it seemed as though the Hermon range overtowered the land and was able to drop its dews across the intervening distance upon the mountains of Zion. Thus, from the glory of His exaltation,

September

Jesus drops the dew of the Holy Spirit as blessing upon the lowlands of our life—that blessing which is life forevermore. Our response to it should be the fertility of our heart's and life's activities.

"Ye have," said the apostle, "an unction [anointing] from the Holy One, and ye know all things." Could that assertion be made of us? If not, let us seek it.

5

If you have found honey, eat only enough for you, lest you be sated with it and vomit it.

Proverbs 25: 16, RSV

He who is sated loathes honey.

Proverbs 27: 7, RSV

HONEY was not used in sacrifices made by fire unto the Lord. Its luscious taste may have made it an emblem of the pleasures of the world. As bees roam from flower to flower, sipping nectar here and there, so does the heart of the worldling roam over the world for satisfaction; settling nowhere for long, but extracting sweets from a variety of attractive sources.

The best way of combatting worldliness is by satisfying the heart with something better. The full soul loatheth even the honeycomb (Prov. 27: 7). When the prodigal gets the fatted calf, he has no further hankering after the husks which the swine eat. The girl who gets real jewels throws away her shams; and the child who has become a man has no taste for childish toys that once seemed all-important. This is the meaning of the old proverb: Love God, and do as you like. Whenever the spirit of worldliness gets into a congregation, you may be sure that the teaching has been defective, and that souls have not been made to sit at the rich banquet of the divine providing.

We are reminded of the words which the psalmist applied to the Word of God: "Sweeter than honey, or the honeycomb." Fill your heart with God and His sacred truth, and the things of the world will lose their charm. Do you know this absorbing love of Jesus? We can at least choose to know it, and present ourselves to the Holy

September

Spirit, that He may shed it abroad in our hearts. Oh, to be full! Full of the more abundant life of which the Lord spoke, of the unspeakable joy, of the peace that passeth understanding—in a word, of Jesus, as the chief and best.

And Jesus answering said unto them, Do ye not therefore err, because ye know not the Scriptures, neither the power of God?

Mark 12: 24

6

WHAT IS there in Scripture that invested it, in Christ's judgment, with such unique authority? What are the Scriptures? It would be difficult to find a reply more satisfactory and Scriptural than that given by the late A. J. Gordon: "Literature is the letter, Scripture is the letter inspired by the Spirit." What Jesus said of the new birth is equally applicable to the doctrine of inspiration: "That which is born of the flesh is flesh, and that which is born of the Spirit is spirit." Educate, develop, and refine the natural man to the highest possible point, yet he is not a spiritual man till, through the new birth, the Holy Spirit renews and indwells him. So of literature; however elevated its tone, however lofty its thought, it is not Scripture. Scripture is literature indwelt by the Spirit of God. The absence of the Holy Spirit from any writing constitutes the impassable gulf between it and Scripture. "*In fine,* the one fact which makes the Word of God a unique book, standing apart in solitary separateness from other writings, is that which also parts the man of God from common men—the indwelling of the Holy Spirit."

And when they had prayed, the place was shaken where they were assembled together; and they were all filled with the Holy Ghost, and they spake the word of God with boldness.

Acts 4: 31

7

THIS fullness must be received. The fullness is in Jesus, but we must *take* it. It is not enough even to pray; we must reverently and humbly

September

appropriate its stores. "Give me this water," must be the cry of each "that I thirst not, neither come hither to draw."

There are three methods by which the filling process may be hastened:

1. Give yourself to holy song; if not with the lip, then in the heart, and with the music of a loving, trustful spirit and the rhythm of a life attuned to the will of God.
2. Give thanks always for all things. Some of God's best gifts come in the roughest cases. When you see your father's handwriting in the direction, kneel down and thank Him for the contents before you unpack them. All must be good that comes from Him.
3. Give submission and subjection to one another, except in matters that touch conscience and the demands of God.

But above all, learn the secret of an appropriating faith, that goes to God with its need, and dips its empty pitcher down into the fullness of Jesus, and takes up at any moment of the day the supply of its thirst, daring to believe where it cannot discern, and to act on its sure reckoning that it does receive that which it asks of God.

Too often God's ships come laden to our wharves, but we are not there to discharge them. Too often His couriers bring love letters, but we are asleep and they pass our doors. Too often, His showers pass over the hills, but we do not catch their blessed fullness to fertilize and enrich our fields.

8 . . . *The Holy Ghost said, Separate me Barnabas and Saul for the work whereunto I have called them.*

Acts 13:2

IN LATER days, following this event, Paul referred to himself as being separated unto the gospel of God. It is a mistake to make the act of separation our own resolve and deed. We will inevitably fall back unless God has come into the transaction and has set us apart for Himself. We must be separated *from* sin and sinners *unto* a holy God.

We are needed for a specific purpose. God blesses men only

September

through men. As once He used the Jews to be the medium of communicating His truth to men, so now He is eager to use His church; if only she will allow Him to deliver her from the taint of sin and the world, and separate her for a peculiar possession unto Himself. Let us individually yield ourselves to the blessed influences of the Holy Spirit, that He may realize in us the purpose for which He has called us.

We are required to satisfy God's heart. He needs love for love. Throughout the world He seeks for those who can afford Him pleasure, as His enclosed gardens, His sealed fountains, His peculiar treasure.

This separation is effected by the Holy Spirit, and is referred to in the word "sealing." "He hath sealed us unto the day of redemption" (Eph. 4: 30).

What an honor this is! To be for God Himself: to do His errands; to fulfill His commands and give Him pleasure! Rejoice greatly when He says, "Thou art Mine." Let us be glad if we know the oil of separation has come on our heads, and let us walk worthy of our high calling, separated to the Holy Spirit, counting it sacrilege to be used for any unholy purpose.

I am the good shepherd . . . [who] giveth his life for the sheep.

John 10: 11

9

THIS CHAPTER is a veritable psalm of Life (see also v. 17). It overflows with the message of the Easter morning. Throughout its verses it is witnessed that He lives; that He will ever live. Indeed the writer to the Hebrews says He lives "by the power of an indestructible life" (Heb. 7: 16, RSV); that He lives after the power of an indissoluble or indestructible life.

Remember all that was done to end His life. Satan spoke to his chief captains, Sepulcher and Corruption, and told them to hold his Prisoner fast. The Sanhedrin affixed their seal, and set the watch, and made the grave as secure as possible. But it was all in vain. His body could not see corruption. His life defied death. All through the

September

Greek mythology there is the wail of infinite sorrow. Laocoon and his sons strangled by the folds of the mighty serpent: day always mastered by night: the year with its wealth of life descending to the abyss. Strive as man might, he would be mastered at last, and primeval night reign once more. But all this is altered in Jesus. Though He gave His life, He is Priest after the power of an endless life (Heb. 7: 16).

And, what is more, that life may be communicated to us by the Holy Spirit. It is not only true that He ever lives; but also that because He lives, and as He lives, we shall live also. In the first creation God breathed into Adam the breath of his life, and he became a living soul; but in the second creation Christ breathes into us the spirit of His life, and our spirit is filled with a property which it had not previously, and in which the sons of men have no share. "The first man Adam became a living soul. The last Adam became a life-giving spirit." See to it that you deny your own life, so that His life may become evermore dominant within you.

10	*And Jesus being full of the Holy Ghost returned from Jordan, and was led by the Spirit into the wilderness.*
	Luke 4: 1

WHAT different circumstances the last Adam experienced compared to the first! Adam began in a garden which the Lord God had planted; but his great Antitype began in a *wilderness,* the thorns of which spoke of that first sin. But whereas the first Adam transformed the garden into a wilderness, the last will convert all desert places into gardens—whether they be in the heart, or the world around—so that they will blossom as the rose.

To Adam the *beasts* came, that he might name them; but at the coming of the last Adam they were wild. "He was with the *wild* beasts" (Mark 1: 13). Yet they were tame to His pure manhood. On His head the crown of royalty over the inferior races, which man had lost, was already placed. Is it not also true that holy men still have power over the lower creation? Certainly Francis of Assisi had. And in the ages yet future, the children shall play, unhurt, amid the wild beasts of the forest.

Again it is true of you, O son of man, that, like your Lord, you are between the wild beasts and *the angels*. On the one side you touch the lower, and on the other the higher. At every moment you are called to choose between them. Your body calls you this way, and your spirit that. Be sure to subdue the lower appetites; rule them; be king and lord in the realm of your soul. Make them crouch around you, as the lions of Daniel's den. Get your Lord to master them for you. If you don't, you will miss the angels of God, who come to encamp around you, and minister to you, as one of the heirs of salvation. Was it here in the wilderness that Christ learned to contrast His homelessness with the lairs of the beasts?

And they were all filled with the Holy Ghost . . . when the day of Pentecost was fully come. . . .
Acts 2: 4, 1

11

THE DISCIPLES were filled on the day of Pentecost with the Holy Spirit. Peter was suddenly and mightily infilled for his encounter with the Sanhedrin (Acts 4: 8). In Acts 4: 31 again they were all privileged, while in the attitude of prayer and praise, to be once more most blessedly infilled. From this we gather that we may claim repeated fillings of the Holy Spirit.

Remember, however, that it is not necessary for the place to be shaken, or for the air to be filled with the outward phenomena of Pentecost as the necessary condition of this heavenly gift. One commentator reminds us that the Lord may be pleased to come softly to our help. He may cause our sinfulness to cease by helping us to sink gently to unknown depths of meekness. Like Naaman, we are full of prejudices. We expect that the Pentecostal gift will come to us with as much ado, pomp, and bustle, as the Syrian general looked for. But the blessed Paraclete often goes counter to our preconceived notions. When we are looking for the hurricane, He comes as the gentle summer breeze. When we are expecting the torrent to pour into and fill the well, He fills it by single drops.

September

But the results will always be the same—great boldness in witness-bearing, much liberty in prayer and praise; great grace and beauty of character; self-denying love for those in need; great power through union with the risen Lord. If the second chapter of Acts had been lost, we would still have inferred something like Pentecost. In no other way could we have accounted for the marvelous change which took place in the followers of Jesus, delivering them from the cowardice, wrangling, and prejudices of former days. Oh, for a similar transforming experience for us all!

And the word of God increased; and the number of the disciples multiplied in Jerusalem greatly....

Acts 6: 7

THE CHURCH grew not simply by addition, but by multiplication (Acts 9: 31). Three added to three make *six;* three multiplied by three, *nine.* That is the Pentecostal ratio of increase. These are the conditions of church growth: "The Church had peace, being edified; and ... was multiplied" (Acts 9: 31).

First, there must be peace.—The Bible says: "Let us endeavour to *keep* the unity of the Spirit in the bond of peace." As far as it lies in our power, let each of us live peaceably with all men. Let all bitterness, and wrath, and anger, and clamor, and railing, be put away out of our hearts, with all malice, and let us be kind one to another, tenderhearted, and imitating God the great Peacemaker.

Next, the church must be edified.—We must build ourselves up on our most holy faith. And, indeed, such growth in grace and the knowledge of God is almost inevitable where the Holy Spirit breaks up the reign or apathy and stagnation. When its foundations are deeply laid in righteousness and peace, the City of God arises into the pure air.

Moreover, the members of such a Christian community must walk *in the fear of the Lord.* To walk means the daily plodding, routine life—full of commonplaces, somewhat prosaic—but always ruled by the fear of grieving the heart that was pierced on Calvary. Lastly, we must walk *in the comfort of the Holy Spirit,* or, as the words might be rendered, in the *paracletism* of the Paraclete. The Holy Spirit is our Advocate, Teacher, Guide; and we should habitually dwell in His radiant and helpful environment. What a difference there is between sea weeds and sea flowers expanding in their rock-surrounded aquariums, and the same when taken into common air! Such is the contrast wrought by the Spirit.

Wherefore, brethren, look ye out among you seven men of honest report, full of the Holy Ghost and wisdom. . . .
Acts 6: 3

13

THE BLESSED characteristic of Stephen lay in his being perpetually *full* of the Holy Ghost. "But he, being full of the Holy Ghost, looked up steadfastly" (Acts 7: 55). It is said of others, even Peter, that they were *filled*, as though they needed some special and overmastering inducement for special service. But Stephen is more than once described as full (6: 5), as though he were always kept brimming, like a lake from the hills.

Those who are full of the Holy Spirit are always looking steadfastly upwards.—They look not at the things which are seen, but at those which are not seen. Across the valleys, they catch sight of the Delectable Mountains, rising like the Himalayas above the plains of India. While others look around for help, they lift up their eyes to the hills whence cometh their help; and to them heaven stands always open.

Those who are full of the Holy Spirit see and are transfigured by the glory of God.—What wonder that those who sat in the Council beheld Stephen's face, as if it had been the face of an angel. The light that shone there was not as when Jesus was transfigured—in that case, the light of the Shekinah broke out from within—but here the glory of God shone from the open door of heaven. So the sunrise smites the highest peaks.

Those who are full of the Holy Ghost see the Lord Jesus, in His glory, as their Priest.—It is the special work of the Holy Spirit to direct the gaze to Jesus. Those who are full of the Spirit may hardly be aware of His gracious presence, but they are keenly alive to their

September

Lord's. The Spirit takes of the things of Jesus, and reveals them to the loving and obedient; specially those that concern His priestly work on the cross and in heaven.

14	*It is the Spirit himself bearing witness with our spirit that we are children of God.*

Romans 8: 16, RSV

IT IS our privilege, not only to be children, but to know that we are such. The world does not know us, but God knows us, and we know Him, and we know that we are His sons and daughters, through regeneration and faith. How do we know?

We believe His Word (John 1: 12).—By faith we have received Him, we do trust in His name; then by the authority of that text, if there were no other, we may claim to have been born into the divine household.

We have the witness of the Spirit (Gal. 4: 6).—The fact that our hearts look to God as Father, and appeal to Him with the infant's cry, Abba, is a proof that we are born again. Do not look for an audible voice in your heart, but notice whether the thought of the fatherly love of God toward you is not becoming more familiar and precious. It is not the perception of your childship, but of His Fatherhood, which will reassure you.

We are led by the Spirit.—If we are led by the Spirit, we will love the things we once hated, and hate those we once loved. Our choices, tastes, methods of life, habits, and companionships, will undergo a radical alteration.

We love the people of God (1 John 4: 7).—The converse is also true, that he who is begotten of God loveth.

We do not presumptuously and habitually yield to known sin (1 John 3: 9).—The apostle is not speaking of some isolated act into which a man may fall under unexpected temptation, but of habitual courses of inconsistency and wrong-doing. Test yourselves, therefore, whether you are indeed born again.

September

Blessed be the God and Father of our Lord Jesus Christ, who hath blessed us with all spiritual blessings in heavenly places in Christ.
$$\boxed{15}$$

Ephesians 1: 3

IN CHRIST the blessings of redemption are stored. All conceivable spiritual blessings needed by us for living a holy and useful life are stored in Jesus. We must therefore be in Him by a living faith to partake of them; as a child must be in the home, to participate in the provisions of the father's care. It is only they who know the meaning of the life hidden with Christ in God, and who abide in Christ, to whom God gives the key of His granary, and says, "Go in, and take what you will."

How can mortal man exhaust the wonderful gifts of our Father's grace? But they are all freely bestowed in the Beloved, in whom we also stand accepted. Who can estimate the meaning of redemption, which begins with the forgiveness of our trespasses, and ends in the rapture of the sapphire throne? But it is to be found only in Him and through His blood. What do we not owe to the sealing of the Spirit, by which our softened hearts get the impress of the Savior's beloved face, and are kept safe until He comes to claim us? But the sealing is only possible to those who are in Him. All things are ours, but only when we are in Christ.

$$\boxed{16}$$

For the kingdom of God is not in word, but in power.
1 Corinthians 4: 20

MAN LONGS for power. The young man will give all he has for love; the older man counts no sacrifice too great for power. He who wields power is the idol of his fellows, even though, like the first Napoleon, he has won it at the cost of the suffering of myriads. We are not wrong in longing for spiritual power, if only we desire it for the glory of our Master and the blessing of man. It is even our duty to covet this great gift, and to take all means to procure it, that we may be strong and able to do exploits.

September

Let us never forget that the power of the spiritual realm is never to be had except in submission to the laws of its operation. All around us in our world great forces are throbbing, prepared to do our bidding, to carry our messages or drive our vehicles; but we must obey them before we can use them. Once we learn the laws of their operation, and yield to them exact obedience, there is nothing they will not do, toiling like another Hercules in notable deeds. And, similarly, we must learn, by prayer and watching, the laws of the operation of the power of God; that we may adapt our lives and methods to benefit by each throb and pulse of it which may be within the reach of man.

We must remember also that spiritual power is not a separate entity, which we may possess independently of the Holy Spirit. The power of the spiritual world is the indwelling and inspiration of the Holy Spirit Himself. We cannot have it apart from Him. We diminish it when He is grieved or quenched. We are most evidently the subjects and vehicles of it, when He resides in His gracious fullness in yielded and loving hearts. We covet the gift, let us then make welcome the Giver. Let us no longer speak of *it,* but of Him.

In whom ye also trusted, after that ye heard the word of truth, the gospel of your salvation; in whom also after that ye believed, ye were sealed with that Holy Spirit of promise.
Ephesians 1: 13

THE HOLY SPIRIT is the special promise of the Father made to those who are one with His Son by a living faith. "Wait," said our Lord, "for the promise of the Father, which ye heard from me"; and immediately on His exaltation to the right hand of God He received the promise of the Holy Spirit, which He poured upon the suppliant church. That promise is still open to as many as the Lord our God shall call. "For the promise is unto you, and to your children, and to all that are afar off, even as many as the Lord our God shall call" (Acts 2: 39).

Upon the yielded soul, the blessed Spirit descends, bearing with Him the likeness of Jesus, which He imprints and fixes, as a stamp will leave its die upon the softened wax. Only melted gold is minted;

September

only moistened clay is molded; only softened wax receives the die; only broken and contrite hearts can take and keep the impress of heaven. If that is your condition, wait beneath the pressure of the Holy Spirit; He will leave the image of Jesus upon you, and change you into His likeness, from glory to glory.

That the God of our Lord Jesus Christ, the Father of glory, may give unto you the spirit of wisdom and revelation in the knowledge of him.
Ephesians 1: 17

18

IT HAS been truly said that every revelation of Himself that God makes to man involves a revelation of what man is in his nature and needs. When we learn that Christ is made to us righteousness, we know that we are unrighteous. That He is our Paschal Lamb teaches us that we are in danger of the destroying angel. The name Comforter given to the Holy Ghost, assures us of our need of one to stand beside us. When, therefore, God describes Himself as God to men who had passed from this earth for centuries, it was conclusive evidence that they were living somewhere, within some warm enclosure of His most blessed and happy-making presence.

There is, therefore, misconception when we speak of the *dead*, as though death were an abiding place, a permanent condition. It is a passage, not an abiding place; an act, not a state; a shadow flung for a moment by the portal through which we enter the other world, where the chalice of life brims over.

Which is his body, the fulness of him that filleth all in all.
Ephesians 1: 23

19

IT IS SAID of Abraham that he died at a good old age, an old man, and *full*. It is a beautiful conception; as though all his nature had

September

reached its complete satisfaction and he could desire and receive nothing more. The psalmist, too, sings of fulfilled desire; and Mary tells how God filled her hungry soul with good things. Can we speak with equal certainty of being "filled"?

Christ is the source of fullness to His church and to individual souls. We have sought to be filled with earthly goods and human love. Away from the mountains we have tried to hew out for ourselves cisterns, to be fed by rushing brooks and falling showers, and be always brimming; but we have been greatly disappointed. In each case a flaw or crack has made our work abortive, and we have seen the waters sinking inch after inch till only drops have remained to quench the thirst of our souls. Not more successful have been the attempts of those who have sought rest in systems of theology, in rites and ceremonies, or in the rush of unceasing engagements. In none of these can the nature of man find its completion or fruition.

All the fullness of the Godhead dwells bodily in Him, and of that fullness we might all receive, and grace on grace; like repeated waves that follow one another up to the furthest reaches of the tide. In Him we have been made full in the purpose and intention of God; and in Him we may be made full by the daily reception of His grace, through the operation of the Holy Spirit.

And you hath he quickened, who were dead in trespasses and sins.

Ephesians 2: 1

HE WILL do more than just forgive us our sins; He will protect, maintain, and quicken into stronger and healthier growth. The Holy Spirit will take charge of the feebly smoking flax and fan its flickering flame into fire. He who hath begun a good work in you will complete it. There shall be a perfecting of the tender purpose, a blossoming of the fragile bud. Is this not included in that nourishing and cherishing which is predicted of the Lord's body? It might be applied as well to a nurse's or mother's solicitude for some flickering baby-life, that keeps standing still and asking whether or not it should continue. "After two days he will revive us: in the third day he will raise us up, and we shall live in his sight" (Hos. 6: 2). The power that raised up Jesus from the dead on the third day, waits to do as much for us, not spasmodically and intermittently, but regularly, certainly, ceaselessly, until it seats us beyond all principality and power beside His own steadfast throne.

And hath raised us up together, and made us sit together in heavenly places in Christ Jesus.
Ephesians 2: 6

21

WHAT Canaan was to the Jewish people, that the heavenly places are to us. When the twelve stones were taken from the bed of the Jordan and placed on the farther side, the whole people were deemed to have entered upon the possession of their inheritance. This in spite of the fact that two and a half tribes elected to settle on the farther side, and their wives and children would probably never cross the Jordan at all. So when Jesus passed to the throne, we passed with Him.

Was He raised? So were we. Was He made to sit at the Father's right hand? *That* is our place. Was every foe made His footstool? Then not one of them can overcome us so long as we are in abiding fellowship with our risen Lord. If the "together" of the inner life is maintained, the "together" of victory is secure. Oh, to tread in the power of the Holy Spirit in these high places!

For through Him we both have access by one Spirit unto the Father.
Ephesians 2: 18

22

"THROUGH Him" we have access with boldness into the presence of God, confident that what we ask was according to His mind to give. Then we could sit at His feet, and be taught in Him, even as

September

the truth is in Jesus, learning the secret of putting away the old man and putting on the new. Then it would not be so hard always to give thanks for all things in His name. An artesian well, fed from heaven's deep joy, would then make perennial gladness in our hearts. Then we should never lack strength, our slender supply being fed from His almightiness, on which we could draw perpetually. Spirit of God —divine anointing which we have received of Him—teach us concerning all things, and especially how to abide in Christ. "But the anointing which ye have received of Him abideth in you, and ye need not that any man teach you: But as the same anointing teacheth you of all things, and is truth, and is no lie, and even as it hath taught you, ye shall abide in Him" (1 John 2: 27).

23	*Let your speech be alway with grace, seasoned with salt, that ye may know how ye ought to answer every man.*
	Colossians 4: 6

THE SALT just needs to be salt. It need not attempt to be a voice, a spark of light, or a thrill of electricity. Let it just be good, wholesome salt, and quietly, unobtrusively, it will fulfill its great mission. A gentleman who travels much among lonely farmhouses told me the other day that whenever a fierce dog ran barking at him, he stooped down and looked at it in the face; and he said that he had never met a dog yet which could stand a steady gaze; so there is something in the look of a really good man that abashes sin. The look of a Charles Finney stayed the blasphemy of a large factory, and brought all the workmen to their knees. In fact, it would be impossible to tell of all the prisons, the frontier settlements, the soldier's camps where the progress to sin has been arrested, and the devil himself has slunk away before the presence of a resolute, genuine man of God. *You* might do the same, only you must be a genuine character. Salt must be good before it can effect its great preventive ministry. But if it is good, it will do it. And if you are really full of the Holy Spirit, and of faith, your very presence will be all that is needed to defeat the evil that cries to heaven.

September

And grieve not the Holy Spirit of God, whereby ye are
sealed unto the day of redemption.

Ephesians 4: 30

24

WE MUST watch carefully our own attitude toward the Holy Spirit. He is not merely an influence; He is a person, and may easily be *grieved*. The dove of God is very tender and gentle; and if there are thorns in the nest, He cannot remain. The things that grieve Him are instantly recognized by the holy soul by an immediate unveiling of the inner light. They are enumerated here as bitterness, wrath, anger, clamor, railing, with all kinds of malice. There is no secret of the inner life more necessary than to retain the inner presence of an ungrieved spirit.

But also let us seek to be *filled* by Him. We have drunk of Him, as Jesus has placed the pitcher to our lips; but we should never rest till He has become in us a spring of water, leading up to eternal life. The Holy Spirit is in every believer; but He cannot be said to fill each. There is all the difference possible between a few drops at the bottom of the bucket and a brimming well; between a few stray flowers scattered sparsely through the glade, and the myriads that make it blue with hyacinths or yellow with primroses.

And be not drunk with wine, wherein is excess; but be
filled with the Spirit.

Ephesians 5: 18

25

TO BE filled with the Spirit was the blessing of Pentecost; but it awaits us all, Christians who seek it today as well as those in Paul's day. Indeed, Paul bids us here to be Spirit-filled. It is a positive command. We have no other option than to obey it. Mentioned in the same paragraph with the love of husband to wife, and the obedience of child to parent, it is as obligatory as either. Let no reader of these lines rest without seeking and receiving by faith this blessed gift, which God is able to make abound toward us. Receive it without emotion by faith: reckon it as yours: and act as if you felt it.

September

It is upon the submissive soul that the Blessed Spirit descends, bearing with Him the image of Jesus which is imprinted upon the life of the believer. This is what it means to be filled with the Spirit— so to live in the love of Christ that others see Him in us.

26	*There is one body, and one Spirit, even as ye are called in one hope of your calling.*

Ephesians 4: 4

THE HOLY SPIRIT is the secret and source of unity. There is one body, the mystical body of Christ; and as the human body, in all its different organs and members, is one living unit by reason of the spirit of life that pervades it, so the church, with its manifold diversities of organization and belief, is one, because animated by the only, the one Holy Spirit.

Many earnest and holy men refuse outward fellowship with those who do not belong to their communion; but they are still one with them, since the Holy Spirit is in them all. And they will recognize this on the shore of eternity.

27	*Which are a shadow of things to come; but the body is of Christ.*

Colossians 2: 17

IT IS as if God stored the whole fullness of His nature in Jesus, that it might be readily accessible by us. The river of God, which is full of water, flows over the low threshold of His humanity, that it may be within the reach of the weakest and smallest in His kingdom.

There is not one, who is in Jesus by a living faith, that may not reckon on being filled by Him. As the life-blood flows from the cistern-heart into each member and part of the body, so do the tides of life and love that emanate from the heart of Jesus pulse against the doors of all believing hearts. He fills all, and He fills all in all. The heart, with its keen power of enjoyment or sorrow. The mind, with its marvelous ability of tracking the footsteps of the Creator. He cannot do otherwise, without robbing or impoverishing Himself. For, as each part of the plant is needed to fill up the measure of its ideal, and as each member is required to fulfill the complete conception of a man; so each one of the members of Christ's mystical body, that Church is essential to the manifestation of His fullness. He needs you and me, or there will be some portion of His fullness which will never be able to manifest itself. But, as sure as we present ourselves to Him, there will be an infilling of our nature with Himself, as the chill morning air, at dawn, becomes suddenly radiant with sunbeams.

To whom God would make known what is the riches of the glory of this mystery among the Gentiles; which is Christ in you, the hope of glory.
Colossians 1: 27

28

A MARVELOUS lift is here! From the grave of mortality to the throne of the eternal God, who only has immortality; from the darkness of the tomb to the insufferable light; from this small world to the center and metropolis of the universe. Open the compasses of your faith to measure this measureless abyss; and then marvel at the power which bore your Lord across it; and know that that same power is toward you if you believe, waiting to do as much for you in your daily experience if you will but let it have its blessed way.

It is a matter of constant complaint with Christian people that they fall so far below their aspirations and hopes. They sigh at the foot of cliffs they cannot scale. The fault is with themselves. As we step into the elevators which are attached to so many factories and offices, and expect them to bear us upward, never doubting for a moment they will do it, so if we would keep an abiding fellowship with the Holy Spirit (i.e., if we would not willfully step out of the range of His blessed help) we should find ourselves mounting with wings as eagles, and going from strength to strength.

September

<table>
<tr><td>

29

</td><td>

Wherefore gird up the loins of your mind, be sober, and hope to the end for the grace that is to be brought unto you at the revelation of Jesus Christ.
</td></tr>
</table>

1 Peter 1: 13

LET US then gird up the loins of our minds and resolve again in the resurrection-grace of the Holy Spirit. Let us dare to register vows of absolute consecration and surrender, laying aside every weight and the sin that doth so easily beset us, and let us follow on with patience to know the Lord; and as we do so we will find ourselves strengthened with all might, according to His glorious power, unto all patience and longsuffering. We cannot expect to snatch so great an attainment with one swift rush; we must follow on, placing it before us as an acquisition which, at all cost, and by any sacrifice, must be ours. And it shall be ours, for though His going forth is as gentle and gradual as the morning, it is as sure. As an old saint said, with a touch of heartbreak in her tone, "The Almighty is tedious, but He's sure." She meant He is sometimes slow-moving, but He is the only One we can count on. This is the Spirit who infills His followers.

<table>
<tr><td>

30

</td><td>

Seeing ye have purified your souls in obeying the truth through the Spirit unto unfeigned love of the brethren, see that ye love one another with a pure heart fervently.
</td></tr>
</table>

1 Peter 1: 22

IN ITS deepest sense love is the perquisite of Christianity. There is something like it, in germ, at least, outside the school of Christ; just as wild flowers recall the rich splendor of the hothouse. But in all such there are flaws, traces of selfishness and passion, which prevent their realizing God's fair ideal. Love, as the Bible uses the word, is the fruit of the spirit. It may be grafted on the natural stalk, but it is essentially His creation. To feel toward enemies what others feel toward friends; to descend as rain and sunbeams on the just as well as the unjust; to minister to those who are unprepossessing and repellent as others minister to the attractive and winsome; to be always the same, not subject to moods or fancies or whims; to suffer long; to take no account of evil; to rejoice with the truth; to bear, believe, hope, and endure all things, never to fail—this is love, and such love is the achievement of the Holy Spirit alone.

October

He shall order the lamps upon the pure candlestick before the Lord continually. And thou shalt take fine flour. . . .
Leviticus 24: 4, 5

1

THE LIGHT of the candlestick and the twelve cakes of fine flour were to be before the Lord continually, as symbols of the twofold office God's people were to sustain, on the one hand to the world's darkness, on the other to God Himself.

We must shine as lights in the world: as a candle in the hands of the housewife who sweeps her house diligently; as a lamp in the hand of the virgin expecting the bridegroom; as a lighthouse on a dangerous and rocky coast. We must dispel the darkness and guide wanderers through the murky night. Light is soft and still, and is thus a fitting symbol of the influence of a holy life, which burns steadily before the Lord continually, and is unaffected by the attitudes of men. If no one seems the better for our consistent testimony, we should aim to satisfy the Lord. The lamps of a holy life are not for man only, but for Him. But they can only be maintained through the constant supply of the pure oil of the Holy Ghost, ministered by Him who walks amid the seven golden candlesticks. "Ye are the light of the world."

We must be as bread to God. In a blessed sense we feed on God, but God also feeds on us. He finds satisfaction in beholding His people's unity and love, in receiving their sacrifices of praise, and in watching their growing conformity to His will. The two rows of six cakes foreshadow the unity and order of the church; the fine flour, its holy, equable character; the pure frankincense, the fragrance of Christian love. There is a testimony in all this to the world; but we often fail to realize what satisfaction is afforded our great God, who made such a costly sacrifice for His church, when He sees our holy lives.

October

2	*Thou art my hiding place; thou shalt preserve me from trouble; thou shalt compass me about with songs of deliverance.*

Psalm 32: 7

IT IS possible that out of sad experiences will come a song. We may say that we will never sing again, that the spring and gladness of our life are gone forever; the flowers have all withered, the joy-notes are broken, and the harp strings jangled. We insist on mourning all our lives, and that each day will only bring added grief. But God says that we *shall* sing. Even though the summer seems gone, there will be an Indian summer, even mellower than the first.

In the days of Israel's youth she sang her glad songs on the banks of the Red Sea. Those notes still seem to hover over the outspread waters: "Sing ye to the Lord, for he hath triumphed gloriously; the Lord is a man of war, the Lord is his name." Those victorious notes were also ours at one time, but does it seem long ago? Never fear, you shall sing again as in the days of your youth. God wants to give you a new revelation of His love, to attract you into His tenderest fellowship and friendship, to make a fence around you which will prevent your following your old paths, to lift you into a life of victory and satisfaction. When all these things come to pass (and they may begin today as you return to Him), you will find that He has put a new song into your mouth and on your lips.

3	*For the sin of their mouth, and the words of their lips let them even be taken in their pride. . . .*

Psalm 59: 12

THE HEART of man is full of pride which shows itself in many ways: There is the *Pharaoh* phase, in which we proudly refuse to renounce, at the bidding of God, that which we claim to have acquired by our own ingenuity or capacity: "Who is the Lord, that I should obey him to let Israel go?"

There is the *Naaman* phase, which starts back in a rage from some simple ordinance to which the Lord claims obedience. There is the

Haman phase that cannot endure the refusal of a Mordecai to stand up or move to him: "All this availeth me nothing, so long as I see Mordecai the Jew sitting at the king's gate."

There is the *Hezekiah* phase, in which we show all the treasures of our home, in the spirit of ostentation and vain display.

There is the *Pilate* phase, which refuses the remonstrances of the Christ who stands to be judged.

Proud of our religious observances, our charities and self-denials, of the positions we hold in the church; of our very humility and courtesies to the poor; impatient of the least slight; quick to take offense; cherishing feelings of dislike for those who beat us; bent on edging our way to front positions; priding ourselves on the successes we have achieved, the talents with which we have been gifted.

What a contrast between us and our Savior! He came to serve and to give His life a ransom for many. Let us emulate Him—not the worst of men!

When I remember thee upon my bed, and meditate on thee in the night watches.

Psalm 63: 6

4

I AM TOLD that it was the habit of Charles H. Spurgeon to recognize the presence of God by uplifting his heart to Him once each quarter of an hour. My informant told me that often, in the midst of his gladdest hours, he noticed him suddenly turn his thoughts, and the thoughts of those who a moment before had been laughing at his wit, into the presence of the Lord.

This habit of meditating on passages of God's Word is also a helpful way of inducing that devoutness of spirit which realizes the Lord's presence. The Bible is like a garden where the Lord God walked. There will be times when the sense of His presence will be more impressive than others. St. Bernard said of Him, "He entered not by the eyes, for His presence was not marked by color; nor by the ears, for there was no sound; nor by the breath, for He mingled not with the air; nor by the touch, for He was untouchable. How, then, did I know He was present? Because of His quickening power.

October

As soon as He entered, He awoke my slumbering soul. He moved and pierced my heart, which before was strange and stony, hard and sick. He began to open the prison-house, to make the crooked straight, and the rough way smooth, so that my soul could bless the Lord."

But at other times, when one is hard and cold, it is a great secret to begin to say, "Thou art here, O Lord. I do not feel Thee or enjoy Thee. My heart within me is desolate, but Thou art beside me." Faith, not feeling, is the realizing faculty. If you say this again and again, in the face of the protest of your feeling, you will soon find it easy to realize He is with you.

Thy way was through the sea, thy path through the great waters; . . . Thou didst lead thy people like a flock by the hand of Moses and Aaron.

Psalm 77: 19, 20, RSV

THIS IS almost the extremity of exaltation; because of the contrast of the majesty and gentleness of God. In the first of these verses you have the former. God is described as wading through mighty oceans as a man might ford some tiny stream. The Atlantic with fathomless depths is no more to Him than a brook to us—not so much. But as the brook hides the footmarks which are imprinted on its soft ooze, so are God's footprints hidden. We cannot detect His great and wonderful secrets. We are unable to gauge His reasons. He marches through the ages with steps we cannot track. For His orbit there is no standard of computation.

But do not fear Him. This mighty God has the tender heart of a shepherd. He leads His people like a flock; not overdriving, but carrying the lambs in His bosom, and gently leading those that are with young. Mightier than the mightiest, but meeker than the meekest! The Lion of Judah, but the Lamb of Bethlehem! Prince and Savior; Fellow of Jehovah; and yet the smitten Shepherd of the scattered flock!

Nor is this all. It is a human hand that leads the flock. God does His work through the hands of human and fallible agents. You did not recognize Him; but had your eyes been opened, you would have seen His leading in the gentle hand of a mother, in the strong grasp of a friend, in the insecure fingers of a young girl, in the tiny hand of a child. Ah, how many good and tender hands have molded and fashioned our lives!—but beneath them all there have been the leadings of the great God, convoying us through deep and dark waters to our fold.

If the Lord had not been my help.
                                     Psalm 94: 17, RSV

| 6 |

HERE IS an If which cannot be an if. It is never a matter of uncertainty whether the Lord is with us. For the Lord Jesus in His incarnation and death has taken His place beside us for evermore. He is always with us, so long as we keep His paths and walk in His ways.

There are in all human lives hours of overpowering anxiety, when we feel as though it were impossible to live another moment—exposed to danger, separated from dear ones, not knowing what an hour may bring forth. Then, as you look up, you find that the Lord is beside you, sharing your anxieties, and affording you His inviolable protection. You cannot see Him with the natural eye, but you know Him to be there, and neither man nor devil can prevail against you.

When we look back on life, as the psalmist does here, we become aware of the myriad instances of divine protection. We were not so vividly conscious at the time; we might even have had fits of depression and counted ourselves abandoned. But if we narrowly consider the perils from which we have been rescued, when we were about to be swallowed up quick, we become convinced that He was there. In life and death and judgment, Jesus, your Advocate, will ever stand at your side and silence all who would condemn. So that with good courage you may say, "The Lord is my helper; and I will not fear what man shall do unto me!" (Heb. 13: 6).

October

7	*How great are thy works, O Lord!*
	Psalm 92: 5, RSV

THE MERCHANT goes forth to seek goodly pearls. Go forth, O Christian heart, to discover fresh jewels in your Savior's character. You will find them in meditation, in converse with other souls, but mainly in the reverent investigation of Scripture.

The theme of the Bible is—the works of the Lord. Its constant affirmation is that they are *great;* that His work is honor and majesty; that He has made His wonderful works to be remembered; that He shows His people the power of His works; and that the works of His hands are truth and judgment. Where better could we study or seek them out?

Consider God's works in creation, as scene after scene is unfolded in the first chapter of Genesis; in destruction, when the Deluge swept the earth; in redemption, when He led His people out of Egypt; in judgment, when He handed His people over to their enemies; in the holy Incarnation, the Passion, the Resurrection of Jesus, and in the coming of the Paraclete. Seek out these great and wonderful works; trace the references made to them in every part of Scripture; find a holy pleasure in reviewing them in all their wealth of significance.

Kepler, when he first turned his telescope to clustered worlds, exclaimed, "I am thinking over again the first thoughts of God." Our attitude, like his, must be one of reverence, patience, and dependence on the revealing Spirit. Probably this will be our employment in eternity; ever passing into deeper and fuller appreciation of the works of God.

8	*It is he who . . . gives food to all flesh. . . .*
	Psalm 136: 23, 25, RSV

GOD knows what you need for the maintenance of physical life and strength. The body is more than meat, and to have given you this is a pledge that He will give you that. The body is the vehicle and organ of the soul; and since God has given such a wonderful instrument into your custody, He is bound as need arises to furnish needful supplies. He could not expect that you should do what He has arranged should be done in your life, without providing for the repair and maintenance of the wonderful machine through which alone your life-plan can be realized. Trust in His faithfulness. He cannot deny Himself. The writer of the Proverbs says He will "feed me with the food that is needful to me" (Prov. 30: 8).

But there is other food which is needful. The daily bread of love, of hope, of holy thought, and fellowship. There are hungers other than that of the body. But these also will be provided, according as each day requires. If the human fails, the divine will takes its place, and God Himself will become the complement of your need. The Chinese Christians often put on the gravestones of their cemeteries the words, "They shall hunger no more," in allusion to the idea of the Confucians that children must constantly be sending on supplies to maintain their ancestors. And may we not say, with unwavering certainty, of those who have learned to be satisfied with God, "They shall hunger no more"?

Notice the alternative rendering of the RV, "The bread of my portion." In God's granaries there is our share of corn already calculated for and provided. Let us ask for and claim it. We have no wish to have more than our share, or to despoil others. As Jesus said, Give us each day the day's supply. O happy child of the great Father, his hired servants have enough and to spare; there is plenty for you!

Surely I have behaved and quieted myself, as a child that is weaned of his mother; my soul is even as a weaned child.

Psalm 131: 2

9

THIS Psalm is perhaps the most exquisite expression of the Christ-spirit before the Incarnation. There is nothing to match it, save the words which tell that the heart of the Redeemer is meek and lowly, and that the childlike and humble are the special subjects of the kingdom He is setting up among men.

October

The Psalm is attributed to David, and there is no reason to doubt his authorship. But this adds new interest to it, for it is clear that it was not natural to his lion-heart to write like this. From his earliest maturity he had been a man of war, compelled to force his way to the throne by intrigue and calumny—too stained with blood to build the temple of peace. His was not the hand we would naturally have credited with this tender and delicate sonnet. It must have come to him after some of the rougher experiences had passed, and he felt the necessity of curbing his strong and impetuous spirit. If this be the case, there is some hope for us whose lives have been stormy, whose natural bent is in the direction of pride and self-sufficiency. We too may be led, as David did, to say, "The days in which my heart was haughty and my eyes lofty are passed. Not now do I exercise myself in great matters, or in things too wonderful for me. I have learned to still and quiet my soul like a weanling upon his mother's knee."

Shall I lift up mine eyes unto the mountains?

Psalm 121: 1

IT IS NOT high enough to look to mountains. They are deeply rooted and permanent in their sockets. They rise like the pillars of heaven. Rivulets gush from their sides, vineyards drape their terraced slopes, eternal snows cap them with crowns of unsullied purity. The ancients thought that the gods had chosen them for their home, as on Parnassus or Olympus. To their towering steeps the eyes of their votaries were frequently directed to catch the first symptoms of descending help.

But the psalmist forbears to look to soaring mountains for his help. He lifts his eyes above and beyond, to the Lord who made heaven and earth. From thence shall His help come.

We are all tempted to look at the mountains, to the creature rather than the Creator; to wealth, talent, or influence; to things and people beneath the heavens, instead of to Him who dwells above the heavens, in His infinite majesty, and to whom all power is given in heaven and earth.

O unslumbering Keeper! O sleepless Watcher! Shade from heat, shelter from cold, protector from assault, transformer of ill to good, escort when we go out, home when we return! You are the complement of our need. We are content to suffer the loss of all things, to find them all in Thee. And therefore we betake ourselves to Your shadow till life's calamities are past.

. . . The Lord is round about his people. . . .
Psalm 125: 2

11

IT IS a beautiful conception. Around the chosen city the mountains stood like sentinels, leaving no part without its barrier. So is God around us; and this enables us to understand how His permissions may become His appointments. It is easy to accept pain and disappointment which come to us direct from His hand; but not so when they approach us from the plotting and malevolence of a Judas or Shimei. It is impossible, however, to arrive at a settled peace, so long as we make a distinction between the afflictions which come to us from the Divine, and those which visit us from the human; and, indeed, the distinction is untenable. For the assaults of our foes are at least permitted by God, and His permissions are His appointments.

This will become evident, if we clearly apprehend that God is round about us, as a rampart to the city, as an envelope to a letter, as the atmosphere to the configuration of our bodies. If then He chooses, He can pass off from us any arrow that might harm us; but if He opens His environing protection, so as to let it pass through to us, by the time it has traversed the atmosphere of His care, it has become His will for us. Put God between yourself and everything. Many put their anxieties between them and God, and see God as the sun through a fog; mind that you put God between yourself and the entire world of men and things.

In a city on the Continent the custodians keep the regalia without

October

iron bars, on what seems to be an open table—but none would dare to touch one jewel, for all around a powerful stream of electricity is perpetually being poured. Invisible, but potent! Such is the encompassing presence of God. Such is the imminence of His coming.

12	*As touching the dead, that they rise; have ye not read in the book of Moses, how in the bush God spake unto him saying, I am the God of Abraham, and the God of Isaac, and the God of Jacob?*

Mark 12: 26

THE FIRE that burned in the bush has generally been taken to mean the tribulations through which the church passes in this world, and which fail to consume her fabric or rob her of one twig or leaf that belongs to her organically. But surely it is truer to the symbolic teaching of Scripture to regard it as a symbol of the presence of God, who is as fire in the purity and spirituality of His nature; who needs no fuel to sustain His eternal being; and who is willing to stoop to the meanest and most despised of His creatures in tender pitifulness. Abide in Him, and let Him abide in you; let Him settle down on you, enveloping you in the luminous garments of His holy presence, so that you are inaccessible to death. All that corrupts and disintegrates shall be rendered powerless to harm you. You shall abide in the secret place of the Most High, and hide under the shadow of the Almighty.

13	*He healeth the broken in heart. . . . He telleth the number of the stars. . . .*

Psalm 147: 3, 4

HOW WONDERFUL that these two qualities should blend in one Being! That God tells the number of the stars is only what we should expect of Him. They are His flock, lying down on the fields of the heavens; and as a shepherd has a name for each of his charges, so

October

has God for the stars. But that He should be able to bend over one broken heart and bind it with His sympathy and heal its flowing wounds, this is wonderful, amazing, divine.

It is said that in a healthy man the clenched fist is about the size of the heart. So in God, His might is the gauge of His mercy; His hand of His heart. The mountains of His strength show the valleys of His tenderness.

Yet, surely, it must be so. The stars are after all only things, great masses of matter; while hearts are those of living, sentient beings which He made, redeemed, and loves. *They* are the adornments of His house, while broken hearts are His children. Would He have names for the one and no care for the other? This text is exquisitely illustrated in Jesus. Through Him God made the worlds; and by His pierced hands tears have been wiped and stifling sobs silenced all through the ages. Is your heart bleeding? He knows, He cares, He loves, He bends over and heals with exquisite sensitiveness and skill. Yes, the stars may fall from heaven as untimely figs; the sun burn out as an extinct volcano; but He will never cease to tend and comfort His own.

. . . As Esau, who for one morsel of meat sold his birthright.

Hebrews 12: 16

14

EVERYONE is born with a birthright which the devil tries hard to make him barter away. In that birthright are included:

The redemption of Jesus Christ. Everyone is born into a redeemed world; the propitiation of the blessed Lord, the blood that flowed on Calvary, the cancellation of Adam's sin are for all. As all the world was affected by Adam's sin, so all are included in God's love in Jesus. But again Satan is eager to induce men to reject and cast away these benefits. He blinds the eyes of those that believe not, so that they refuse to "behold the Lamb of God, which taketh away the sin of the world."

The grace of the Spirit. Everyone may build up a strong and beautiful character by yielding to the Holy Spirit's gracious prompt-

October

ings. That grace knocks, like sunshine, at the windows of every soul; but how often it is sold for a mess of pottage! The choice between the two roads is constantly being presented to us. God help us always to choose, the divine, the spiritual, the eternal as we come before Him in worship and surrender.

| 15 | *Thy dead men shall live, together with my dead body shall they arise. Awake and sing, ye that dwell in dust. . . .* Isaiah 26: 19 |

ISAIAH must have overheard some angel minstrel sing this strain of resurrection hope. Normally, those who dwell in dust are the last persons to be bidden to awake and sing. Yet what is impossible to men is the ordinary experience of the sons of God. This was our Lord's experience. As He went down to the dust of death He could sing: "Thou wilt not leave my soul in hades, nor suffer thy holy one to see corruption. Thou wilt show me the path of life: In thy presence is fullness of joy; at thy right hand there are pleasures forevermore" (Ps. 16: 11).

Sing, because God has brought you into the dust of death for a great purpose. It is He who has permitted your plans to fail. It is He who has allowed you to witness the wreck of your most cherished hopes. It is God who has shut up every avenue of escape. You have tried repeatedly, but every effort has ended in disaster. Believe it or not, God has been behind it all, with infinite tenderness, watching and waiting His time. All these experiences were needed. You were proud and vain; you did what seemed to be for God's glory really for your own glory; you evaded life's discipline by seeking other means of comfort. Madame Guyon was a bright and beautiful girl, who at sixteen married a man twenty years her senior. This man, with his mother and her maid, submitted Madame Guyon to every form of torture; but as she reviewed it afterwards, this was the only discipline that could have availed to open her soul to God's love. So, awake and sing!

The wilderness and the solitary place shall be glad for them;
and the desert shall rejoice, and blossom as the rose.
Isaiah 35: 1

16

THIS SONG was prepared to be sung when the exiles left Babylon, on their weary six weeks of desert journey until they reached the oasis of Damascus. Isaiah saw that his people would be carried into exile, that they would pine there for a period, and that they would come again to the land of their fathers. On one glad day, when the soft wind was breathing through the garden of his heart, he prepared this triumphal song.

Suppose that we had been present at Ahava when Ezra led the first detachment of exiles toward home; and suppose we had started with them on the march, with this song in our mind? Do you think we should have seen those wastes literally carpeted with flowers? Do you think that strips of meadow grass would have spread a carpet for our feet, or that the songs of spring birds would have filled the air? We should certainly have been disappointed. When the exiles were returning there was possibly not a single additional flower, not a spring of water, not a song of welcome, that would not have been there in any case. What then—was it a false prediction? Where were the songs and flowers of Spring? They were in the *hearts of the exiles*. It was not a false hope; it was not a mere mirage; it was literally true. When finally they returned to Zion they saw Spring everywhere, because they carried it in their hearts.

. . . That take, and give unto them for me and thee.
Matthew 17: 27

17

FOR ME and thee!" As Jesus enters the wilderness of temptation, His sufferings culminating in three tremendous shocks of assault by Satan; as He repels the insinuation and resists the solicitation; as He treads lion and dragon underfoot, in all the glory of His divine manhood, He seems to turn to us and say: "This take for me

October

and thee." As in Gethsemane, His forehead is bedewed with clammy sweat, or as on the cross, He drinks the cup of death, amid all the midnight darkness of that hour, He doesn't forget to turn to us and remind us that it is not for Himself alone—"It is for me and thee."

We stand by the grave on Easter morning and watch Him issuing forth as He passes radiant with triumph. Amid the rending rocks and the tremors of earth, He says, "This victory over death and the power of the grave is for me and thee." As He ascends from the Mount of Olives, His voice falls back to us: "My ascension is for Me that I may go to My throne and be glorified with the glory I had with the Father before the worlds were; but it is for thee, My beloved, for where I am, thou also must be, and with My glory thou shalt be glorified." We must appropriate the unsearchable riches of Christ or they will not profit us. We must receive that we may give out.

18	. . . *His mercy endureth for ever.*

Psalm 136: 26

TWENTY-SIX times in Psalm 136 we are told that God's mercy endureth for ever. The psalmist had been reviewing the history of the past. As far back as the Creation his eye had traveled, and all through the stormy, troublous days he could detect the silver thread of mercy. Oh, that we had his eyes to see always the love of God! Amid the murky gloom of chaos there is a silver gleam; it is His mercy. When sun and moon appear, there is a brighter light than theirs; it is His mercy. Above the roar of the Red Sea and the rattle of the thunderstorms, are the flutelike notes of His mercy. Through all the strife and horror of the conquest of Canaan there glides the white-robed angel of His mercy. Deeper than the darkest shades of sin, higher than the highest floods of transgression, is the love of God, in the hand of which the round world and all its inhabitants lie, as a drop on the palm. Look back on your life, and say whether you cannot see the thread of mercy linking all its beads.

October

And do you suppose that such mercy is going to fail you? It endures for ever! You fret and chafe like a restless little child; but you cannot fall out of the arms of God's mercy. Lie still, it hovers over you like a mother's face; it breathes about you as a mother's embrace. O love that will not let us go! O mercy that has neither beginning nor end! O God, who has loved, who now loves, and who will love, when the sun is no more, and the things that are now shall have passed away as a dream! O grace of God, exceeding in abundance the highest mountains of our sin!

By faith Jacob . . . worshipped. . . .
Hebrews 11:21

19

OUR GREATEST victories are sometimes the fruit of pain, purchased at the cost of the humbling of the flesh. Jacob learned that the secret of prevailing with God and man was not in the strength but in the weakness and suffering of the flesh: "And when he [the angel] saw that he prevailed not against him, he touched the hollow of his [Jacob's] thigh" (Gen. 32:25). It must ever be so. The Victor Lamb still bears the scars of Calvary and appears as One who had been slain.

The shrunken thigh counteracts pride. So high a spiritual achievement as to prevail with God might have tempted Jacob to arrogance and pride. But God anticipated the possible temptation by this physical infirmity which was constantly present to Jacob's consciousness. This reminds us, too, of Paul's "thorn in the flesh."

The crippled thigh was the secret of victory. Had it not been shriveled by the angel's touch, Jacob would have continued to resist in the pride of his strength—and would never have clung convulsively to the angel, crying, "I will not let thee go." It was only in that act that he became Israel, the Prince.

The shrunken thigh makes us think little of this world and much of the next. From this moment Jacob takes on more of the pilgrim attitude. He finds that for him, at least, the pace will have to be slower; but it is well, for he relaxes his hold on the seen to become more involved with the unseen—the realm of faith.

October

<table>
<tr><td>20</td><td>That in the dispensation of the fulness of times he might gather together in one all things in Christ, both which are in heaven, and which are on earth; even in him.
Ephesians 1: 10</td></tr>
</table>

CHRIST is our center of unity. It is the evident purpose of God to finish as He began. He began by choosing us in Christ. He will end by summing up all things in Him, both the things in the heavens and the things upon the earth. All the landscape focuses in the eye; all creation finds its apex in man; and all the story of the ages will be consummated in our Lord, the Divine Man.

That unification is now in process. The sheep are gathering up the mountainsides to stand together as one flock, beneath the care of one Shepherd. Those who were far off are being made nigh. Those who were at enmity are being reconciled, because the middle wall has been broken down. Those who were strangers and foreigners are recognizing each other as fellow members, fellow partakers of the promise, and fellow heirs. Amid the many churches, the one Church which Jesus purchased with His blood, is being formed. For the ruins of many structures the one Temple is being built.

<table>
<tr><td>21</td><td>For we are his workmanship, created in Christ Jesus unto good works, which God hath before ordained that we should walk in them.
Ephesians 2: 10</td></tr>
</table>

CREATE is one of the greatest words of the Bible. It is its peculiar possession. Other religious books have their cosmogonies, and attempt to explain how all things came to be. The process of production is traced as far back as possible; but they dare not speak this wonderful word. It is left to the Bible to inscribe the name of God on all things visible and invisible, and append to it the word *create*. "In the beginning God. . . . In the beginning God created. . . ."

It is, however, not with the material but with the spiritual creation that I want to deal. When we first knelt at the cross of the Lord Jesus, we were made new creatures (2 Cor. 5: 17). But there is an older creation than that. If we read the Apostle's thought correctly, he takes us back beyond the limits of our mortal life to the eternal past and reveals to us the workings of God's thought before even the earth or the world was made. We were created in Christ Jesus, in the purpose and intention of God, before an angel sped through the newly created ether, or a seraph raised his first sonnet of adoration. Our creation at the cross was the realization in our experience of an eternal thought of God.

But now, in Christ Jesus, ye who sometimes were far off are made nigh by the blood of Christ.

Ephesians 2: 13

22

WE WERE in Christ in the marvels of His death. In Him we paid the debt; in Him we lay in the grave, and broke from death, and sped on the heavenly track home to the bosom of God. In Him we sat down at the right hand of the Majesty on High, and sit there still.

Time is the elaboration in actual fact of the thoughts and purposes of God. Slowly the Divine conception has taken shape in the formation and education of the church; just as of old it took shape in the making of the world. And it is a great help to us to catch a glimpse of the direction of the Divine movement. The explorer who, from a commanding headland, is able to make out the set or lie of a country, confers a lasting benefit on all who follow him by mapping the terrain; and it is one of the inestimable benefits of Revelation that it removes the obscurity which drapes our mortal lives so closely, and makes all men see the dispensation of the mystery. This is the quickening power of the Holy Spirit.

For through him we both have access by one Spirit unto the Father.

Ephesians 2: 18

23

HE IS the Inspirer of prayer. However diverse the saints are, in birth or religious customs, they become one in the exercise of true prayer.

October

Because as suppliants they pass into the presence of the Father through the One Mediator; and because their prayers emanate from the same Holy Paraclete.

There are two Advocates or Paracletes. One is on the throne—Jesus Christ the righteous; the second is in our hearts—the Holy Spirit (1 John 2: 1; Rom. 8: 26). And because He pervades all holy hearts, as the wind the variety of organ pipes, He makes them one. Men as wide apart as Jew and Gentile have access by one Spirit unto the Father. They are therefore, no more strangers, but fellows.

"If two of you agree on earth," said our Lord. The Greek word is *symphonize*. A symphony is a consonance or harmony of sounds in which there is perfect agreement. Not necessarily the same notes in different keys, but different notes in the same key. Struck by a master hand, they make delightful music. So, when souls are touched by the Holy Spirit, though in many respects they differ, yet they may accord in the same prayer. Peter and Cornelius, Saul of Tarsus, and Ananias, though far apart and totally diverse in temperament, respond to each other in perfect harmony. And such accord indicates the purpose of God.

24	*. . . I chose you and appointed you that you should go and bear fruit and that your fruit should abide. . . .* John 15: 16

OUR MASTER is abounding in life, and longs to pour that life upon the world. But He can only do this through chosen and appointed vessels. He has therefore chosen and appointed us. That latter word might be rendered *placed*. He has placed us where we are, that at that very spot He might have a suitable outlet for His abundant vitality.

The way in which He communicates His life to the world is very noticeable. He does not attempt to stir up the remote energy of any number of individuals, as though each carried a supply of vitality in himself, but He speaks of Himself as a mighty storehouse or reservoir of energy, waiting to pour into all who are united with Him by faith, that through them, as channels or branches, it might reach the fainting sons of men, and He has a purpose in the exact situation where He places each individual branch. Don't complain about your lot in life. Always remember that He has appointed it and placed you there. Go and bear fruit!

That Christ may dwell in your hearts by faith; that ye, being rooted and grounded in love, may be able to comprehend with all saints what is the breadth, and length, and depth, and height; and to know the love of Christ. . . .
Ephesians 3: 17–19

25

IT IS ONLY as we love that we apprehend Christ's love. The Revised Version is very emphatic. The apostle asks that his Ephesian converts might be strengthened with power through the Spirit in the inner man; that Christ might dwell in their hearts through faith; to the end that, being rooted and grounded in love, they might be strong to apprehend, with all saints, the love of Christ. How remarkable this stress on strength; why is it so necessary in connection with love?

Is it that we should be strong to obey the least promptings of the gracious Master, Christ? Is it that we need strength to suppress ourselves in favor of the new passion which has entered our hearts, until it shall have become all-powerful? Is it that the bud of Divine love in its most perfect form can only be grafted on a strong stalk? Any of these suppositions may meet the case. But we must be strengthened before we can receive the fullness of the indwelling Lord; and one chief result of His presence within, is to make us strong to apprehend His love.

With all lowliness and meekness, with long-suffering, forbearing one another in love.
Ephesians 4: 2

26

LOVE should be the atmosphere of our church relationships. The unity or oneness of the Spirit is a divine reality, which we have not

October

to make, but to keep. Try as we will, we cannot make it a bit more perfect than it is. No agreements, conferences, or conventions can do this. But we are called upon to give all diligence, that the divine ideal may be realized, as far as possible, among the saints. There never will be uniformity; but there may be unity. The pipes in the great organ will never be all of the same length or tone; but they may be supplied by the same breath, and conspire to utter the same melody. It must be our endeavor to guard against anything that would jar with the inner unity of the Spirit. Jealousy, bickering, harsh words—these must be under the ban of the loving soul. We must forbear one another in love.

When a minister told the sainted M'Cheyne that on the previous Sunday he had preached the awful doom of the ungodly, M'Cheyne replied, "I hope you preached tenderly." Oh, for more of the Spirit of the apostle who spoke with weeping of those who were enemies of the cross of Christ.

It is when there is perfect love between us and our fellow-believers, that the grace of God can pass easily from one to another. If we are out of fellowship with any, to that extent we cannot impart to them or they to us. But, when love pervades the body as the genial spring warmth of the woodlands, there is an up-building and out-flowering in love. Each gives to another, and gets as he gives.

27	*And walk in love, as Christ also hath loved us. . . .*
	Ephesians 5: 2

HUMAN love should be modeled on the divine. It is no ordinary love to which we are summoned. Whether in the home circle, where man and wife live in each other's presence, or in the daily walk and conversation of life, we are to imitate God, as His dear children. It is not enough to love as our fellows do. We must love as Christ did. Our one ideal must be, "as Christ loved."

To love foes, to make them friends; to love in the teeth of censure and blame; to love to the point of self-giving and blood; to love the foul till the pollution gives place to purity and beauty—such is the love of Christ. Let us sit at His feet and learn of Him until we reflect Him, and are changed into the same image from glory to glory. Oh, to love like Thee, blessed Master! And that we may, fill us with Thy love until our cup runs over.

Grace be with all them that love our Lord Jesus Christ in sincerity. Amen.

Ephesians 6: 24

| 28 |

OUR LOVE must be sincere. There are plenty who say, Lord, Lord, but who do not the things that He says. It is easy to be profuse in our expressions, and readily swayed by gusts of emotion, and yet to be heartless and loveless. But, such do not love with sincerity. They resemble the shallow soil, where the seed soon dies, because there is only rock beneath. For such, the apostle had no words of benediction.

But, wherever there is sincere love to Jesus, however weak and ignorant the disciple, there is a member of the mystical body, the church, and one on whom our benediction may alight. You may not speak our language or accept our creed; but if you sincerely love Jesus, we bid you welcome and wish you *grace*.

Spirit of God, baptize us in God's holy fire, that we may begin to glow with the sacred flame, and be burning ones indeed.

And the very God of peace sanctify you wholly; and I pray God your whole spirit and soul and body be preserved blameless unto the coming of our Lord Jesus Christ.

1 Thessalonians 5: 23

| 29 |

THERE IS a note of confidence in these words which reveals the unwavering faith of the Apostle Paul in the faithfulness and power of God to do for these primitive Christians what indeed is needed by all of us: first, to be sanctified wholly, and secondly, to be pre-

October

served blameless until the coming of our Lord Jesus Christ. We can hardly realize how much this meant for men and women reared amid the excesses and abominations of those days, when religion was another name for unbridled indulgence. Blamelessness of life, the stainless habit of the soul, self-restraint, were the attributes of the few whose natures were cast in a special mold; while they mocked ordinary people much as Alpine peaks defeat the invalid and the cripple. And yet how strong the apostle was in stating that, in the face of insurmountable difficulties, the God of Peace would do even this for them. Note this, however. Blamelessness and faultlessness are not the same. The latter can only be ours when we have passed the Gate of Pearl and are presented faultless in the presence of His glory with exceeding joy; the former, however, is within the reach of each of us, because God has said that He will do it. Our spirit, soul, and body may be preserved blameless. Let us understand the distinction.

30	*In whom ye also are builded together for a habitation of God through the Spirit.*

Ephesians 2:22

HE INDWELLS the church. Other passages clearly teach that He indwells the individual believer. He does this, that each several Christian community, fitly framed together, may grow into a holy temple in the Lord. The high and holy One, who inhabits eternity, makes His home with humble and contrite hearts. He lives in you and me, if only we could realize it. But, in addition to this, when a company of believers is gathered in the name of Jesus, there is a habitation of God. "There am I in the midst of them."

This gives each company of disciples the mysterious power to bind and loose. Their acts receive divine sanction and achieve eternal results, because they are determined beneath the prompting of the Holy Spirit, and therefore, in the presence of the living Savior. The Spirit conveys the will of God to the saints, and bears back their prayers and decisions to God. Thus, the church keeps in step

with heaven and utters, though sometimes unconsciously, the purposes of God.

A merry heart maketh a cheerful countenance.
Proverbs 15: 13

31

WE CAN PROMOTE a cheerful heart by dwelling on the bright
things of our lot; by counting up the mercies which are left, rather
than dwelling on what we have lost. When the heart is full of the
light and love of God, can it be other than cheerful? How can this
be obtained except by a living union with Jesus Christ?

Acid dropped on steel and allowed to remain will soon corrode
it. And if we allow worries, anxieties, care-worn questioning to
brood in our hearts, they will soon break up our peace, as swarms
of tiny gnats will make a paradise uninhabitable. There is one thing
that we can do. We must hand them over to Jesus just as they occur.

God seeks to mold us by circumstances, and you must believe
that God has put you down just where you are because your present
position is the very best place in the universe to make you what He
wants you to become.

The Thankful Life

November

<table>
<tr><td>

1

</td><td>

And God said, Let us make man in our image. . . .
Genesis 1: 26

</td></tr>
</table>

ONE OF the greatest words of the Scripture tells us that man was made "in the image of God." From that phrase, throbbing with hope, we gather that our moral and spiritual nature was planned on the same model as God's; and that in our original constitution, there was an identity in quality, though not in quantity, between us and our Creator. This thought lies at the basis of all our reasonings about God. If truth, holiness, and mercy mean one thing when referred to Him, and another one applied to us, we know nothing of Him amid the blaze of revelation and the clear teachings of our Lord. Of course, there must always be the limitations of the finite, the shadows of mortality falling thick and dense, the wilting effect of sin; but nevertheless there is so great a similarity between God and us, that we can reason from what we know of ourselves to the nature of Him who is eternal, immortal, and invisible.

This is particularly true of *love*. We use the term for the mysterious affinity between parent and child, friend and friend, husband and wife. It is the strongest factor in our nature, which bridges distance, defies time, triumphs over impassable barriers, and irradiates with golden light the prosaic circumstances of ordinary people. We cannot explain it. We only know that when this passion takes possession of us, it eliminates self, and makes another's interests the pivot of thought and effort and life. Then turning from ourselves to God, we cry, "It is thus that God feels toward man." "God so loved the world." "He loves me."

November

They beheld God, and ate and drank.
$$\text{Exodus 24: 11, RSV}$$

2

IT IS a beautiful combination, which we would do well to emulate.

Some eat and drink, and do not behold God. They are taken up with the delights of sense. Their one cry, as the children of this world, is, What shall we eat, and what shall we drink, and how shall we be clothed? But the God in whose hand their breath is and whose are all their ways, they do not glorify. Let us beware; it was of the enemies of God that Paul said, "Whose God is their belly" (Phil. 3: 19).

Some behold God, and do not eat and drink. They look on God with such awful fear that they isolate Him from the common duties of life. They draw a strict line between the sacred and the secular, between Sunday and weekday, between God's interests and their own. This divorce between religion and life is fatal to true religion, which was meant to be the bond between the commonest details of life and service of God.

Some behold God, and eat and drink. They turn from the commonest pursuits and look up into His face. They glorify God in their bodies as well as in their spirits. They obey the apostle's injunction: "Whether therefore ye eat, or drink, or whatsoever ye do, do all to the glory of God" (1 Cor. 10: 31). Oh, for the grace to be able to combine the vision of God with every common incident—to live always beneath His eye in the unrestrained gladness of little children in their Father's presence!

The Lord reigns, he is robed in majesty; the Lord is robed, he is girded with strength.
$$\text{Psalm 93: 1, RSV}$$

3

TELL IT out! The message is too good to warrant silence. That the Lord is King is the secret of jubilation and blessing for all the world.

Nature is glad, because His rule will emancipate her from the

November

bondage under which she has groaned too long. When the kingdom is established in the hand of the Son of Man, the long travail of creation will be over; the new heavens and earth will have emerged. Therefore the psalmist depicts the outburst of thanksgiving from seas, and fields, and trees. "Let the heavens rejoice, and let the earth be glad; let the sea roar and the fulness thereof. Let the field be joyful . . . then shall all the trees of the wood rejoice" (Ps. 96: 11,12). The world of men may be glad also, because the reign of Jesus means equity for the oppressed, equal-handed justice for the poor, peace among the nations (Ps. 96: 13).

But, above all, gladness becomes the saints. If the Lord Jesus has become King of your heart, and has brought blessing to you, do not hesitate to give voice to your allegiance. In private, sing unto Him a new song; in public, show forth His salvation, and declare His glory. Tell it out, tell it out!

---

4   *May God be gracious to us and bless us. . . .*
            Psalm 67: 1, RSV

THIS PSALM is full of yearnings for the salvation of mankind. The selfish desire for the exclusive blessing of the chosen people is lost sight of in the universal yearning that all the earth should fear Jehovah. "God shall bless us; and all the ends of the earth shall fear him" (Ps. 67:1). Indeed, this is the ground on which the psalmist rests his personal claim for the divine blessing. It is as though he said, "We only ask for gifts of grace, that through us they may be transmitted to all mankind." Turn us again, O God, that times of refreshing may come from Your presence to all men; our one desire is that the peoples may praise You.

Are we infected with this noble passion? Do we echo from our hearts the repeated prayer of this psalm: "Let all the peoples praise Thee"? Do we ask for blessing from our own God, that we may be able to be a greater blessing to others? It is because God is "our own God," that we are so anxious to make Him known. Oh, that we might be carried out to sea on the tide of God's purposes, and yearnings, and pity; and long as the psalmist did that His saving health might be known among all nations!

The king's wrath is as the roaring of a lion; but his favor is as dew upon the grass.

Proverbs 19: 12

5

HAVE YOU ever, on a spring morning, gone forth from your home to find every blade of grass with its coronet of dew-drops flashing in the sunlight? Each drop has been a prism for the sun's rays. O my soul, if you can only get down as low as the herbage, you will come to the place where the Spirit of God can most easily reach you. It is not on the tall cedar, or the spreading oak, or the fruit-bearing tree that the dew descends most lavishly. Rather, it is on the tender grass, sprouting after the King's mowings. It is on women, whose lives have been one long disappointment, and men who have lived to see their hopes blighted and dead, that there rests the sparkle of the dew of the Holy Spirit.

Thank God for the humble, broken-hearted people. As the dew on the grass refreshes the whole creation, so does the grace of the Holy Spirit, resting on such, bless the church and the world.

Jude, a servant of Jesus Christ and brother of James, to those who are called, beloved in God the Father and kept for Jesus Christ.

Jude 1, RSV

THE WORD *keep* rings like a refrain through this brief letter. It reappears in verse 6 (twice) and in verse 21: "And the angels that did not keep their own position but left their proper dwelling have been kept by him in eternal chains . . . until the judgment of the great day. . . . Keep yourselves in the love of God, looking for the mercy of our Lord Jesus Christ unto eternal life." Another Greek

November

word is used in verse 24: "Now to him who is able to keep you from falling. ..."

The word *kept* is more than *keep yourselves*. It suggests a power which originates in the divine will and operates through the Spirit's energy within us. Behind our willing and working, behind our choosing and electing, behind all the influences that are brought to bear on us, there is a gracious and divine movement, by which we are being "kept for Jesus Christ." Our spirit is being kept by His Spirit, so that His Spirit can indwell us; our soul is being kept that His mind may energize it; our heart is being kept as a fountain out of which His pure love may flow in and out; our body is being kept that He may have the use of its members. Let us realize how much Christ needs us, and how much we will miss if we neutralize the very purpose for which we were born and sent into the world.

| 7 | *Where there is no vision, the people perish. ...*
Proverbs 29: 18 |

WHAT A difference lack of vision makes in our teaching and preaching! The people perish for want of seers of those who can say with the apostle, "That which we have seen and heard, declare we unto you also, that ye may have fellowship with us." It is not difficult to know whether a poet or painter has a vision. Vision adds a glow and passion to his work. And it is no more difficult to detect the excitement of vision in the speaker on divine things. It is obvious whether he is speaking second-hand truth, or the convictions of direct vision.

This vision of God was given to Elijah, and the Apostle Paul. Concerning the latter God said, "He shall be a minister and a witness of things which he has seen." This is our only qualification for teaching others; not intellect, or imagination, nor rhetoric, but to have had a vision of the King and His glory. For such a vision, on our part, there must be humility, patience, and faith, a definite withdrawal from the life of sense, and a definite concentration of the gaze on the things that are unseen and eternal. On God's part there must be revelation. "It pleased God," said the apostle, "to reveal His Son in me, that I might preach Him."

The apostle said, "I could not see for the glory of that light." A party of tourists was divided one dull morning in Switzerland; the majority thought that it was useless to attempt the mountains. A few started, soon got beyond the low-hanging clouds, spent a day in the heights under marvelous skies, and returned at night, radiant, overflowing with what they had seen. Ah, speaking is easy when one has *seen!*

And they sing the song of Moses, the servant of God, and the song of the Lamb, saying, "Great and wonderful are thy deeds, O Lord God the Almighty! Just and true are thy ways, O King of the ages!"

8

Revelation 15: 3, RSV

THIS REMINDS of the deliverance from Pharaoh on the shores of the Red Sea. Here John translates it into the imagery and language of eternity. The hosts of God will emerge before long from their long oppression; by suffering they shall conquer; they will be victorious over the beast, and his image, and the number of his name. Behind them shall be spread out the sea of time, so calm and still, so hushed from all its tumult and storm, that it will seem to be like sheets of glass; and as the morning of eternity breaks, it will be drenched with fire. Fire here is probably an emblem of the holiness and the judgments of God.

Israel broke into rapturous thanksgiving, as the people saw their enemies dead upon the shore. "Sing unto the Lord, for He hath triumphed gloriously!" But those triumphant notes, though chanted by an entire nation will be a whisper compared with the song that will thunder down from the saints of all the ages. Those who were brought up under the dispensation of Moses, and the followers of the Lamb in the present dispensation, together with all holy souls who have overcome, will constitute that one vast choir.

But search the song of Moses as you will, you will fail to find one note that equals this in sublimity. Here are the saints of God, trained

November

in distinguishing the niceties of righteous and holy government and behavior, enabled from their vantage-ground in eternity to survey the entire history of the divine dealings, adoring Him as King of the Ages, and acknowledging that all His ways are just and true. What a confession! What an acknowledgment!

---

9   *Of the increase of his government and peace, there shall be no end. . . .*

Isaiah 9: 7a

THE ORDER of the divine procedure and government should provoke us to song. The world around us is full of the attempts and triumphs of high-handed wrong. The pride and will-worship, the lust of the flesh and of the eyes, the downtreading of the weak by the strong, the spoiling of the defenseless by the arrogant oppressor, the apparent success of those who set at naught God's Law—these facts are apparent to us all. They accost us in every street, and flaunt themselves before our eyes. And the waters of a full cup are wrung out for us as we ask with one of old, "Why do the wicked prosper?"

But when we turn our thoughts heavenward, we are arrested by the order, regularity, prevalence of God's statutes—this, that light is stronger than darkness, and Christ than Satan; this, that holiness and purity always bring blessedness; this, that falsehood and wrongdoing carry with themselves the seeds of disintegration and decay; this, that those that love their lives lose them, while to those who seek first the Kingdom of God all else is added.

As we consider the certainty that ultimately God will justify Himself before the eyes of the universe, and establish righteousness and justice, vindicating the oppressed and punishing the wrongdoer, we seem to be standing on the sea of glass, hearing the harps of God, singing the song of the redeemed: "Great and marvelous are Thy works; just and true are Thy ways, Thou King of Saints." Thus the order and procedure of the divine government may become our songs in the house of our pilgrimage.

November

10

Be glad in the Lord, and rejoice, ye righteous. . . .
Psalm 32: 11

ARE YOU glad in your Christian life? Gladness is the reward of children and childlike hearts, and there is nothing which is more distinctively characteristic of the work of grace in the heart than Christian gladness. The world may simulate it, but it is a dreary failure. Often faded worldlings will come to the true Christian, saying, What is the secret of your perennial gladness?

The glad heart is conscious of the love of God; knows that it is reconciled through the blood of the cross; realizes that there is nothing between itself and the light of the Father's smile; is conscious of integrity of intention and tenderness of yearning love and pity. In every difficult circumstance it recognizes the Father's appointment; in every archipelago of rocks it is aware of the presence of God aboard the vessel, holding the helm and keeping the keel in the deepest current.

O souls, get right with God! Take advantage of the perfect righteousness of Christ; watch that there be nothing between you and Him; walk in the light as He is in the light; cultivate the habit of considering what has been given rather than what has been withheld—and you will find that He will make you glad in proportion to the days in which He has afflicted you, and the years in which you have seen evil. The sad heart tires in a mile. The glad one mounts up with wings as eagles.

11

I am like a green olive tree in the house of God.
Psalm 52: 8

IN ITS dress of evergreen, the olive is at all times a beautiful object. There are many reasons why we should resemble it. Three ways of becoming like a green olive tree are mentioned in this and the following verses:

November

Trust in the mercy of God.—To trust when the light has burned to its socket in the house of life, and the heart is as lonely as Job's amid the wreck of his home. To believe that the mercy of God is not clear gone, nor His tender mercies failed. To know that all is well, that seems most ill. This keeps the heart from withering.

Thanksgiving.—"I will give thee thanks for ever." There is always something to thank God for. When someone condoled with the old slave woman, because she had only two teeth left, she replied quickly, "But I thank Him, honey, all the time, that they are opposite each other." Find out with Paul something to be happy about, even when arraigned before a judge, on trial for your life. "I think myself happy, King Agrippa."

Waiting on God.—Not always talking to Him or about Him, but waiting before Him, till the stream runs clear; till the cream rises to the top; till the mists part, and the soul regains its equilibrium. This keeps the soul calm and still. The name of God is good, a wholesome theme for meditation, because it includes His nature. To meditate on it is soul-quieting and elevating. O troubled one, get away to some quiet spot and wait on God! Look away from the wind and waves to the face of Jesus. The Divine Name is written on those dear features; and heaven looks forth from those true, deep, tender eyes. The house of God is a safe and sheltered place for His olive-trees!

12	*I will meditate in thy precepts, and have respect unto thy ways.*

Psalm 119: 15

GOD'S precepts yield song. Shakespeare says that music is "the consent of sweet sounds." But it is more, just as poetry consists of harmonious words. Music is the language of the Unseen and the Eternal; and song is the accord of the heart with this, the utterance of Eternity. Of course there are evil songs, which show that the singer is in accord with the dark netherworld of evil; but good and worthy songs show that the heart of the singer has caught the strains and chords of the bright blessed world of God and the Holy Angels.

But how should we know the thoughts and principles of the Unseen and Eternal world, if it were not for the divine precepts? God has set them up on earth that we might know through them the order of the Divine realm, and might by obedience, bring ourselves into accord with it. Take, then, the precepts of the Bible, especially those given by our Lord, His reiterated commands to love, to pray, to sacrifice self. Embody them in every act of the life in every phase of thought; learn them, obey them, follow them; and when the life is married to them, as noble music to noble words, there will come a new gladness into the heart, and a new song into the life. What rapture there is in obedience! What comfort and joy in the Holy Spirit! What singing of the conscience void of offense toward God and man! Thus God's precepts become our songs in the house of our pilgrimage.

And now, brethren, I commend you to God and to the word of his grace, which is able to build you up, and to give you an inheritance among all them which are sanctified.
Acts 20: 32

13

WHEN AN immigrant first received the title deed of the broad lands made over to him in the far West, he had no conception of what had been conveyed to him by the government. And though acres vast enough to make an English county were in his possession—rich and loamy soil, stored with mines of ore—yet he was not sensibly the richer. For long days he traveled toward his inheritance and presently pitched a flimsy shanty upon its borders. But even though he had reached it, many years must pass before he could understand its value, or compel it to minister to his need.

Child of God, your estate has been procured at the cost of blood and tears; but you did not buy it! Its broad acres have been made over to you by deed of gift. They became yours in the counsel chamber of eternity, when the Father gave Himself to you in Jesus. And they became yours in fact, when you were born at the foot of the cross. As soon as your eyes were opened to behold the crucified Lord, you became all unconsciously heir to the length, breadth, depth, and height of God.

November

14	*Even as David also describeth the blessedness of the man unto whom God imputeth righteousness without works.*

Romans 4: 6

MEN MAY sneer at the doctrine of imputed righteousness, but it is unquestionably an integral part of the apostle's teaching. More than once we are told that as righteousness was reckoned to Abraham because he believed, so it is reckoned to all that believe in Him who was delivered for our offenses and raised again for our justification. It were easier to take the sun out of the heavens than to take the doctrine of reckoned righteousness out of the Epistles of the New Testament.

There are two railway lines to the Crystal Palace—the Low and the High Level. If you travel by the one, you must climb numberless stairs before you reach the Palace; but with the other, you have only to pass easily across the road. The first illustrates the efforts of men to obtain a righteousness of their own; the second, God's method of justification. He not only forgives us, but by the act of His grace puts us on the level of the righteousness of Christ—His obedience unto death, His resolute conformity to the Father's will—and bids us live on that level by the power of the Holy Spirit.

15	*For sin shall not have dominion over you: for ye are not under the law, but under grace.*

Romans 6: 14

WE ARE under law when we have transgressed law. Adam was under the law when he had taken the fruit; and Joseph's brethren, when his words aroused their consciences, and made them remember their sin, which lay half-hidden under the dead leaves of the years. The murderer is under the law when, fleeing from justice, he trembles at each snapping twig. So long as our sins are unconfessed, and faith is not exercised for the transference of their burden to Jesus, we are under law.

But as soon as we believe, we enter upon the privileges of that

November

union with Jesus which is best described as "in Him." We see that in Him we have met the deserved penalty of a broken law, that in Him we have exhausted the curse which was due to us, that in Him we have met the demand that the sinner should die. The law has had all it can ask, and is satisfied; we are no longer under its thrall or power; we have passed into the realm where God's grace is supreme.

To the praise of his glorious grace which he freely bestowed on us in the Beloved.

Ephesians 1: 6

| 16 |

GOD'S love flows to us through the channel of the Beloved. We must not think that the Father loves us because our Savior interposed between His wrath and us, and made Him love us. To think this is heresy indeed. We cannot separate between the Father and the Son, for God is one. As is the Son, so is the Father. It was the one purpose of Jesus to dissipate these untrue and terrible conceptions of the Father, and to make man see that His own life and love were a true reflection of the depths of His Father's heart.

The love of God was not caused by the death of Jesus, but caused it. God did not love us because Jesus died: but Jesus died because God loved us so much as to give Him up to the death for us all. God loved us from eternity; but before His love could have its blessed way with us, it was necessary for Him to satisfy the claims of a broken law, to vindicate His righteousness, to be just: and therefore He gave Himself to us in Jesus, who manifested God in the flesh, put away sin by the sacrifice of Himself, and entered into the Holiest of all to become a merciful and faithful High Priest.

Though God's love was not caused by the Beloved, it comes to us in Him. The ocean fullness pours itself through the channel of the man Christ Jesus. It has therefore all the abundance and wealth of the Divine, and all the adaptation and tenderness of the human. The Only-begotten and Beloved Son is the reservoir in which the great love of God is stored. In proportion therefore as we abide in Him, we will realize its blessed fullness.

November

<table>
<tr><td>17</td><td>But he that is joined unto the Lord is one spirit.
1 Corinthians 6: 17</td></tr>
</table>

WE ARE in Him as He is in us. We are joined to the Lord, and are one spirit; we are members of His body, of His flesh, and of His bones. This is not only a matter of present personal experience, but we learn that it is the realization of a divine conception and purpose. We were, indeed, chosen in Him before the worlds were made. We suddenly awake to the fact of our union with Jesus, but that union was present in the mind of God in the distant ages of the past.

The Holy Spirit, in the Epistle to the Hebrews, founds an argument on the fact of Levi being in Abraham when the latter paid tithes to Melchizedek and was blessed by him. Since the less is blessed by the greater, he argues, the Levitical priesthood was clearly inferior to that of Melchizedek, on the model of which Christ's was constituted. Thus we may be said to have done in Jesus, what Jesus did as our Representative and High Priest. We are, and we were, in Him, that is true. We died in Him, rose with Him, ascended when He left Olivet beneath His feet, and sat down with Him when He took His seat at the right hand of the throne of God.

<table>
<tr><td>18</td><td>Who hath also sealed us, and given the earnest of the Spirit in our hearts.
2 Corinthians 1: 22</td></tr>
</table>

WHY IS it that some of God's children live lives so much fuller and richer than others? You must seek it in the differences of their appropriation of God. Some have learned the happy art of receiving and utilizing every square inch of that knowledge of God which has been revealed to them. They have laid all God's revealed character before them. They have raised harvests of bread out of the Incarnation; vintages of blood-red grape from the scenes of Gethsemane and Calvary; all manner of fruit out of the mysteries of the Ascension and the gift of the Holy Ghost. In hours of weakness they have drawn on God's power; and those of suffering, on His patience; and those of misunderstanding and hatred, on His vindication; and those of apparent defeat and despair, on the promises that gleam over the smoke of battle as the cross stands above the battlefield; in death itself, on the life and immortality which find their home in the being of God.

So we, being many, are one body in Christ, and every one members one of another.

Romans 12: 5

| 19 |

WE REPEAT such words without emotion; but there was a time when they could not be uttered save at the cost of much that men hold dear. It is as if we were passing over a battlefield, once raked with shell and soaked with blood; or were handling a banner torn and ragged, around which the conflicting warriors fought for half a day. Let us not forget the brave hearts that were martyred in Scotland and other places, rather than confess that any but Christ might assume the title of head of the church. The church, as a whole, must take its commands from Him. If He bids her advance, protest, or suffer, she has no option but to obey.

This position of our Lord is as much for each member of the church as for the whole body. Because, as in the natural body each several muscle, nerve, and vein as well as more prominent members have direct double communication with the head from which they derive their unity, direction and energy; so in the spiritual body of which Christ is head, there is not one single redeemed spirit who is not directly connected with its Lord. It would not be in the church at all if that relationship had not first been formed. We are related to one another, only because we are related to Him. We are first members of Christ, then members of each other in Him. First Christ, then the church.

November

20

Which is the earnest of our inheritance until the redemption of the purchased possession, unto the praise of his glory.
Ephesians 1: 14

THROUGHOUT the Old Testament there runs the double thought of our inheritance in God, and God's in us. This twofold aspect of that one deep conception interpenetrates the heart of Paul's teaching in Ephesians (Ps. 16: 5,6; Deut. 32: 9).

The Holy Spirit is given to us as the earnest of *our* inheritance. Obviously, inasmuch as God is the earnest, nothing less than God can be the inheritance. In the same verse, the apostle describes the saints as God's possession, which is not yet fully acquired by Him, though fully purchased; but which is waiting its full occupation in that day of glory, when not a fragment of the purchase of Calvary will be left in the power of the grave, but body, soul, and spirit will be raised in the likeness of the glorified Savior.

In the first clause of this verse, he therefore speaks of that inheritance which is ours as heirs of God, and joint-heirs with Christ. In the second, he speaks of ourselves as that inheritance upon which the Son of God so set his heart as to be willing to obtain it by the sacrifice of the glory that he had with the Father before the worlds were made. We are therefore in turn *inheritors* and an *inheritance*.

21

Which He wrought in Christ, when he raised him from the dead, and set him at his own right hand in the heavenly places.
Ephesians 1: 20

CHRIST sits there. Is it not wonderful to find the second Person in the Holy Trinity seated far above all rule, authority, and power, every name that is named? But it is even more wonderful to find Him there as Man, wearing our nature, identified forever with our race. The Mediator between God and man is Himself man (1 Tim. 2: 5). The vision of Ezekiel is a literal fact: this Man, robed in fire, upon the likeness of the throne—a sapphire stone.

We need not, therefore, anxiously inquire what "the heavenly places" are, or where. It is enough to know that they are where Jesus is, and that they are open to us, just in proportion as we live in communion with the Lord. Abide in Him, and you are by necessity an inhabitant of these heavenly places, wherever your earthly lot may be cast. They are the hallowed meeting ground, where the saints of earth come to the spirits of those just made perfect. It was of them that Bunyan spoke when, describing the land Beulah, he said, "Here they were within sight of the city they were going to; also here met them some of the inhabitants thereof, for in this land Shining Ones commonly walked, because it was upon the borders of heaven." This is where we can walk if we are walking with Him.

This is a great mystery; but I speak concerning Christ and the church.

Ephesians 5: 32

| 22 |

THE LOVE of Christ to His church is inexpressible, saved by the tenderest human relationship. Here is a mystery indeed that seen in Eden is also a parable. It was not good for Christ to be alone. He needed one to love and to give love. But there was none among unfallen angels who could answer to Him. Therefore God the Father sought a bride for His Son from among the children of men; yes, He took the Second Eve from the wounded side of the Second Man, as He lay asleep in the garden grave.

Redeemed men compose that bride. The Savior loves them, as a true man who for the first time loved the pure and noble woman. He does not love them because they are fair, but to make them so. He has approved His love by becoming man, and giving Himself to death. By His blood, and word, and spirit, He is sanctifying and purifying them for Himself. The process is long and severe; but He nourishes and cherishes them, as a man does his wounded flesh. Before long, when the bride is complete, the mystery that now veils her shall be flung aside, and amid the joy of creation, He will present her to Himself, without spot or wrinkle or any such thing; bearing His name, sharing his rank, and position, wealth, power, glory, forever and ever.

November

<table>
<tr><td>23</td><td>To the intent that now unto the principalities and powers in heavenly places might be known by the church the manifold wisdom of God.</td></tr>
</table>

Ephesians 3: 10

IT IS through the church that God's wisdom is made known. Men learn God's manifold wisdom in creation; in the eye that is able to adjust itself immediately to the waxing or waning light; in the hand, so marvelously adapted to its myriad purposes, its dexterity a convincing assurance of the being of God. But angels learn the manifold wisdom of God by studying the adaptation of His grace to the very needs of His saints. As students discover the wonderful resources of the surgeon who passes through the wards of the hospital adapting to the need of each sufferer; so do angels in the lofty spirits of heaven learn secrets they had never known, but for the infinite variety of sin and need and sorrow with which God has to deal, in which becomes so many prisms to break up the white ray of His character into its varied constituent hues.

<table>
<tr><td>24</td><td>And walk in love, as Christ also hath loved us, and hath given himself for us an offering and a sacrifice to God for a sweetsmelling savor.</td></tr>
</table>

Ephesians 5: 2

GOD'S love was expressed in a supreme Sacrifice. Wherever there is true love, there must be giving, and giving to the point of sacrifice. Love is not satisfied with giving trinkets; it must give at the cost of sacrifices; it must give blood, life, all. And it was so with the love of God. He "so loved the world, that He gave His only begotten son." Christ also "loved and gave Himself up, an offering and a sacrifice to God. . . ."

And this was very gratifying to the Father. It was as the odor of a sweet smell, reminding us of the sweet-savor offerings of the ancient Levitical code (Lev. 3: 5, etc.). To us the anguish of the cross seems one awful scene of horror; but it pleased the Lord to bruise Him. In love, so measureless, so reckless of cost, for those who were naturally so unworthy of it, there was a spectacle which filled Heaven with fragrance and God's heart with joy.

November

For this ye know, that no whoremonger, nor unclean person, nor covetous man . . . hath any inheritance in the kingdom of Christ and of God.
                                                    Ephesians 5: 5

25

LET EVERY reader mark this, the difference that obtains between Christians is not one of grace, but of the use we make of grace. Supposing two men obtained a grant of an equal number of acres. If other things were equal, their wealth would be in exact proportion to the amount of use each had made of his special acres. If one learned a swifter art of appropriating the wealth open to his hand, he would be actually, though perhaps not potentially, richer than his neighbor. All of this is a parable.

There will always be a vast difference between those who have five talents and those who have two, in the amount of work done for the kingdom of God. But as far as our inheritance of God's *grace* is concerned, there are no preferences, no stepchildren, no arbitrary distinctions. It is not as under the laws of primogeniture, that one child takes all, while the younger children are dismissed with meager portions. Each soul has the whole of God. God gives Himself to each. He cannot give more; He will not give less.

Husbands, love your wives, even as Christ also loved the church, and gave himself for it.
                                                    Ephesians 5: 25

26

GOD'S love is as the love of the bridegroom to the bride. In Eden man needed one to answer to him (Gen. 2: 18). There was none such among the animal creation, and his nature yearned for the reciprocity of love. Then God made woman. Either sex without the other is incomplete. Together the twain are one. This is a great mystery; for our Maker, the Lord of Hosts is His name. God needs us, as we need Him. The Son of God yearns for the redeemed who will answer to Him, and give Him love for His love. Augustine said that God made us for Himself, and that we could never rest till we found rest in Him. We may reverently add that Christ Himself cannot rest satisfied until He has cleansed and sanctified the church,

November

and presented it to Himself in a union which eternity shall only strengthen. Marvel of marvels, He wants my love! He seeks it of me and offers His love in exchange.

27	*In whom all the building fitly framed together groweth unto a holy temple in the Lord.*

Ephesians 2: 21

THE CHURCH is also a building. Deep in the overwhelming floods that surged around the cross, God laid the foundation stone which none but He could lay, which is Jesus Christ. He had laid it on purpose for He set the foundations of the hills, but He laid it then in fact. On Him souls have been built through the ages, one by one. They were lifeless indeed when they first touched Him; but coming in contact with the Living Stone, though dead they began to live, and thus the building grew.

A building is for an inmate; and the church is for God. Without Him it has no reason to exist. The universe cannot contain Him; but the spiritual house whose stones are redeemed souls is His pavilion, habitation, and home.

28	*Peace be to the brethren, and love with faith, from God the Father and the Lord Jesus Christ.*

Ephesians 6: 23

GOD'S love passes into human hearts. "Love with faith, from God the Father and the Lord Jesus Christ." The stream issues from the common throne of God and of the Lamb; from thence it flows downward to redeemed hearts and through them to a dying world.

Love and faith are inseparable. We trust before we love. We love and find it easy to trust. Faith is the open channel down which God's love passes into our nature; and love in its passage hollows out the channel down which it came. Like burnished mirrors that face each other, they flash the sunbeams to and fro. And thus as we live near God we are filled with love, not ours, but His—His love reflected back on Himself—His love flung toward men.

Who gave himself for us, that he might redeem us from all iniquity, and purify unto himself a peculiar people, zealous of good works.

Titus 2: 14

29

WE ARE NOT to work up to the new life, but from it. The good works we do before regeneration are not even reckoned to our account. The apostle calls them *dead* works. They are the automatic convulsive movements of a corpse. The only works that please God, and are accepted through the mediation of Christ, are those which emanate from that new life which He imparts in regeneration by the Holy Ghost. We are created unto good works. "He gave Himself for us, that He might redeem us from all iniquity, and purify unto Himself a people for His own possession, zealous of good works." Cain's gift of fruit may be both fair and fragrant; but it is rejected because it is an attempt to purchase God's favor instead of being the outcome and flower of his faith.

It is blessed to know that our good works have been prepared for us to walk in. Walking implies a *path,* whether through the corn field, or over the meadow, or beside the sea; and we may think, therefore, of our life course as a path which starts from the cross, where we entered on our real life, and ends, as Christian's did, at the gate of the Golden City.

But when once we have learned to believe that the pathway of our good works was before prepared for us by God; that He created for us the prepared path, endowing us with all the qualities it might demand; and that He prepared the path for us whom He created, to afford scope for our special powers—we come to rest in the perfect adaptation between God's creation and His preparations. Fear not: Go forward! He gives what He commands, and then commands what He wills.

November

30	*Whereby are given unto us exceeding great and precious promises.*

2 Peter 1: 4a

CHRIST'S promises are conducive to song. Is your life undergoing change? Listen to His promise that He will abide the same forever. Is your life perilous? Remember that He has promised to go before to prepare the path and to follow after as our re-reward. Is it lonely? Have lover and friend stood aside? Have companions of early years dropped away? Are all the faces growing strange and unfamiliar? Still, recall His promise that He will never leave nor forsake.

Let us scan the promises, remembering that they are ordered in all things and are sure—that they touch every possible phase of life, that they are the bank notes of Heaven, each bearing the signature of the Almighty—that they are Yea and Amen in Christ; and as we meditate and pray, there will be a sense of security and wealth breathed into us which will awaken songs. God's promises will become songs in the house of our pilgrimage.

December

I waited patiently for the Lord; and he inclined unto me, and heard my cry.
                                                      Psalm 40: 1

1

AMID THE evil of the world, it is necessary for us to hope and quietly wait for God's salvation. There is a sufficient explanation for the present condition of the world, if we only knew it. God will justify Himself before the whole universe of moral being and intelligence. Therefore, judge nothing before the time, but be of good cheer, establish your hearts, for God will come and not keep silence. Before long the groans of a prevailing creation will be hushed, the long agony of her sin and sorrow will be ended, and angel voices will proclaim that the kingdoms of this world have become the kingdoms of our God and of His Christ. In the meanwhile let us keep the word of His patience and manifest the patience and faith of the saints. And when the heart sinks and it seems all were lost, ask that you may receive a fresh supply of the patient endurance of the Christ of God who stood as a Lamb before His shearers and opened not His mouth.

O God, the Lord, the strength of my salvation, thou hast covered my head in the day of battle.
                                                      Psalm 140: 7

2

ALL DAY long the fight has been waging fiercely against the hard-pressed soldier. The very sky has seemed darkened with danger, and the enemy has raged like a tornado amid the reeds on the river's

December

brink. The fiery darts of venomous sarcasm have been like a storm of hail, and yet the lonely warrior has not succumbed. To himself, and to all others, his escape has been marvelous. How could it be accounted for, except that an unseen shield had been around him, covering his head in the day of battle?

Ah, beloved soul, God is not only the strength of your salvation, but He is also the covert, the panoply, the shield on which the malice of the foe expends itself in vain. Be quiet. Let not your heart be troubled, neither let it be afraid. No weapon that is formed against you shall prosper. There is but one matter for which you need to care. Always be sure that you are ranged on God's side.

> O Holy Lord, who with the children three
>   Didst walk the piercing flame,
> Help! in these trial hours, which, save to Thee,
>   I dare not name;
> Nor let these quivering eyes and sickening heart
> Crumble to dust beneath the tempter's dart!

This is our prayer as we await His soon coming!

3

Thy kingdom is an everlasting kingdom. . . .
Psalm 145: 13

THESE WORDS are engraved on the door of a mosque in Damascus, which was formerly a Christian church. Originally they were plastered over by stucco; but this has dropped away, and the words stand out clearly defined. They seem to be contradicted by centuries of Mohammedanism; but they are essentially true. Just now the kingdom is in mystery; but soon it will be revealed.

Jesus is gone to the Father to be invested with the kingdom, as a Roman official might have gone from the provinces to Rome for his investiture on the part of the emperor as pro-consul or governor. And Daniel tells us that when He comes to the Ancient of Days, He will receive from Him dominion, and glory, and a kingdom that all the peoples, nations, and languages should serve Him; and His dominion is an everlasting dominion which will not pass away, and His kingdom will not be destroyed. It will break in pieces, and consume all other kingdoms. The iron, clay, brass, silver, and gold, will be broken in pieces, and become like the chaff of summer threshing-floors; but it will become a great mountain and fill the earth.

We are called to receive a kingdom that cannot be shaken. Each faithful servant is to rule over his allotted cities. We are to reign with Christ for a thousand years in this world, sharing His throne and empire. We have been made kings unto God, and we shall reign for ever and ever.

For yourselves know perfectly that the day of the Lord so cometh as a thief in the night.
1 Thessalonians 5: 2

4

THE SECOND Advent will come on men generally suddenly and unexpectedly. When they say, Peace and safety, then sudden destruction shall overtake them, as travail a woman with child, and they shall not escape (1 Thess. 5: 4). With the rapidity of the lightning flash; with the suddenness of a flood or avalanche; with the surprise of the midnight robber—Christ will come. When men are asleep, when every bolt and fastening refuses admittance, when the streets are still and hushed, behold the Judge will stand before the door. "Behold, I come as a thief. Blessed is he that watcheth" (Rev. 16: 15).

As Lightfoot, quoted by Dr. Macduff, suggests, the allusion may be to a Jewish custom in the service of the temple. Twenty-four wards or companies were appointed night by night to guard the various entrances to the sacred courts. One individual was appointed as captain or marshal over the others, called the "Man of the Mountain of the House of God." His duty was to go round the various gates during the night to see that his subordinates were faithful to their charge. Preceded as he was by men bearing torches, it was expected that each wakeful sentinel should hail his appearance with the password, "Thou Man of the Mountains of the House, peace be

December

unto thee!" If through unwatchfulness and slumber this were neglected, the offender was beaten with the staff of office, his garments were burned, and he was branded with shame.

It was in contrast with these slumbering Levites that Jesus pronounces a blessing on His own people who watch and keep their garments, and are saved from the reproach of spiritual nakedness. Let us, therefore, wait for the promise of His coming, looking for and hasting unto the coming of the day of God.

And it shall be said in that day, Lo, this is our God; we have waited for him, and he will save us: this is the Lord; we have waited for him, we will be glad and rejoice in his salvation.

Isaiah 25: 9

THERE ARE three things that make us glad. (1) *The sense of God's Presence.* We know that He is near, though the woods are bare and the frost holds the earth in its iron fist and the wind blows together the dead leaves; but we feel Him nearer when every hedgerow is clothed with flowers, every bush burns with fire, every tree claps its leafy hands, and every avenue is filled with choristers. (2) *The optimism of an illimitable hope.* Spring is the minstrel of hope. She takes her lyre and sings of the fair Summer, which is on its way. Life pours through a myriad of channels, and shows itself stronger than death; for Spring is victorious over Winter as good shall prove to be over evil. (3) *The exuberance of love.* Spring is the time of love. The whole creation is attracted by a natural affinity, and love rules in forest and field.

These three elements met in the hearts of the returning exiles, and made the world seem young again. The heart views the outer world in lines borrowed from itself. When life is young and carefree, all the echoes ring with joy notes; but when the joy of life is fled, what mockery comes back on us from even the tenderest outward scenes! The lesson is clear. Cherish the sense of the presence of God, cultivate an illimitable hope, be conscious of a love flowing toward you and from you. Rejoice in the lovingkindness and tender mercy of God, and be glad in His salvation.

December

Jesus answered and said unto them, Ye do err, not knowing the Scriptures, nor the power of God.
Matthew 22: 29

6

WHATEVER God has promised in the Scripture, He is prepared to make good by His power. It is necessary to know each. Abraham believed that what God had promised He was able also to perform. He looked from the promise to the Promiser, from the world to the eternal power of the Godhead, to which nothing was impossible, not even difficult.

This must be our attitude also. In the proper balancing of these two—in the study of the Scriptures on the one hand, and in the adoring contemplation of God's power on the other—we shall find our best preservative against the errors of our age, and may await the time when God will vindicate Himself, fulfilling every promise and prediction of Scripture with the might of His stretched-out arm.

Do you ask how the dead are raised up, and with what body they come? Do you fear that somehow in the crowd you may miss elect and beloved spirits? Be still and wait; these fears would be annulled if the veil were torn from our eyes, and we knew the Scriptures and the power of God. Not the Scriptures without the Power, or you arrive at dry-as-dust Phariseeism. Not the Power without the Scriptures, or you drift into the ineptitude of mysticism and fanaticism. Always combine the Scriptures and the Power of God; and is not the commanding proof of the unique position of the Scriptures as the inspired Word of God, that through them, as through no other book whatsoever, the Divine Power travels and works? And this is the same Word that promises His soon return.

And to offer a sacrifice according to that which is said in the law of the Lord . . . two young pigeons.
Luke 2: 24

7

THESE WERE the offerings of the poor, of those whose means did not allow them to buy a lamb. All these offerings pointed to the one great Sacrifice to be offered on Calvary.

December

The blood of Christ is within the reach of the poorest and feeblest. None can say that it is beyond them, that they cannot afford it, that they are too poor. To the poor the gospel is preached. The divine call is to those who have no money. Salvation is to him who cannot work for it, but believes on the One who justifies the ungodly.

The faith that understands but a part of the Savior's work saves. The pigeon may stand for the meager understanding of Christ that is the portion of the faltering and timid; but it saves equally with that fuller conception of His saving work which might be compared to the bullock of the priest. The question is not as to the quantity but the object of faith. Is it fixed on Jesus? All faith directed to Him cannot but be genuine. It may touch but His garment's hem, yet it saves.

The beneficence of God's law. What tender touches there are through this strong ancient code! There is such a one here, framed partly in anticipation of the mother of our Lord, who gladly took advantage of this provision. What a glimpse into our Master's humiliation! He owned the cattle on a thousand hills, yet He so emptied Himself that His parents were compelled to bring the poorest offering the law allowed. He stooped that we might rise; emptied Himself that we might be full; became poor that we might be made rich; was made human that we might be made divine; is coming again that we might reign with Him.

This is now the third time that Jesus showed himself to his disciples, after that he was risen from the dead.
John 21: 14

JESUS will not only come to you amid the scenes of natural beauty and daily toil. He will come to you most of all when you are mourning over your failure in His service. Have the weary hours passed with you doing your small best, without one tiny fish entering the net? Does it seem as if your hand has lost its cunning, and you think sadly of how you are going to disappoint others? This is the likeliest moment of all to meet Jesus. He always comes to men who seem to

December

have failed, who have meant great things but have fallen short, who have toiled greatly and taken nothing. Such are dear to Christ. Nothing touches His heart like patient and steadfast endurance. Nothing will so surely bring Him within reach as those empty nets and light keels. Look out for Him as the night is passing, and the day breaking, when strength is gone and exhaustion paralyzes you. Your heart will awake, smitten by the gleam of His face, and you will say softly to yourself, "This is my God; I have waited for Him. He is come to save me. This is the Lord. I will rejoice in His salvation. It is the Lord!" The promise of His return for His own is no less certain than the assurance of His resurrection.

Finally, my brethren, be strong in the Lord, and in the power of his might.

Ephesians 6: 10

9

THE POWER of God equips us for conflict. We are seated with Christ above the power of the enemy, but we are still assailed by it in our daily experience. We wrestle not against flesh and blood, but against principalities and powers. The darkness of the world, and especially of heathen lands, is the veil beneath which evil spirits set themselves against the Lord and against His Christ. What are we, that we may hope to prevail, either in our own temptations, or in our efforts to dislodge them from human wills, unless we have learned to be empowered in the Lord, and in the strength of His might?

By His own conflicts, and notably by the mighty act of His ascension, our Lord Jesus has become in His human and representative capacity, the storehouse of spiritual force, which has proved itself more than a match for all the power and graft of Satan. He holds in Himself abundant spiritual power, which is destined finally to issue in the binding of Satan and the destruction of his realm. That power is not yet exerted to its full measure. But it is nevertheless in Him, and in Him for us. We may be strengthened with might by His Spirit in the inner man (Eph. 3: 16). We may become strong in the Lord, and in the power of His might; and able to do all things through Christ who strengthens us.

December

10

But God be thanked, that ye were the servants of sin, but ye have obeyed from the heart that form of doctrine which was delivered you.

Romans 6: 17

THE IDEA IS borrowed from the smelting furnace, where the metal is brought to fluid shape, so that it may take on the shape of the mold in which it was poured. At a given signal, the contents of the furnace are discharged and obey the form of the pattern which awaits them. Some time elapses during which the metal cools. Then the mold is destroyed, but the pattern is fixed forever on substances that yielded itself to its shape.

This process furnishes the apostle an illustration of the effect produced upon his converts by his teaching. They had been the bondslaves of sin, presenting their members to uncleanness after iniquity, having no fruits to show for years, which as they reviewed them gave them nothing but regret. Yet these people have become saints, walking with God in purity and righteousness all their days, because their hearts melted in penitence and contrition, had assumed the shape of His teaching, and so had become conformed to the image of the Son of God. If we were to obey from our hearts that same type of teaching, might it not bring about in us a similar transformation?

11

Being then made free from sin, ye became the servants of righteousness.

Romans 6: 18

LET US comfort ourselves with this assurance. As He is, so shall we be. Can you not imagine the reluctance and questioning of the metal when first it leaves the heart of the furnace and begins to pour along its appointed channel toward its destination? How cold, dark, and perplexing it is. And when the mold is entered and the dividing streams part company, to take their several ways into the dark passages, how regretfully they must regard their happy past—how they must wonder what is happening. They must be prone to murmur at that point regarding their exclusion from light and air. But if they refuse to take on the prepared pattern, they will only expose themselves to added pain, because they will be broken up with ruthless hammers, plunged again into the furnace, and compelled to retrace their way. Better far to immediately and gladly accept the pattern to which they have been delivered. When that is achieved and the mold is broken, and the finished work brought to light, the metal will be satisfied. The founder will also rejoice with exceeding joy.

God ... hath raised us up together ... that like as Christ was raised up from the dead by the glory of the Father, even so we also should walk in newness of life.
Ephesians 2: 6; Romans 6: 4

12

IN THE STORY of the Deluge, the ark bore Noah and his family from the old world, where corruption and sin had reigned, to the new world of resurrection and life, as it emerged from its watery grave; even so the Lord Jesus, the true Ark of Safety, has borne us through His death and resurrection into the world of Life. It is on this thought that the apostle bases the appeal, "If ye then were raised with Christ, seek those things that are above."

This is the beginning of sanctification: to feel that in Jesus we no longer belong to the world that cast out and crucified Him, but to that in which He reigns forevermore; to know that His cross and grave stand between us and the past; to realize the power of His resurrection in its daily detachment from sin and attachment to God.

13

... which veil is done away in Christ.
2 Corinthians 3: 14

THAT VEIL was rent when Jesus died, the Holy Spirit signifying that from that moment access was free into the Holiest. All believers

December

are now welcome to draw near and live in the perpetual presence of God, their Father, even as Jesus did in His earthly life, and as He does now in the Heaven of heavens. This is the clear teaching of Hebrews 10: 19–22, "Having therefore, brethren, boldness to enter into the holiest by the blood of Jesus, by a new and living way, which he hath consecrated for us, through the veil, that is to say, his flesh; and having an high priest over the house of God; let us draw near with a true heart in full assurance of faith, having our hearts sprinkled from an evil conscience and our bodies washed with pure water."

But there is a deeper significance still. The new and living way was opened up through the rending of the flesh of Jesus Christ. As His flesh was torn on the cross, the Temple veil was rent from the top to the bottom. And it is only when we have chosen the cross, with its shame and death, as the lot of our self-life, that we can enter into that immediate fellowship with God which is described as "within the veil."

How many there are who never get beyond that dividing veil! They know the brazen altar of Atonement, the layer of daily washing, the golden altar of intercession; but they are never admitted to that blessed intimacy of communion which sees the Shekinah glory between the cherubim and blood-sprinkled mercy seat. O Spirit of God, apply the blood to sprinkle our consciences, and the water to cleanse the habits of our daily life; and lead us where our Forerunner and Priest awaits us. He is coming again to remove the veil from our eyes forever.

And what is the exceeding greatness of His power to us-ward who believe, according to the working of his mighty power.

Ephesians 1: 19

WE ARE bidden to follow our Master and His upward track, and to sit with Him in daily happy experience, where He is already seated at the right hand of God. But this is as impossible to our unaided energy, as for the swallow to follow the majestic flight of the golden eagle, soaring sunward. So strong is the gravitation that holds

December

us to earth, so dissipating our cares, so fickle our resolution, that naught but the divine power and grace can lift us to the level of the divine life.

But God waits to realize in us all He has prepared for us; and the third item in the apostle's prayer for his converts is that they might know "the exceeding greatness of His power to us-ward who believe." It is *power;* it is *His power.* It is *great power:* nothing less would suffice. It is *exceeding* great power, equivalent to "the energy of the strength of His might," which He energized in Christ, when He raised Him from the dead, and seated Him at His own right hand in the heavenlies.

In the body of his flesh through death, to present you holy and unblameable and unreprovable in his sight.
Colossians 1: 22

| 15 |

CHRIST is the ideal Man. The Man, Christ Jesus, was before the first man Adam, so far as the thought and purpose of God are concerned. When the great Potter took in hand the red clay to make a man, He made it in His own image and after His likeness. And what could these be but the nature and lineaments of that blessed Son of His love, who was His fellow—Himself? The Incarnation and Ascension were only possible on these conditions. How could the Son of God become incarnate unless the nature He was to assume had already been made after the model of Himself? And how could our human nature be taken into the ineffable glory of His throne, unless, in a sense it had belonged there before the worlds were made?

But Adam fell from his original type. He shared morally in that aptness toward sin which runs through nature. In his fall, we all fell. All who are one with him by the bonds of natural relationship shared in that sad act of disobedience and its results.

But Adam begat a son in his own likeness, after his image, and the second Man possesses the same glorious power by which He is able to fashion anew the body of our humiliation, that it may be conformed to the body of His glory, according to the working whereby He is able even to subject all things to Himself.

December

<table>
<tr><td>16</td><td>Having abolished in his flesh the enmity, even the law of commandments contained in ordinances; for to make in himself of twain one new man, so making peace.
Ephesians 2: 15</td></tr>
</table>

BY HIS death, the Savior has made an atonement and propitiation for men as men. Not for the Jew in one way or the Gentile in another; but for all on the same terms. By one death, and one body on the cross, which is common to the whole world of men, and by His intercession, through which both have access to one Father, He has brought to an end the divisions of the ages.

But He has done more. In His resurrection, He has constituted the origin and head of a new race. The race of regenerate men! The race of His resurrection-life and power! The race of the new heavens and the new earth! All who believe in Him are born into that new humanity. It is the one new man, which is composed of all nations, kindreds, peoples, and tongues. He fulfilled the law so perfectly— not for Himself, but for all—that it had no more to ask. Its claims were met and satisfied; and therefore the Jews could not insist on them, on the one hand, nor the Gentiles chafe beneath them on the other.

<table>
<tr><td>17</td><td>Unto him be glory in the church by Christ Jesus throughout all ages, world without end.
Ephesians 3: 21</td></tr>
</table>

THE CHURCH'S end is the glory of God. At the close of this sublime doxology, in which the burning heart of the apostle rises to an almost unparalleled ecstasy of thought and expression, he seeks for voices that will give utterance to the glory which is the due of such a God and, according to the Revised Version (which accurately renders the best reading of the original Greek), he finds them in the church and in Christ Jesus; "Unto *him* be glory in the church and in Christ Jesus."

The juxtaposition of these two is very wonderful and suggestive. The thought seems to be passing from the comparison between the church and a building or body, to trace a parallel between it and the bride, lifted by the love of the bridegroom to stand beside Him on the same level with Himself. We know, of course, that glory must accrue to the Father, for ever and ever, from the work of the Lord Jesus. A revenue of glory will ever ascend from the cradle, the cross, the grave. The ages are to see repeated harvests accruing from the sowing of His tears and blood. But, we had not realized, except for these words, that a similar wealth of glory was to accrue from the church from the first-born. The church of the redeemed shall stand beside Christ and raise her voice, in unison with his, as the voice of one ascribing glory to the Father. And as the ages pass they shall not diminish, but increase, the sweetness of her song and the volume of her voice.

He that descended is the same also that ascended up far above all heavens, that he might fill all things.
Ephesians 4: 10

18

THIS POWER to fill was won by Christ in His death and resurrection. He did not ascend till He had first descended. Always death before resurrection; stooping before rising; the garden and the cross before the Ascension Mount.

But as surely as these come first, the others follow. He who condescended to the fashion of a man, and thence to death, even the death of the cross, must ascend by the very laws of that spiritual world which He obeyed. He could not be held by death. "Wherefore God highly exalted Him." "Thou art worthy, for Thou wast slain."

And being by the right hand of God exalted, He received of the Father the promised platitude of the spirit. It had been His before, as the Second Person in the Holy Trinity; but it became His now as the representative and High Priest of His people. It was entrusted to Him as their trustee. As we receive the fullness of forgiveness from His death, so we may receive the fullness of the Spirit from His life.

There is no soul so low in its need but He can touch it because He has descended into the depths of Hades; now from the zenith throne

December

of His ascended glory He can reach the furthest and remotest points of spiritual need; as the sun can cover a wider area when it sits regnant in the sky at noon, than when pillowing its chin upon the western wave.

19	*And hath put all things under his feet, and gave him to be the head over all things to the church.*

Ephesians 1: 22

NO CONGREGATION, or set of congregations, can realize the sublime conception of the Church that rises before our vision in Ephesians. It is as if the apostle had been able to anticipate the glorious spectacle which John beheld in the Apocalypse. Though he had founded more churches in the great cities of the Roman Empire than any other one in the apostolic band, yet none of these alone, nor all of them together, could realize Paul's fair ideal of that one mystical body, the Church, the bride, the Lamb's wife.

Ephesians is preeminently the epistle of the church; we must enter into God's thought when we speak about the church—not as she now is, in broken bits like shards of painted glass; but as she is to be when the mystery of God is finished, and she is presented to His Son, worthy to "answer to" Him, according to the ancient word of the Creator, when seeking a bride for Adam (Gen. 2: 18). Be assured of this: He who is the Head of the Church is also coming again to claim His bride, the Church.

20	*For the husband is the head of the wife, even as Christ is the head of the church; and he is the savior of the body.*

Ephesians 5: 23

EACH MEMBER is united to the head by nerves that carry impressions from the surface of the body to the head; and there is nothing that happens to any one of us which is not instantly com-

December

municated to our Savior. Each member is also united to the head by nerves that carry volitions from the brain to the extremities of the body—withdrawing the foot from the thorn, or compelling the hand to avoid the flame. Thus we should also receive our life impulses from Jesus Christ; He bears our griefs and carries our sorrows; He is touched with the feeling of our infirmity. The glory with which He is surrounded is not like an insulating barrier between Him and the weakest and meanest of His members.

In Ephesians 5: 23 the headship of Christ to the church is compared to that between husband and wife; we are reminded of one of those deep verses that reveal the unities of creation as they were present to the apostle's thought. As God is the head of Christ, the glorified Man, and as man is meant to be the head of woman, so is Christ head of each redeemed man, as an individual, and of all such together, in the church. Thus, amid the discord and the anarchy of creation we are learning the divine concords, and shall yet find harmony emanating from the church to soothe, to still, and to unify creation. This event will be crowned by His triumphant return for His own.

Let this mind be in you, which was also in Christ Jesus.
Philippians 2: 5

21

A LITTLE crippled boy in the east of London, who had heard snatches of the gospel in the ragged school, refused to be moved from his miserable home to the children's ward of the neighboring hospital, because he said, "I don't want to die easy when He died hard." Our Lord did die hard. He needn't have died at all, since He was sinless, but He might have stepped into paradise from the snow-white brow of Hermon, where He was transfigured. Or He might have died at Bethany with Mary and Martha ministering to Him; or He might have died in some easy, painless way. But He chose the death of the cross—the most degrading and painful death known.

December

Let this mind be in you, says the apostle; think His thoughts; follow in His steps. The church's most glorious days have not been those when she has attracted fashion, wealth, and learning; but when she has been a fugitive in the catacombs and an outcast on the moors. If ever she is to sit with Christ on His throne, to bear His name, and to share His glory, she will have to renounce these sources of influence on which she is apt to rely, and to associate herself with the sorrowful lot of the masses of the people whom she desires to help. The most urgent matter for each of us to consider is not whether we are orthodox in our creed, though that is not unimportant; but whether at any cost we are manifesting the love of God to a dying world.

22	*But made himself of no reputation, and took upon him the form of a servant and was made in the likeness of men.* Philippians 2: 7

JESUS refused to avail Himself of the homage due His original nature. He had been in the form of God, and did not think it necessary to grasp at equality with God. When the wife is not sure of her husband's love, she grasps at every opportunity of testing and asserting it. But when she knows herself to be supreme in his affections, she takes her position as a matter of course. So when our Lord lived visibly among men, there was no theophany like that of Sinai or Horeb—nothing to startle or frighten but everything to woo and win. He veiled His glory, and was content with the form of a servant and the fashion of man.

He refused to use the attributes of His intrinsic deity. Once they flashed out for a moment when His foes came to arrest Him, but they were immediately replaced at His command. It was as though a man were to fight life's battle with one arm held voluntarily behind his back. He emptied Himself in the babyhood of Bethlehem, the boyhood of Nazareth, the voluntary limitations of His earthly ministry, and the weakness of His cross. *There* was the hiding of His power.

December

But made himself of no reputation, and took upon him the form of a servant, and was made in the likeness of men.
Philippians 2: 7

| 23 |

OUR WORLD is in revolt. Wars and rumors of wars surround us, as they have since the distant past. Conflict exists between man and himself, man and his fellow man, and man and God. Is there no help? Cannot God bring peace and goodwill into these troubled scenes? Yes, for Paul says that "God also hath highly exalted him (Jesus), and given him a name which is above every name: that at the name of Jesus every knee should bow, of things in heaven and things in earth, and things under the earth" (Phil. 2: 9,10). Thus, God will be glorified and become all in all.

But notice the process by which this consummation will be secured. Our Lord Jesus will effect it without the aid of much that we expected, and through means that we do not expect. He will become a servant and a sacrifice, through which He will manifest the love of God in the most conspicuous and convincing manner; that He might bear away the guilt of the world, and might work out and bring in an everlasting righteousness. Therefore, He is exalted and bears evermore the name of Jesus—the Savior.

. . . Now is our salvation nearer than when we believed.
Romans 13: 11

| 24 |

NOW IS our salvation nearer than when we believed. Not our salvation merely, but salvation generally. Jesus is about to appear the second time, without sin, unto salvation. The bodies of the saints are to be set free from the power of death, and raised in the likeness of the body of Christ's glory: The creature is to be emancipated from the bondage of corruption; the last remains of Satan's rule over our world are to be destroyed. The golden ages are to return. From the watchers and holy ones the song of redemption is yet to ascend:

December

"Salvation to our God that sitteth on the throne, and unto the Lamb forever and ever."

We look back to the hour when we first believed. It is a definite moment in the vista of the past, but we look forward to indefinite degrees of light and glory. The light will grow ever to a more perfect day, the results of the Savior's death will become ever more appreciated, the circles of influence that radiate from His throne will reach to further limits and be more than ever prolific of blessing to unknown races of beings at the uttermost limits of the universe.

25	*May the Lord direct your hearts into the love of God, and into the patient waiting for Christ.*
	2 Thessalonians 3: 5

THE KING James rendering of this verse is manifestly inconsistent with the accurate rendering of the Greek, which is clearly *"the patience of Christ."* The word *direct* is the same as is used in the first Epistle, where the apostle asks God to direct his way to Thessalonica. As that city was his goal then, so God's love and Christ's patient waiting must be ours now, but it cannot be gained at once, and only after many a day's weary trudge along the path marked out for us. Not at a single bound, but by successive steps, do we appreciate and appropriate the love of God. Only gradually do we attain to that patient waiting with which our Lord anticipates the completing of the Divine program.

Our Lord waited patiently from all eternity, until the fullness of the times had come, and the hour of the Incarnation struck. He waited patiently for thirty years in Nazareth, while preparing for His life work, filling His mind with Scripture and His heart with compassion. When He returned to the Father He sat down at His left hand until His enemies were made His footstool. Throughout the ages He quietly waits, in sure expectation of the destined end when all rule and authority and power shall be put down. All the anguish of the world lies on His heart and He bears them with unfaltering patience, because He sees the end from the beginning, and knows that at the last God will be all in all. It is into this love and this patience that we are to be led.

December

. . . them which believe and know the truth.
                              1 Timothy 4: 3

IT IS a blessed thing to be sure that we have passed from death
unto life, and are the children of God by faith in Christ Jesus. True,
our eternal destiny does not hinge on it. Many will doubtless be
saved at last who have spent their lives between hope and fear. But
it is very necessary for our comfort and growth in grace to be able
to declare our assurance, and to know that we have been translated
into the Kingdom of God's dear Son.

The Gospel of John was written that we might *believe;* the First
Epistle that we might *know.* But many seek this knowledge in the
wrong way and are exposed to endless questionings. They try to discover the date, place, or experience in the past, when they were in-
corporated into the divine family; and because they cannot point to
these, they imagine that they are still outside. Now for every one who
has had a definite experience of the new birth, there are perhaps a
score who entered the divine family almost as a sailor passes the
line of the equator. Yet it is possible for you to know that you are
born again, though you may not be able to pinpoint your spiritual
birthday.

If you are trusting Jesus, if the Spirit witnesses with your spirit
that God is your Father, if you are full of a holy fear of grieving
Him, if you are becoming like Him, if you love the brethren—you
may certainly declare yourself His child and rejoice in the knowledge that He is coming again!

*For the grace of God that bringeth salvation hath appeared
to all men. . . .*
                              Titus 2: 11

27

IT IS well to be reminded that we have no claim on God. All He
does for us and gives us is of His own free grace. By grace we have
been saved, through faith, and that not of ourselves: it is the gift

December

of God. There certainly was nothing in us to merit eternal life before our conversion; and it is equally sure that there has been nothing since to merit the continuance of His favor. Indeed, as we remember and review the past, to us belong shame and confusion of face for our repeated acts of disobedience. Oh, the depth of the riches of His grace!

If we were not saved for our goodness, we shall not be lost for the lack of it. When we have been betrayed into sin, in the keenness of our remorse, the fear is suggested lest God should put us utterly away. And there would be ground for the fear if we had been chosen because of our righteousness. But since our original acceptance with God did not depend on works of righteousness which we had done, but on His mercy in Christ Jesus, it will not be undone by our failures. This thought does not lead to carelessness and indifference, but to the holy fear of sinning.

If our justification was apart from our merit, our sanctification will be. The one was a gift, so must the other be; the hand of faith must receive each from Christ, and her voice must render thanks for each, as the unmerited gift of divine love. Where is boasting then? It is shut out. We can claim nothing but emptiness and need. Handfuls of withered leaves! The Lord Jesus is our only hope, pleading for us in heaven, living within our hearts, and coming again for us in great glory. Of ourselves we are nothing; only in Him are we complete.

28

But this man, because he continueth ever, hath an unchangeable priesthood.

Hebrews 7: 24

THE DEATH of other high priests only brings into greater prominence the encouraging contrast in the case of our blessed Lord, who ever lives, and has, therefore, an unchangeable priesthood.

Christ ever lives; what an encouragement to the penitent sinner! All that He ever was, He is; all that He ever did for others, He is willing to do for you. The records of His earthly life, with His tenderness for those who were out of the way, are leaves and specimen pages of the diary of His life. Therefore, you need not hesitate to come to Him.

Christ ever lives; what a blessing to the saint! "I am he that liveth" (Rev. 1: 18). He bent over His fainting apostle and said, in effect, "You remember what I was when you leaned upon my bosom, followed me to the shore on which I had prepared your supper, and assured you of My never-faltering affection. I am that still. Through death I have come to a life which can never decay; because I live you shall live also." Let us rest our souls on this sweet word—from His heart there will ever stream to us rivers of incorruptible life. Let us keep all the channels of our being open toward the fountain of eternal life, that there be no slacking in our reception by Him.

Christ ever lives; what a warning to the church! There is no need, therefore, of the human priest to transact matters between God and man. The Son is Priest and King in His own house, and He is coming again in the power of an endless life; and human mediators are no more necessary than flickering night lights at noon.

How much more shall the blood of Christ, who through the eternal Spirit offered himself without spot to God, purge your conscience from dead works to serve the living God?
Hebrews 9: 14

29

WHEN WE are told that on the cross that our Lord offered Himself to God through the Eternal Spirit, it opens to us a profound concept, because it is clear that the element of the eternal was in the "wondrous cross." And what is the meaning of that great word *eternal*? Too often it is employed as though it were synonymous with *everlasting*. But the two words stand for very different ideas. *Everlasting* conveys the idea of the duration of time, whereas *eternal* stands for the quality and character of the existence referred to, which is absolutely timeless.

It is this attribute of timelessness which gives the cross its perennial power. It was because it was present to God in the earliest ages that He was able to pass by iniquity, transgression, and sin. And as to the future, "Dear Dying Lamb, Thy precious blood shall never lose its power." Of course, the crucifixion of our Lord was a definite

December

fact in the history of redemption; but it was more, it was the revelation of the timeless and eternal fact in the nature of God. Calvary was an inlet into human history of something which has always been in God, but which creation could never reveal.

30

And they overcame him by the blood of the Lamb. . . .
Revelation 12: 11

NO RELIGION that ignores this elemental fact in human consciousness is destined to permanence. To say with Buddha, "You can wipe out your sins with good deeds," or with Mohammed, "God is good, and will not be hard on you," is not enough. The religious creed that deals most radically and drastically with sin is the one which will ever appeal most strongly to the human heart, and it is because Jesus Christ has not treated sin lightly, but has loosed men from it by His blood, that He shall be enthroned forever when the names of all other teachers shall have faded as stars at noon.

Whatever else the blood of Christ may mean, it means that Christ has viewed our sin as of tremendous gravity. With Him it is no slight illness to be cured by a regimen of diet and exercise. It is deep-seated, radical, perilous, endangering the fabric of our soul's health and the scope of our soul's outlook on the future. This is He who came by water and blood; not by water only, but by water and blood. He hath loosed us from our sins in His own blood. And He is coming again to take us unto Himself forever!

31

And he made us to be a kingdom, to be priests unto his God and Father; to him be the glory and the dominion forever and ever. Amen.
Revelation 1: 6

THE POSITION they assigned to Him was superlative. They said with one voice, "To Him be the glory and the dominion until the

December

ages of the ages." An age of days is long, an age of years incomputable, but an age of ages is eternity; and it was their desire and belief that through uncounted eons, every star would shine, every jewel would flash, every wave break, every voice sing, and every creature live to promote the everlasting radiance of His crown, the glory of His name. That His rule should outlast the sun, that it should embrace all beings, in all spheres, for all ages, without rival or successor; that the Man of Nazareth and Calvary should be the only Ruler; that the Lamb should be seated in the supreme place of authority—such was the confident expectation and the desire of the church as reflected here. But on what ground did the early believers base their estimate of our Savior's superlative claims? Whatever else might have been urged, *this* was their supreme consideration, that "He had loosed them from their sins in his own blood" (v. 5). This was His greatest contribution to the world's need; and it was for this that they ascribed to Him "blessings and honors and glory and might, unto the ages of the ages."

Scripture Index

Since the pages of this daily devotional book are not numbered, a code indicating day and month has been devised. For example, 1/11 designates January 11, 11/1 designates November 1, and so on.

Index

Index

Index